5th

Mount Allegro

New York Classics
Frank Bergmann, *Series Editor*

Mount Allegro

A MEMOIR OF ITALIAN AMERICAN LIFE

Jerre Mangione

Foreword by Eugene Paul Nassar
Introduction by Dorothy Canfield

Foreword copyright © 1998 by Syracuse University Press
Syracuse, New York 13244–5290
Copyright © 1942, 1952, 1963, 1972 by Jerre Mangione
"Finale" copyright © 1981 by Jerre Mangione

First Syracuse University Press Edition 1998
10 11 12 13 14   9 8 7 6 5

This book is published with the assistance of a grant
from the John Ben Snow Foundation.

Published by Harper & Row in 1989.

The paper used in this publication meets the minimum requirements
of American National Standard for Information Sciences—Permanence
of Paper for Printed Library Materials, ANSI Z39.48-1984. ∞™

Library of Congress Cataloging-in-Publication Data
Mangione, Jerre Gerlando, 1909–
Mount Allegro : a memoir of Italian American life / Jerre Mangione ;
foreword by Eugene Paul Nassar ; introduction by Dorothy Canfield.
— 1st Syracuse University Press ed.
p. cm. — (New York classics)
Originally published: New York : Perennial Library, 1989,
© 1981. With new foreword and introd.
ISBN 0-8156-0429-7 (alk. paper)
1. Italian Americans—New York (State)—Rochester—Social life and
customs. 2. Mangione, Jerre Gerlando, 1909– . 3. Italian
Americans—New York (State)—Rochester—Biography. 4. Rochester
(N.Y.)—Biography. 5. Rochester (N.Y.)—Social life and customs.
I. Title. II. Series.
F129.R79185 1998
974.7'8900451073'092—dc21
[B]   97-50547

Manufactured in the United States of America

To My Mother and Father

CONTENTS

Foreword

JERRE MANGIONE'S *MOUNT ALLEGRO* DID FOR
Italian Americans in its time (1943) what William Saroyan's
My Name is Aram did a little earlier (1937) for Armenian
Americans: it gave a literary visibility and identity, amiable
and appealing, to a poorly-understood ethnic group in Amer-
ica, and did so at a very high level of artistry. *Mount Allegro*
has endured, as has the Saroyan volume, as a minor classic of
American literature, through seven different editions; it has
an almost iconic status in Italian American literature specifi-
cally, and in ethnic American literature generally. During
the period of the late Thirties, there also appeared Pietro Di
Donato's *Christ in Concrete* (1937) and the early work of
John Fante (*Wait Until Spring, Bandini*, 1938, and *Dago
Red*, 1940), but there is little question that the early Italian
American community would find in Mangione's book their
choice of the one volume to represent them: "Jerre Mangione's extended family is our family, our people." And the
reason would not be hard to articulate. The delineation of
his people has a sweetness, a sympathetic understanding, and
yet an accuracy (cf. Richard Gambino's later study, *Blood of*

My Blood) that seems a distillation of an ethnic neighborhood at a given time and place, Rochester, New York, from
the Teens through the Thirties, and yet also at the same time
a paradigm of the general ethnic experience in America.

I grew up (and still live) as a Lebanese American in the
Italian American enclave of East Utica in Upstate New York,
a neighborhood that was even more densely Italian than
Mangione's, though less Sicilian, more Calabrian. The eminent sociologist, Herbert Gans, in an introduction to the fifth
separate edition of *Mount Allegro,* could have just as well
been speaking of my people as Mangione's:

> The mainstay of Mount Allegro social life and the heart of
> the book are the "stories" that family members told each
> other during their nearly nightly gatherings. Some are dra-
> matic renderings of neighborhood gossip; others are similar
> gossip from the old country now transformed into folk tales.
> A handful are or were once true; many have always been
> apocryphal. Some are tragic, most are funny, but virtually all
> are morality playlets which uphold and defend the immi-
> grants' major values against real or imagined subverters.

I remember one evening as a teenager in the 1950s hearing an old Sicilian gentleman who lived on our block tell us a
story that I had heard many times from my mother's repertoire of Lebanese folktales told around our kitchen table. I
was sure that he must have heard it from my mother or one
of her peers and embellished it with Sicilian detail. But I
have since found that both tellers had wonderfully adapted
folktale motifs that had circulated from country to country
through oral transmission at the level of peasant village society, there where people of different countries are most alike.

It is this well-spring, this vital source of central, enduring human values that Mangione keeps tapping in *Mount Allegro*. One can do some scholarship in Sicilian folklore, in the work of Giuseppe Pitre, Salvatore Salomone-Marino, and Italo Calvino, as I have tried to do, and one will continue to admire Mangione's easy and courtly grace in treating of his peoples' attitudes and predilections, their songs and stories.

Mangione's Sicilians are the inheritors of a rich culture: the evening *sirinatas,* as described in *Mount Allegro*'s chapter 2, the family feasts at table detailed in chapter 7, with Mangione's father toasting with improvised verses each family member—a scene that seems an uncanny reflection of evenings in my Lebanese tradition in our home in the Fifties (and a scene beautifully captured in Robert Cimbalo's cover illustration), the story telling competitions of chapter 7 (of, say, Baron Albertini) and chapter 10 (of Giovanni and Giuseppe Scalla).

Jerre Mangione makes clear the right way to understand Sicilian folktales:

> To hear a recital of them, you would have imagined that Sicilians were a bloodthirsty lot . . . But if you examined the stories and listened to them carefully, you would realize that each story expressed some profoundly noble sentiment and was always told with the proper amount of moral indignation.

To be sure, the folktale or the toast-at-table may poeticize or romanticize real experience, but so be it. In a postscript to *Mount Allegro* written in 1980 that he calls "Finale," Mangione describes his initial purposes for this memoir:

Perhaps the overriding motive in writing *Mount Allegro* was to recapture the world from which I had escaped while it was still fresh in my memory. There was also the hope that I could produce a work that might help dispel some of the more spurious clichés pinned to the image of Italian Americans by an uninformed American public.

In "Finale" Mangione also expresses his feeling that with the benefit of hindsight, he might have shown more of a darker chiaroscuro in the life of Mount Allegro, but it is my feeling that few readers would want the book to be otherwise than what it is: the capturing of a warm tonality of a world, now lost, as felt and imagined by a young, talented writer who had left it not very long ago.

Jerre Mangione was born in Rochester in 1909 and left the ethnic neighborhood to attend Syracuse University from 1928–31. Thereafter, in the depths of the depression, he worked at various jobs with the writers' profession always in mind, especially when he worked as national coordinating editor for the Federal Writers' Project from 1937–40. Besides *Mount Allegro,* he is the author of *The Ship and the Flame* (a novel), New York: A. A. Wyn, 1948; *Reunion in Sicily,* Boston: Houghton Mifflin, 1950; *Night Search* (a novel), New York: Crown, 1965; *Life Sentences for Everybody,* New York: Abelard-Schuman, 1966; *A Passion for Sicilians: The World Around Danilo Dolci,* New York: Morrow, 1968; *America is Also Italian,* New York: Putnam, 1969; *The Dream and the Deal: The Federal Writers' Project, 1935–43,* Boston: Little, Brown, 1972 (reprinted by Syracuse University Press in 1996); *Mussolini's March on Rome,* New York: Franklin Watts, 1975; *An Ethnic at Large: A Memoir of*

America in the Thirties and Forties, New York: Putnam, 1978; *La Storia* (with Ben Morreale), New York: Harper-Collins, 1992.

He was professor of English and creative writing at the University of Pennsylvania from 1961–77. His many awards include Guggenheim, Fulbright, and National Endowment fellowships, research grants from the Rockefeller Foundation and the American Philosophical Society, and Italy's *Premio Nazionale Empedocle.*

English editions of *Mount Allegro* are: Boston: Houghton Mifflin, 1943 (illustrations by Peggy Bacon); New York: Knopf, 1952; New York: Hill and Wang, 1963 (introduction by Dorothy Canfield); New York: Crown, 1972 (introduction by Maria Cimino); New York: Columbia University Press, 1981 (introduction by Herbert Gans); New York: Harper & Row, 1989.

For a comprehensive Mangione bibliography and recent articles on Mangione's career, see *VIA* 4:2 (1993). See also Fred Gardaphe's *Italian Signs, American Streets: The Evolution of Italian American Narrative,* Duke University Press, 1996, and John Reilly, "Literary Versions of Ethnic History from Upstate New York," in *Upstate Literature,* ed. Frank Bergmann, Syracuse University Press, 1985. The Jerre Mangione Archive is housed in the Special Collections Department of the University of Rochester.

Eugene Paul Nassar

Professor of English
Director of the Ethnic Heritage Studies Center
Utica College of Syracuse University

Introduction

AN AMERICAN OF MY AGE AND EXPERIENCE, even one for whom the book-world has always been home, knows as well as anybody else that a large number of the books published should not remain too long on our shelves. They should quietly dry up and blow away, go permanently out of print.

This does not mean that they had no value when published. On the contrary, many of those which should imperceptibly evaporate to make room for others, gave, when they were new, that special fresh pleasure which is apt to accompany newness, were read with delighted laughter, or with equally delightful tears of sympathy. But later generations need only those books which prove to have a certain vibrating life, hard to define, hard to recognize when they are just off the press, but which the passage of time brings clearly to view. After a few years it becomes possible to know which volumes have lasting value, not only as a product (major or minor) of the great art of literature, but as a contribution to the growth of that attitude towards human life which is rightly called the national tradition.

Mount Allegro was such a contribution. When, due to the pressure of war-time conditions, it went out of print, it was a loss to our tradition because it not only had ineffable charm, but also because it was one of the first valid expressions in print of the special qualities poured by Americans of Italian parentage into our richly diversified American tradition.

When it appeared, its cheerful good-humor, so infectiously portrayed, enchanted its American readers. This description of a Sicilian family living in Rochester, New York, brought us two literary pleasures seldom found in the same book—novelty and strangeness, but also the "joy in recognition" of the familiar, essential, and lastingly human. Most of those who read the book had had neighbors like these Rochester Sicilians, but had not known them, because their ways of life seemed so strange to us. And yet we saw now they were like any other family group, made up like ours of parents, children, kinsfolk, and neighbors. *Mount Allegro,* when read aloud, held the sympathetic attention of American listeners —any listeners, that is, who liked to chuckle, for there was a light-hearted gaiety in the life portrayed on its pages, which was always ready to break into a laugh.

Yet there was nothing shallow about this portrait of European wage-earners in the U.S.A. They were painted with the light, skillful, unself-conscious touch which suits a genre canvas. None of the sombre tensity which for so long has been a literary fashion: but also no prettifying. The chapter called "A Man and His Vice" deals honestly with tragedy. The book is genuinely moving at the end, authentically human throughout, and fortifies the hope in all our hearts that life is not necessarily a martyrdom, but is often a variegated delight.

That sort of contribution to our taut, strenuous, and now apprehensive American tradition is too valuable to lose. We need it, even more than when the book was written. In bringing *Mount Allegro* back to circulation in this new edition, the publisher has deserved well of the republic.

Dorothy Canfield

Arlington, Vermont
April 1952

Mount Allegro

When I Grow Up . . .

'WHEN I GROW UP I WANT TO BE AN AMERICAN,'
Giustina said. We looked at our sister; it was something
none of us had ever said.

'Me too,' Maria echoed.

'Aw, you don't even know what an American is,' Joe
scoffed.

'I do so,' Giustina said.

It was more than the rest of us knew.

'We're Americans right now,' I said. 'Miss Zimmerman
says if you're born here you're an American.'

'Aw, she's nuts,' Joe said. He had no use for most teachers. 'We're Italians. If y' don't believe me ask Pop.'

But my father wasn't very helpful. 'Your children will
be *Americani.* But you, my son, are half-and-half. Now
stop asking me questions. You should know those things
from going to school. What do you learn in school, anyway?'

The world, my teacher insisted, was made up of all the
colored spots on a globe. One of the purple spots was
America, even though America wasn't purple when you

looked at it.   The orange spot was Italy.   Never having
been there, that wasn't so hard to believe.   You never used
this globe as a ball, even after Rosario Alfano gave you one
as a birthday present.   You just spun it, while some near-by
grownup told you that Columbus discovered the world to
be round.

You pretended to believe that because it was hard to
argue with grownups and be polite at the same time, but
you told yourself that any grownup who swallowed that
must be nuts.   It was confusing when your own father said
it because you liked to think he was right about everything;
but when your Uncle Sarafino said it, the uncle from Boston
who promised to give you a dollar for eating some hot
peppers raw, and then refused to give you the money, you
were sure he was nuts and the world wasn't round.

Then one day one of your new teachers looked at you
brightly and said you were Italian because your last name
was Amoroso and that too was puzzling.   You talked it
over with some of the boys in the gang.

First with Tony Long, who was the leader.   Tony said
his father changed his name when he came to America because he got tired of spelling it out for a lot of dopes who
didn't know how to spell.   I showed Tony my globe and
he pointed to a red spot on it and said that was where his
mother and father came from.   That's all he knew about
it.   Tony couldn't speak Polish and his mother hardly
knew any American.   He looked angry when she spoke
to him in Polish in front of the other kids.

Then there was Abe Rappaport, who went to a synagogue every Saturday.   Abe wore glasses and knew a lot.
He said his parents came from Russia and pointed to a

big gob of blue on the globe. It was close to Poland but Abe looked more like me than he did like Tony, who had blond hair. Abe was one of those who like to read and argue. We spent a whole day once asking each other, 'How do you know I ain't God?' until the other guys said we were crazy.

The other boys in the gang claimed they were Americans even though their parents didn't know how to speak American well. When I showed them my globe and asked them to point to the country where their parents came from, they said they didn't know. They didn't care either.

I showed my globe to a guy who belonged to another gang. His name was Robert Di Nella and he had blond hair and blue eyes like Tony Long. None of us liked him because he was always trying to boss us around, and we called him the Kaiser. He pointed to Italy on the globe, even though his mother didn't speak Italian the way mine did. Then he pointed to a tiny orange splash at the end of the Italian boot and called me a lousy *Siciliano*. I hit him on the jaw and, because he was taller and bigger, ran to safety with the globe tucked under my arm like a football.

This incident marked the beginning of a long and violent feud with the Kaiser. He ambushed me at every possible opportunity and preceded each attack by calling me a Sicilian. From the way he hissed the word at me, I soon realized that while being a Sicilian was a special distinction, it probably was not one that called for cheers and congratulations.

The Kaiser must have been descended from a Borgia.

He was a talented fiend and would lie in wait for me on Sunday mornings just as I was coming out of church. With my soul just whitewashed for the week, he could hardly have picked a better time to bully me. There I stood, without any of my gang around, hopelessly overflowing with peace and the religious ecstasy I had achieved by singing in tune with the rest of the choir boys.

As I saw the Kaiser waiting, his face ugly with a leer, the forces of good and evil would come to grips within me and before the good could gain enough strength, the Kaiser had already spat out his insults. In a lot behind the church, where we staged our battles, my conscience would make one last futile effort to persuade me to turn the other cheek, but by that time the Kaiser, quite unhampered by a conscience, had already landed the first blow and forced me to retaliate.

From anyone else the name *Siciliano* might not have been so insulting. From the Kaiser it rankled and assumed diabolical meaning, especially when he followed it up with such invectives as 'blackmailer' and 'murderer.' For a time the boys in the gang used this propaganda against my brother and me whenever they became angry with us. As a result, Joe and I, who were usually at war with each other, began coming to one another's rescue when one of us was defending the honor of Sicilians and getting the worst of it.

By such teamwork we usually won our fights. But we soon learned that the odds were hopelessly against us. There were grownup Robert Di Nellas all around who were too big for us. There were also the newspapers, which delighted in featuring murder stories involving persons with foreign names. My father would read these accounts carefully, anxious to determine, first of all, if the killer was an Italian; if so, whether he hailed from Sicily. 'It is bad enough for an Italian to commit a murder, but it is far worse when a Sicilian does,' he would say.

In the event the murderer turned out to be a Sicilian, my father would solemnly announce that the criminal undoubtedly came from Carrapipi, a small town in Sicily which — according to my relatives — produced nothing but a population of potential thieves, blackmailers, and murderers. Few of them had ever seen Carrapipi, but the unpleasant experiences they had had with some of its natives were enough to convince them that all Sicilians in the United States found guilty of serious crimes were born in Carrapipi.

My relatives developed a beautiful legend to substantiate this idea. The villain of the piece was a judge in Carrapipi who, in his zeal to save the state the expense of maintaining dangerous criminals in jail for many years, would send them to the United States instead of prison. His tactic was to pronounce a heavy sentence on finding a criminal guilty, and then inform him that a boat was leaving Palermo in a few days for New York. He would then blandly suggest that if the prisoner was found in Italy after the boat left, his sentence would be doubled.

'Naturally,' my Uncle Nino explained whenever he told the story, 'most of the criminals preferred to catch the boat. Going to America, where the streets were said to be lined with gold, certainly seemed more pleasant to them than spending their lives in jail. That pig of a judge, however patriotic his motives were, is undoubtedly to blame for the miserable reputation we Sicilians have in this unhappy land.'

To call anyone *Carrapipanu*, whether or not he actually came from that town, was to insult him, for the name symbolized nearly everything that was villainous or ungracious. One of the most frequent charges made was that a native of Carrapipi could not even speak the Sicilian dialect properly. Instead of saying 'Please come in,' for instance, he would snarl the words — his tongue was likely to be as crooked as his soul — so that the invitation sounded like 'Please do not come in.'

For a long time I believed everything my relatives said about Carrapipi and imagined the town to be an island cut off from civilization and inhabited wholly by desperate characters whose chief ambition was to get to Rochester and prey on the Sicilians there. Joe and I went so far as to draw up careful plans for invading the place with powerful slingshots and rescuing our favorite movie queen from the clutches of the natives. It was a shock to discover a few years later that Carrapipi was a very short distance away from Girgenti, the city where most of my relatives were born, and that the people of Carrapipi considered the natives of Girgenti responsible for the bad reputation Sicilians had here. They had no legend to support their theory, but a nasty little couplet instead which they delighted in repeating every time Girgenti was mentioned:

> Girgenti
> Mal'agente

My feud with the Kaiser might have died a natural death if I had been able to disregard his name-calling, but already the thought that *Siciliano* implied something sinister had become implanted in me by dozens of small incidents and casual remarks.

Even before the Kaiser came along, my father had indicated that there might be some doubt about the good standing of Sicilians, by being on the defensive about them and by forbidding Joe and me to carry knives because of the unpleasant association they had in the public mind with Sicilians. He enforced this rule so thoroughly that we eventually came to accept it as though it were a self-imposed one. And although it prevented us from joining the Boy Scouts, it gave us great satisfaction to tell non-Sicilians who wanted to borrow a knife from us that we never carried one.

My father's edict came on the heels of an episode in our lives which was of such an unpleasant nature that Joe and I were ready to do anything, even accept his ruling, to prevent him from brooding over it too much. The incident involved Donna Maricchia, our Sicilian washerwoman, and her son, Angelo, and it had the effect of making my father worry as to whether or not knifing was a peculiarly Sicilian expedient which had been inherited by his sons from some vicious ancestor he did not know about.

Donna Maricchia probably weighed less than ninety pounds, but she was an excellent washerwoman who attacked dirty clothes with the fury of a hellcat. Constantly angry with her husband or some of her eight children, she seemed to hoard her anger during the week, so that she could release it in a torrent of complaints and curses on the day she washed for us. With each curse she would give the clothes she held in her fists a savage twist, as though she actually had her husband or one of her children in her grasp. The electric washing machine, which eventually supplanted her, was less noisy and not nearly so dramatic.

Joe and I were her best audience because my mother was too busy making certain that Donna Maricchia did her work properly to care what she was saying. When it came to housework, my mother trusted no one, and stubbornly held to the notion that only she could make things clean. Donna Maricchia, who was almost stone deaf, politely pretended to understand my mother's elaborate instructions and then proceeded to do things her own way.

Donna Maricchia had grown up in a town that was only three or four miles from Realmonte, my mother's home town, but her pronunciation was harsher, and her stream of talk more rapid. Her deafness caused her to speak of the most casual matters in a roaring tone of voice. She was always mourning the death of some relative, here or abroad, and never wore anything but black. Joe and I, under the recent influence of some of Grimm's grimmer fairy tales, called her the Witch, and she figured in some of our more remarkable nightmares.

We were less afraid of her son Angelo. He accompanied his mother on all her washing expeditions because she did not trust him out of her sight. Angelo was chubby and a few years older than either of us. Although he would not permit us to play games with him at first, he taught us how to smoke and what to look for in girls and, of course, generally regarded us with contempt because, compared to him, we were such amateurs in worldly matters.

For a long time we hero-worshiped Angelo; then one day we saw his mother give him a wonderful whipping. Her slaps and his yelling could be heard in the next block. Since we had never been accorded such treatment by our parents, it made us feel quite superior to him. From then on, his attitude toward us improved, and it wasn't long before we were playing games with him on a footing that might have been regarded as equal if you didn't know how clever he was at cheating.

One Wednesday when Donna Maricchia had come to do the weekly wash, we quarreled fiercely with Angelo because we caught him trying to cheat us in a very obvious manner. One threat led to another, and in a few minutes we were both pummeling Angelo. As we tried to hold him down and extract from him the promise to 'give up,' he squirmed away and ran to a near-by rock pile. Picking up a large stone, he hurled it at Joe. It struck him just above the eye, making a deep gash which bled immediately and profusely. For a horrible moment I thought he had lost his eye, and I let out a screech that frightened Joe into screaming louder than ever. The screams were even heard by Donna Maricchia, who came running from the kitchen dripping with soapsuds. When she saw the blood, she threw up her hands in despair and sprinted toward Joe, invoking the names of her favorite saints as she ran.

Joe mistook her despair for violence and ran around her into the kitchen, where he locked the door. My

mother was the only one who kept her head.   She caught
him in her arms and led him to the sink.   As she washed
and bandaged the wound, she talked to him quietly and
soothingly until he stopped crying.   But though the bleeding and tears had stopped, his feelings toward Angelo had
developed to a state of determined violence.

'Mother,' he said in a deadly calm voice, 'please give
me the kitchen knife.   I'm going to get even with Angelo.'
The seriousness with which he made this unusual request,
and the hate in his eyes, shocked my poor mother into
tears.   She seldom cried; when she did, she usually tried
to hide her tears from us.   Her unrestrained sobbing
scared both of us, and we felt we had committed some
terrible crime.   Joe's mood changed completely and, as
he begged her to stop crying, he himself burst into tears
again.   It was more than I could bear and I joined in too.
When Donna Maricchia saw us through the kitchen window, the tears were running down both sides of her nose,
and she was begging admittance, and forgiveness for her
son.   Angelo was nowhere in sight.

That evening there was a family council and it was
decided that Donna Maricchia was never to bring Angelo
with her again if she wanted to continue washing clothes
for us.

The discussion centering around Joe's request for the
kitchen knife presented problems that were more difficult
to solve.   My father gave us both a long lecture on the
absurdity of seeking revenge, and blamed us as much as
Angelo for the fight.   That was to be expected, for he
was always threatening to punish us if we got into fights
and got the worst of them.   He never carried out his
threat, but if we came home with stories of fights we had

lost, it was useless to expect any sympathy from him.

In this instance we could see that this fight worried him more than the others. First he wanted to know from Joe where he got the idea of knifing anyone. We were both too scared to attempt any explanation. Worried that we might be acquiring criminal habits from sources about which he did not know, my father persisted with his fiery cross-examination. Because I was the elder, I got the brunt of it, despite my protests that I was not the one who had asked for the knife. There was no relenting on my father's part. He was determined to get to the source of Joe's homicidal rage, but he was even more determined to learn why he had chosen a knife as the weapon. I think he would have felt much better if Joe had asked my mother for a revolver instead.

All through the questioning, Joe preserved the most golden of silences, while I sweated under the glare of my father's eyes. After a while I became panicky and threw caution to the winds. I said the first thing that came to my mind.

'What he was really looking for was a hatchet,' I said brightly. My father frowned and looked interested. My brother gave me a look that meant he would try to beat me up the first chance he got.

My mother said, 'What in the world do you mean?'

I didn't really know, but I found myself saying: 'Well, our teacher told us that Washington used a hatchet to cut down a tree. But we don't have one. I mean we don't have a hatchet. I guess we have plenty of trees,' I finished lamely.

This was all my father wanted to know. Unacquainted with either the cherry tree legend or its beautiful moral, he went into an oratorical rampage and delivered a blistering tirade against the American educational system, polishing it off with his inevitable conclusion that our teachers were 'making pigs' of us. We knew no manners, we had no tact, and now, by the holy God and the sainted Devil, we were being taught to revenge ourselves on people we didn't like by scalping them with hatchets.

Porca miseria! What kind of system was that, pray tell him? And why should he pay taxes for American school-teachers who were no better than murdering savages? Etc., etc. Under the fury of his castigation it would have been futile to talk to him about the father of our country. When he had exhausted himself and his repertoire of blasphemies, we all withdrew in respectful silence, quite convinced that school was a bad place for us. But the next morning my mother was screaming at us to get out of bed at once if we didn't want to be late again.

The incident had far-reaching consequences. It left Joe with a permanent scar over his eye, and it provided my father with a deep concern for the criminal tendencies of his sons as well as a new and lurid justification of his contempt for American schools. And, thanks to my mother's perspicacity, it deprived us of the joy of thrilling to the serial movie we used to follow on Saturday afternoons.

Dissatisfied with my father's analysis of the affair, my mother quizzed me further on the hatchet story. She was obviously relieved to learn that my father had misinterpreted it, and was thoroughly charmed with the full account of Washington and the cherry tree. Then she asked me what movies we had been seeing lately. I had barely begun to warm up to some of the exciting weekly episodes in the life of our favorite hero when she interrupted me, in the very middle of a scene where the hero has his back to the wall and the crooks are creeping up to him with knives in their teeth, and announced that we were not to attend the movies any longer on Saturday afternoons. Hereafter, if we must go to the movies it would be on Friday after supper in the company of my Uncle Luigi, who was a habitual movie-goer.

Life without our Saturday afternoon serial seemed rather dull to us for a while, but we soon began to find the adventures of Theda Bara, Mary Pickford, and William S. Hart just as alluring. I think my mother would have been disconcerted to know that there were just as many characters in those movies who won their arguments by the use of knives.

Family Party

BEFORE THEY BECAME AMERICANIZED ENOUGH
to learn poker, my father and three of my uncles used to
play briscola on Sunday afternoons. It was a fine game
to watch because it was played with partners, and the
rules permit the partners to signal each other throughout
the playing. The more talented the players were, the
more frequent and surreptitious were their signals.

You would have had to go a long way to see a signal
system as complicated as the one my father and Uncle
Nino used. They would tweak their noses, belch, purse
their lips, scratch their heads as though they really had
lice — in fact, go through any gesture, permissible or not
in decent company, that would tell their partner what
cards they held and at the same time confuse their opponents to such an extent that they could not keep their
thoughts straight.

The same partners always played together and were so
familiar with their signal systems that they could talk
about the European War or the high price of food without
ever losing track of the game. Briscola had the added

advantage of being sufficiently complicated that none of the wives sitting around ever knew enough about the game to make slurring remarks when their husbands played recklessly.

The women sat near the card table, sewing and gossiping about the women who were not present, and staring anxiously at their husbands whenever the partners abused each other for mistakes. The men often used invectives that were so loud and so vile that it seemed certain there was going to be a fight. There seldom was. The men would get exhausted after a while trying to outdo each other with blasphemies and go back to their briscola as though nothing had happened.

We children made the most noise, each one trying to surpass the other with earsplitting shrieks. Our only concern was to steer clear of adults who might become irritated enough to cuff us. The disadvantage of playing with children who were related was that any of the mothers sitting within striking distance felt she had the prerogative of delivering stinging slaps with the back of her hand, regardless of whether the target was her own child or not. Of course, if your own mother reached you, the slap was likely to be twice as stinging because she loved you more.

As if our yelling and chasing each other under the table and between adult legs was not enough, there was always Caluzzu, that Verdi fiend of a second cousin who played opera after opera on an asthmatic phonograph. He must have had an extraordinary ear for music, because the blare of the children and the thunderous blasphemy usually coincided with the climax in *Aïda, Il Trovatore,* or

Rigoletto, the operas he favored most. Caluzzu never seemed to hear anything else in the room but the music, and when the clamor was the loudest he would shut his eyes halfway in ecstasy, smile like an idiot, and murmur: 'Beautiful music enchants my soul and lifts it to heaven. My soul is enchanted. Shall I play this plate over again?' He might as well have *been* in heaven for all the attention he got.

Toward sunset, when the wives got hungry and tired of gossiping, they would give due notice that it was time to set the table. Since the same table was used for eating and playing cards, it was a polite way of telling the men to stop their game. After a great deal of skillful procrastination, the men would play their 'last' game and settle their accounts. This was a distinctive moment in our lives because one of the winners would be sure to give us pennies, or someone would drop a coin on the floor. Whenever that happened, one of the men would always say, 'Let the servants have it.' This was a standing joke among my relatives which they had inherited from their fathers and grandfathers, who, like themselves, had never had enough money to afford servants.

The losers would dispatch one of us to the neighboring saloon for a bucket of beer, and the women would spread a white tablecloth over the table and pile it high with fried Italian sausages, *pizza* made with cheese and tomatoes, and fried artichokes if they were in season. Finally there would come a great silence, the silence of hungry people eating tasty food, broken only by the children, whose interest in food was still undeveloped. At such occasions we could hold the center of the stage, for then and only then was it possible to risk the impropriety of speaking at the table while food was being eaten.

Ordinarily, of course, a meal was more than a meal; it was a ritual and only adults were allowed to carry on any conversation. They were the high priests, and if a child dared open his mouth without first being addressed by one of them, it would surely cost him a scolding and possibly a meal. But on Sunday nights speaking during meals was a special dispensation — and we made the most of it. Many of our questions would go unanswered, but we asked them anyway, just for the joy of talking at meals without being reprimanded.

It was futile to expect any intelligent responses until the fruit and coffee were served. Then the men would take out their pipes and cigarettes and deign to talk at us. They talked in adult language, without any regard for our ages. Much of it we could not understand, but it was such a rare privilege hearing them chatting pleasantly, without scolding or dictating, that we listened closely and pretended we understood everything they said. My mother, who saved everything, even the talk of people, could always be counted on the next day to translate the answers they made to our questions.

One Sunday night stands out clearly. That morning, after church, I had again fought the Kaiser because he called me a Sicilian and a few other things less mentionable, and I felt an urgent need to know more about Sicily if I was going to continue taking beatings for it. I wanted to know what the difference was between Sicily and Italy, and whether Sicily was a nation or a city. From the way my relatives usually talked about it, Sicily sounded like

a beautiful park, with farmland around that produced
figs, oranges, pomegranates, and many other kinds of fruit
that refused to grow in Rochester.   The air was perfect
in Sicily, neither cold nor damp as it was in Rochester
most of the time.   The wine tasted better, and you could
pick almonds and olives off the trees.   In the summer the
men strummed guitars and sang in rich tenor voices, and
the women went on picnics in the country.   Everyone was
much happier there.   My Aunt Giovanna claimed it was
because God lived closer to Sicily than he did to America.

'*Santa Maria!*   You mean to tell me you don't know
what Sicily is?'   My Uncle Luigi was shocked by my
question.

'What do they teach you in school, anyway?   At your
age — how old are you, anyway?   Nine?   Why, when I
was nine I knew all about the United States.   Can *you*
name the forty-six states in the Union alphabetically?'

'There are forty-eight states, *Ziu*.'

'There were forty-six when I learned them, and I
learned them right.   Don't contradict me.   Don't they
teach you the meaning of respect in school? . . . Well,'
he rambled, reaching for his snuff, 'Sicily was never as
large as the United States but once it was the world's
garden of culture.   Those were the days before the popes
and priests got a stranglehold on it.   The Greeks, the
Romans, the Saracens, the Normans, and even the Arabs
were among those who planted their seeds in that garden.
From there you came — or rather, your father and mother
did.   One has only to look at your Roman nose, your
Arab complexion, and your Saracen disposition to realize
the truth of what I'm saying.   You, Gerlando Amoroso,

are merely a transplanted seed, and it is too soon yet to tell whether you will bloom ínto a flower or a cucumber.'

'Don't fill the child's head with a lot of nonsense about culture,' said my redheaded Uncle Nino, who was more cultured than any of my relatives. 'Sicily is beautiful, yes. So beautiful, in fact, that I should like nothing better than to return there. But it is also terribly poor. It lies at the end of the Italian boot and some government clique in Rome is always kicking it around. Some Sicilians got tired of that treatment and finally left. That, Gerlando, is the chief reason most of us are in this *maliditta terra,* where we spend our strength in factories and ditches and think of nothing but money. All that journeying and all that work just so that we might live and die with our bellies full.' He dug his fork into another piece of sausage by way of punctuation. As a matter of fact, he had never worked in either a factory or a ditch or done a stroke of hard work, but we were all too polite to point that out to him.

'Your Uncle Nino is right about Sicily's poverty,' my father said. 'Sicily is not far from Rome, only a day or two by slow train, but few Sicilians ever had the money to go there.' He looked sad. 'Most of them have never seen any part of Italy except the town where they were born. Those of us who left for America were luckier; we at least got a glimpse of the city where we embarked. Englishmen and Germans have seen more of Sicily than most Sicilians have.'

'*Ma chi dici!*' Uncle Luigi exploded. 'I often went to Palermo when I was a young man.'

'Yes, but you didn't go out of choice, the way real

travelers go. You went because your inamorata **was** there.'

Uncle Luigi shut up.

'Some day, my son, you will go and see Sicily for your-self,' my father said. 'You will see many lovely women and golden sunsets on a blue sea. You will see olive trees that look as old as the world itself. My father, *bonarma*, once told me that God must have once decided to make Sicily the Garden of Eden and then changed his mind abruptly. You will see what he meant when you go. But you must also expect to see *la miseria*. It is all around like a sickness. Your mother may not like to have me tell you this, but in many parts of Sicily, even in Porto Empe-docle, people are so poor that they will follow a donkey, hoping he will move his bowels, and they will squabble over the manure the moment it hits the earth.'

'You are filling the child's head with a lot of crazy ideas. Sicily is one of the most beautiful lands in the world.' My mother was vehement. No one dared answer her. 'Sicily,' she continued defiantly, 'has fruits and flowers beyond the imagination of Americans and, besides, it is the place where your father and mother were born. Most of us did not have much schooling, but we have as much culture and courtesy as Italians who weren't born in Sicily. Don't forget that.'

My mother could always be depended on for her com-mon sense.

'You won't forget, will you?' she repeated.

'No, I won't,' I promised, lapsing into English.

'Don't speak American to me,' she snapped. 'I don't want to hear anything but Italian in this house. You will

never learn it anywhere else. I don't want *my* children
to grow up into *babbi* who can't speak the language of
their parents.' This rebuke was obviously intended for
her brother Luigi, whose children knew so little Sicilian
that he was seldom able to converse with them.

Uncle Luigi began to squirm in his chair, trying to
decide whether to lose his temper or not. At that point,
my Uncle Nino, who had once gone to the university and
studied diplomacy, changed the conversation by suggesting another round of briscola.

There were seldom less than fifteen men, women, and
children at those Sunday sessions; on the Sundays when it
rained, there would be as many as thirty. It was obvious
that no one else in Mount Allegro had as many relatives
as I did; it was also true that no one else's relatives seemed
to seek one another's company as much as mine did. Sundays or weekdays, they were as gregarious as ants but had
a far more pleasant time. There were always relatives
and friends present or about to arrive. And when they
finally left for the night, they occasionally came back for
a surprise visit which they called a *sirinata*.

On these occasions they brought food, as well as their
mandolins and guitars. They stood under our bedroom
windows and sang gently until some member of the household awoke; and when they saw a light go on their singing became louder and more joyous, breaking into an up-
roarious crescendo as the door was opened to them. The
only neighbors who ever minded were those who were
not Sicilians. The others would call out greetings from
their bedroom windows, obviously hoping that they would
be invited.

The explanations for the serenades were invariably the same: 'There were so many stars out tonight that it seemed a pity to go to bed,' or, 'So-and-so couldn't get to sleep and thought you might enjoy a little music.' It was unnecessary apologizing because everyone was very happy to see each other again, after an interim of almost two hours, but my relatives could always be counted on to observe the amenities, especially when they seemed most unnecessary.

Since there were never any rules against children's staying up as long as they wished, we joined these revelries. It was impossible to sleep anyway. The joking and the singing of our elders were too much to resist, and we sat on the edges of the room in our nightshirts watching them solemnly, a little shocked to discover that they could be as noisy and carefree as we could. Those with good voices sang mournful solos about love and death; the relatives with ordinary voices sang bawdy ditties that made the women giggle and the children blush, even though we understood only an occasional double-en-tendre.

The party was punctuated by my father's trips to the wine cellar, and his emergence with more wine and a new set of amazing puns. Every half-hour or so one of the women would dutifully remark that it was getting late, whereupon my father would shush her with the proposal for another drink and another song. Finally, even he be-came tired and the company would start saying good-bye. These farewells were as lingering as the death scene in an opera, and were couched in such terms of endearment that no one could possibly suspect that these same persons would be seeing each other again in a couple of days, if not sooner.

D. H. Lawrence, who lived among Sicilians, once said that Sicilians 'never leave off being amorously friendly with almost everybody, emitting a relentless physical familiarity that is quite bewildering. . . . They hang together in clusters and can never be physically near enough.' He was writing of Sicilians in Sicily, but he might as well have been writing about my Sicilian relatives here. Where they derived their magnificent talent for gregariousness and their pathetic dread of being alone is hard to say.

My most learned uncle, Nino, who had never heard of D. H. Lawrence, believed there was something abnormal about people who were not so gregarious as Sicilians. My Great-Uncle Minicuzzu, who drank a quart of wine a day and lived to be eighty-seven, explained it all on the ground that 'Misery loves company. The people of Sicily had such a miserable time for so many centuries that they naturally acquired the habit of consoling each other. *Bedda Maria*, what better means of consolation are there than people and wine? Will you have a glass with me?'

A sociologist once wrote that it was living on a volcanic island that made Sicilians crave each other's company. All I know is that my relatives seemed happiest when they were crowded in a stuffy room noisy with chatter and children. Their passion for human company probably accounted for their relentless urge to produce children (even when they already had more than they could support properly) and the deep pity they expressed for parents who only had one or two.

When their children were infants, they could hardly wait for them to grow into adults who would drink and eat with them, and in their impatience to see them grow, they would feed them bits of spaghetti and, sometimes, sips of wine on the remarkable theory that wine-drinking not only stimulated the appetite but actually created blood. 'Vivi, figlio mio,' a mother would urge her youngest child. 'U vinu ti fa sangu.'

Only the family clannishness of my Jewish playmates approached that of my relatives. Yet, whereas my Jewish friends were content to see their relatives occasionally, my relatives were constantly seeking each other out to celebrate the existence of one another. The cult of American individualism eventually dampened their exuberance, but when they were still untouched by the refrigerating social habits of those foreigners, l'Americani, almost any event was the signal for family festivities.

There were so many relatives that it was physically impossible to make the gatherings complete, but they took place frequently and there was always a careful account made of those not invited, so that they would not be left out the next time.

The impossibility of getting all the relatives together under one roof (except at weddings celebrated in huge halls) sometimes resulted in bitter family quarrels. Some relative would decide to take offense because he had not been invited to a family gathering and the quarrel would be on. The chances were that it would continue over a long period of months and get increasingly worse, eventually reaching the point where no one could recall the original cause of the quarrel and everyone would offer dozens of reasons to prove that it was entirely justified and should probably go on forever.

But it was far less painful to see a quarrel continue than to watch the antics of some relative who would decide that God had chosen him to negotiate a peace between the two parties. This self-appointed busybody, who considered himself neutral but was thoroughly disliked by nearly everyone, operated most successfully at such important events as births, weddings, or deaths. Funerals were by far the most ideal occasions for peace negotiations. The negotiator could take advantage of the solemnity of such occasions, without the slightest opposition, to employ such propaganda as, 'We are here today, gone tomorrow,' or, 'The moral of living is clear. We should all be dear friends while we are still here to enjoy life. Who knows what will follow?'

If he found he was getting nowhere with such moralizing, the negotiator would approach each of the quarreling parties separately with such a speech as, 'Just a few days before he died, our dear departed relative, *bonarma*, told me how grieved he was to learn that you and So-and-So had not patched up your little quarrel yet. He made me promise that I would try to bring you two together. A promise is a promise. I know you will feel much better once you have embraced each other.'

Everyone present knew that the deceased, not caring a fig whether the quarrelers made up or not, had made no such declaration. But in deference to the respect they had for any relative who died, it would be accepted as the gospel truth. No one in his right mind would have dared refute a quotation attributed to a dying man; that

would only be tempting God.   If my Aunt Giovanna was
about when the peace negotiator was at work, she could
always be depended on to assert that what he said was
true.   From the number of conversations she claimed to
have had with dying persons, I got the impression that
no one would think of dying without first discussing his
problems with her.

When finally effected, a reconciliation would result in
another reunion, a noisy celebration of the peace where
the risk of not inviting some other sensitive relative would
again be incurred.

Most quarrels added to the zest of living.   They provided a subject of conversation that was far more stimulating than the news and more diverting than the weather.
And they divided my relatives into two and often three
factions.   The third faction ostensibly sympathized with
the two who were *rifridati* (cooled) but could be counted
on to sprinkle enough salt on the wounds to keep the
quarrel alive.   The quarrels used to remind me of the
gang wars we played on the block, except that none of my
relatives ever had anything more than his sensibilities
hurt.

The chief fighting techniques used were gossip, snubbing, and hospitality.   When the *rifridati* accidentally
met at some gathering, they carefully avoided each other
and left as quickly as possible; and if conversation was
forced on them, it was conducted with exaggerated po-
liteness.   The most difficult technique to combat was
hospitality.   I was once the victim of that kind of treach-
ery when my parents were *rifridati* with their cousin Don
Antonio Ricotta and his family.

Don Antonio met me one day on my way home from school and after greeting me most effusively, invited me to stop by his house and have some ice-cream with his children. Having an abnormal passion for ice-cream, I finally accepted his invitation and spent more than an hour in his parlor being deluged with attention and two kinds of ice-cream. It was all I could do to tear myself away and, before I left, Don Antonio and his wife made me promise to come back again soon.

By an unlucky slip of the tongue I mentioned the ice-cream I had eaten at Don Antonio's house when my mother asked me why I wasn't hungry. The reaction was horrifying. My father called me an imbecile. My mother screamed some fierce Sicilian invectives at me which I had never heard. Even my Aunt Giovanna, who usually sided with me and was always saying, quite affectionately, that I must be an angel because I had such small buttocks, was plainly disgusted. By letting my scheming relatives shower me with hospitality I had done nothing less than permit the family's honor to be besmirched.

My behavior was that of a traitor, my father claimed, and he promised to give me the beating of my life if he ever found out I went anywhere near Don Antonio's house again. My cousins were nothing but treacherous villains to take advantage of an innocent fool like me, but at my age I should have known better. The storm lasted nearly a week, and during all that time I could hardly bear the thought of ice-cream.

As bitter as these quarrels were, the inevitable reconciliations seemed to inspire the most quarrelsome of relatives with a greater love for each other than ever before.

As soon as there was peace, there was an overwhelming desire, on both sides, to make up for the long separation. Some
of the longest and finest meals I have ever eaten were the
results of quarrels that had recently been settled.

Some of these post-war manifestations of affection took a
very practical turn. My father, who was an excellent
plumber, carpenter, paperhanger, cook, and pastrymaker,
would offer his former enemy free services in any of his
fields. He made the offer with great delicacy, of course, so
that his motives would not appear too obvious. When
visiting a relative with whom he had recently declared
peace, he would casually call the host's attention to the
cracks in the wallpaper or to a door that needed fixing,
and volunteer to do the necessary work. In all likelihood
the relative would be a mason by trade, for that was the
trade of most of my relatives, and the next time he visited
our home he, in turn, would casually make some suggestion for improving the sidewalk or the driveway and offer
his services. None of the offers made in this spirit were
ever turned down for fear of causing offense and starting
another quarrel.

The most painful estrangement that ever took place was
between my father and my Uncle Nino. It resulted from
an incident that frightened Joe and me so much that we
were sick for several days thinking about it. We were
playing cops and robbers in the yard with our friend
Tony Long, while my father was in the cellar rubbing the
sides of his wine barrel with the leaves of a mysterious
plant that would prevent his new wine from going sour.
I didn't want to play cop any longer and we were arguing

about that when we heard my Uncle Nino coming up the street. His red hair shot out in a dozen different directions like long sparks. He was running part of the way, and he was shrieking blasphemies at the top of his lungs.

All this, except the blaspheming, was very surprising. My Uncle Nino was a man who took his time about things. He was against hurrying, on principle, and never bought a car because he could never see the logic of getting anywhere quickly. Also, whatever his other faults might be, he was not a drunkard and never drank more than three glasses of wine at a time. Joe, who was Uncle Nino's godson, knew immediately that something was drastically wrong.

'Pop,' he yelled, 'Uncle Nino is coming up the street and he's running!' That was enough to get my father out of the wine cellar and up the trapdoor leading into the kitchen.

When Uncle Nino came rushing into the yard, he was still screaming foul words against God and the Virgin Mary. 'Where is your father? I'm going to teach him a lesson.' The question was directed at me but I was too frightened to say anything. I was always frightened when any of my relatives lost his temper completely because they had never been taught to fight with their fists and it was hard to tell what they would do. Moreover, Uncle Nino was much taller and broader than my father.

'He's not home,' Joe lied.

Uncle Nino gave him a blank look and went toward the kitchen door. Joe and I tried to close in on him but he brushed us aside. We followed him inside. My father was at the sink washing his hands.

'*Porca Maria!* I'm going to teach you a lesson you won't forget,' Uncle Nino yelled at him. With that, he reached for a flatiron sitting on the window-sill. My father watched him, paralyzed with amazement. He had been with my uncle only a few hours before and they had been perfectly friendly. He watched my Uncle Nino as though he were in a trance.

Joe, fortunately, had all his wits about him. He realized something was wrong with his godfather but he also sensed that my father was in danger. As Uncle Nino lifted the flatiron with a motion to hurl it at my father, Joe sprang into action. He tackled my uncle from behind like a football player, yelling at the same time: 'Gerry, help me! Tony, get the cops!'

We both fell on my uncle as he tried to get up on his feet. But he shook Joe and me off like flies and reached again for the flatiron, which had fallen near by. By this time my father had regained his senses. While Joe was tackling him again, my father grabbed Uncle Nino's arm and tried to pull his fingers off the handle of the flatiron. It was futile; they were clasped around it like iron braces. Then the three of us piled on him. While I pulled at his hair and Joe grabbed his head in a stranglehold so that he couldn't bite, my father managed to get him down to the floor.

'Get me the clothesline,' my father said as we all sat on him. I knew exactly where it was and got it for him. My father wound the cord around my uncle's wrists, then around his ankles. In a few minutes, my poor uncle was completely helpless.

'What in Christ's name has happened to you?' my father

asked. His shirt was nearly all torn off and he was still breathing hard. My uncle only stared at him, as though he were a perfect stranger, and said nothing. I felt sorry for both of them and wanted to cry. We all felt badly when we saw the policeman coming up the walk. My father greeted him at the front door.

'Sorry we bodder you, Mr. Polissaman. Everything o.k. now. My friend doan know what she do. Now she o.k.'

After the policeman went away, my father told us to untie Uncle Nino. He did not say a word while we worked on my father's complicated knots. When he was free, he rubbed his wrists to get the blood circulating again and looked at us as though to say, 'What happened?' Instead he muttered, 'I'm going home now.' My father had his back turned to him and made no comment.

When my mother came home we were in the kitchen trying to figure out Uncle Nino's behavior. 'Your brother-in-law tried to kill me with your flatiron,' my father said. 'He probably would have succeeded if it hadn't been for your sons.'

My mother was horrified and burst into tears while we were telling her the details. 'Oh, my poor sister, my poor sister,' she kept repeating, meaning Uncle Nino's wife Giovanna. Then she dried her tears and prepared a drink with rhubarb in it, which she insisted the three of us take so that we wouldn't suffer any ill effects from the fright. In spite of the rhubarb drink, Joe lost the next three meals he ate and, within a few days, I broke out with boils.

According to Aunt Giovanna, my uncle remembered nothing of his attack on my father. After he got home, he asked her to prepare him some spaghetti with oil and garlic sauce, and then went to bed. He woke her during the night, complaining of sharp pains. My aunt sent for a doctor. It developed that for several weeks Uncle Nino had been unable to urinate properly. The undischarged urine had poisoned his system and brought on the fit of insanity. The doctor claimed that a few more days of the poison would have driven Uncle Nino permanently mad.

When all this was explained to my father he said: 'I am sorry for him, but I can't have him in my house again. How do I know that he will not have another mad fit? Besides, why was it that he turned against *me* in his madness? Surely he must have had some venom in his system for me, besides the venom found by the doctor.'

This pronouncement left my mother and my Aunt Giovanna in tears. With Uncle Nino exiled, it meant that the two sisters could not see each other every day as they had. In view of my father's stand, my mother did not dare go to Aunt Giovanna's house; she in turn was instructed by Uncle Nino, who had taken offense at my father's attitude, not to come to our house. The sisters met secretly at the home of relatives, at first to console each other, then to plot a peace offensive. It was not an easy peace to plot. My father was so much in the right that no ordinary tactics would do. A funeral might have been useful then, but it was a particularly healthy period in the lives of my relatives, and the sisters did not have the patience to wait for Nature to take its course.

They finally decided to enlist the services of Vittorio Marini, a man in his thirties who was admired by both my uncle and my father. Vittorio, who was distantly related to both of them, was the proprietor of a successful shoe-repair shop. Whenever any of my relatives wanted to cite a model man they named Vittorio Marini and told how, virtually on a shoestring, he had set up a shop in a totally American neighborhood and after two years built up a clientèle of such proportions that he employed two assistants, who spoke English flawlessly. Whenever he visited us we would greet him with joy, for it meant that he was willing to take time off from making money just to sit and talk with us. A better choice of a peace nego-tiator could hardly have been made.

The instructions Vittorio received were most explicit. In a few days he was to drop in after supper on the pre-text that he happened to be near Mount Allegro deliver-ing a pair of shoes to a customer. After he had chatted pleasantly with my father for about a half-hour, he was suddenly to become very serious and use all his powers of persuasion in convincing my father that he should for-give Uncle Nino. As soon as my father was won over, they were to adjourn to Vittorio's house, where Uncle Nino would be waiting for both of them with some of Vittorio's own fine wine to seal the reconciliation. In return for all this, my mother and my Aunt Giovanna promised Vittorio they would say a dozen prayers apiece to Saint Joseph (with whom they had considerable influence); this would, of course, help ensure Vittorio a place in heaven.

On the evening of the peace offensive my mother used all the tricks she knew to put my father in a good humor. For supper she served his favorite fish dish, boiled squid soaked in lemon juice, and for dessert she brought out her

best peach preserves.   To make certain his mood would
be mellow, she broke one of her strictest rules and suggested that we drink a bottle of his five-year-old wine
'before it spoiled.'   This was an extraordinary concession,
for she usually guarded those bottles of old wine as though
they were gold, and only permitted them to be used on
rare occasions, like births and weddings, and in times of
illness to drink with raw eggs and other unpleasant foods
difficult to take alone.   Then, to amuse him, she gossiped
about the two old Sicilian women who lived on our street
across the way from each other.

Donna Nunziata was nearly ninety but looked much
younger than Donna Michela, who was seventy-five.
Both of them were intensely superstitious, and both were
fond of my mother and often confided in her.   Suspicious of one another, each old lady was convinced that
the other possessed the 'evil eye.'   That morning both
Donna Michela and Donna Nunziata complained to my
mother of severe headaches and insisted they were caused
by the evil eye of the other.   My mother suggested to
each one that a pair of glasses might prevent the headaches, but they had both ridiculed the idea as American
nonsense and Donna Michela pointed out that her mother,
who was more fortunate in her neighbors, lived to be a
hundred and two without ever wearing glasses or complaining of headaches.   The two old ladies were particularly afraid of each other on Fridays because that was the
day when the Devil operated most efficiently.

Vittorio arrived at that point in her gossip.   My mother
moved the men to the front room, away from the noise of
the dishwashing, and served them with another bottle of

old wine. My father seemed delighted at Vittorio's visit and kept plying him with more wine.

When a half-hour had passed, my mother gave up her dishwashing to eavesdrop on their conversation. They were comparing their wine-making techniques and Vittorio was divulging a secret formula for making alcohol out of the grape stems. At the end of another half-hour, she heard my father giving Vittorio the details of a secret formula for making a fine Italian cordial known as *Caffe Sport.* At the end of two hours Vittorio was telling my father about some of the beautiful American blondes who came to his shop to have their soles fixed.

When after three hours they were still talking on the same subject, my mother lost her patience. As soon as my father went down to the wine cellar for another bottle, she summoned Vittorio into the kitchen.

'*Ma como fini?*' she demanded. 'Have you forgotten what you came for?'

'I came, *cara Zia Margarita,* because I happened to be in the neighborhood delivering a pair of shoes to a customer and I thought how pleasant it would be to pay *Lu Ziu Peppino* and his family a visit.' His eyes were dancing brightly. She could not tell whether that was from the wine or the talk about the American blondes.

'But have you forgotten what you were to tell him about Nino? There is your *Ziu Nino* waiting at your house. What will he think?'

It was obvious that Vittorio had forgotten all about his mission and about Uncle Nino, but he would not dare admit that. 'How could I possibly forget, *cara Zia?*' he asked with a deep sigh. 'I have only been waiting for the

golden moment. After all, *Zia Margarita,* this is a most
delicate matter you and *Zia Giovanna* have asked me to
handle.' He was about to deliver an oration on the delicacy of the matter when my father's footsteps were heard
on the cellar stairway.

'Now, Vittorio, you will taste a wine you will never forget. God took a personal interest in the keg where this
came from. Where is your glass?'

After fixing Vittorio with a hard stare, which clearly
stated that the 'golden moment' had better come along
soon, my mother withdrew. Around midnight the two
men came reeling out of the living-room.

'We,' my father announced importantly, 'are going to
Vittorio's house to taste some of his wine. I don't imagine
you would be interested in coming along,' he added hopefully.

'Your husband has a beautiful talent for making wine,
Zia Margarita,' Vittorio was saying, 'but I want him to
taste some of my own wine.'

As they were going out the door Vittorio, conscience-
stricken by my mother's angry eyes, turned and stage-
whispered, 'The golden moment is about to come.'

About three in the morning there were heavy footsteps
on the porch. My mother, who had not been able to
sleep from worry because it was most unusual for my
father to stay out late at night, went downstairs and be-
held her husband with a beatific smile all over his face
and one arm over the shoulders of my Uncle Nino! Torn
between the desire to lose her temper and the desire to
laugh with relief, she began to scold both of them roundly.
Uncle Nino, who was quite sober, apologetically explained
the circumstances.

He had waited until midnight; then, having despaired of seeing Vittorio or my father, was about to go home when he saw both of them looping up the street. Vittorio was saying, 'I am waiting for the golden moment' and my father was saying, 'Everything comes to him who waits.' This dialogue, my uncle explained, continued all evening. Neither of them paid much attention to him, except to offer him wine, which he refused.

About two in the morning Vittorio fell on his bed in a heap and Uncle Nino took off his clothes and put a sheet over him. Then he turned to my father and said, 'I can't very well take you home until you have forgiven me for that crazy thing I did to you a few weeks ago which, I swear to you, I can't remember.' And my father stopped saying, 'Everything comes to him who waits' long enough to say, 'I'm perfectly capable of going home by myself but I forgive you, though it is difficult for me to believe that you can't remember the incident.' Then they both shook hands and had a glass of wine together. As they were leaving Vittorio turned over on his bed and said, 'I am waiting for the golden moment,' and then went to sleep again.

The most pleasant thing about the incident was that my father remembered all its important details the next day. As for Vittorio, I don't know whether my mother and my aunt ever prayed to Saint Joseph in his behalf. My guess is that Saint Joseph got most of the credit for the reconciliation.

Mr. Michelangelo's Spite Wall

MOST OF MY RELATIVES LIVED IN ONE NEIGH-borhood, not more than five or six blocks from each other. That was about as far apart as they could live without feeling that America was a desolate and lonely place. If it could have been managed, they probably would have lived under one roof. My Uncle Luigi was the only rene-gade; he lived several miles away. My relatives bravely accepted that fact, explaining to each other that, after all, Luigi was a non-conformist and a Baptist.

As numerous as my relatives were, the neighborhood never became known as 'Little Italy,' for the simple reason that the Jews and the Poles by far outnumbered the Italians. The Jews outnumbered everyone else. At one time I had so many Jewish playmates that one of them told my mother I must have been left on her doorstep by a Jewish mother. My dear mother hurled a broom at him for that, not because she was anti-Semitic but because I was her eldest son, her pride and joy.

'Mount Allegro' was the nickname my relatives gave the neighborhood. They liked the sound of it and, even though it was an exaggeration of the topography of the place, it served to express their affection for older neighbors like Mr. and Mrs. Michelangelo who were born in the Sicilian hill town of that name. Uncle Nino, who was sometimes a stickler for accuracy, was the only one who ever objected to the nickname. When he was feeling low he insisted the neighborhood should be known as Purgatory, and when he was cheerful he tried to promote the name Macaroni Town. Neither of these ever became as popular as Mount Allegro.

There were no commercial establishments on the street we lived on — but all the turbulence of the city could be heard and smelled from it. There was a large and roaring laundry less than a half-block away. Two blocks away the biggest optical company in the world sat on the grimy banks of the Genesee River drawing sustenance from its dirtied waters. When the wind was blowing in the direction of our street, you breathed the stench of the river and the smoke of the factory. The wind had a great affinity for the direction of our street.

Sometimes, at night, the sickly yellow glow of the factory was in the sky like a smouldering ceiling of sulphur. Underneath it my relatives sang and played guitars and, if they noticed the sky at all, they were reminded of the lemon groves in Sicily. They were stubborn poets.

Scattered through Mount Allegro was the buzzing and whirring of several tailor factories. From some of them I lugged home half-finished coats and suits for my mother to sew on. 'You aren't strong enough to work in a factory,' the doctor had said. So my mother worked at home.

The blackest smoke of all came from the direction of

the New York Central Station; a five-minute walk from our house. At night it sounded closer when I listened to the sad locomotive whistles and the endless freight cars grumbling their way through the dark.

We lived near the center of the block, a few feet away from a large street light. The boys in Mount Allegro liked to gather under the light to argue and play games, regardless of the time of day or night. But we had to fight for our place under the light. A rival gang of boys living at one end of the block tried to make it their meeting place too. We fought them by day and night, with stones, snowballs, and fists. The Kaiser was the leader of the rival gang. Tony Long was our leader. The most satisfactory victory we ever won was on the day the Kaiser's mother was giving a lawn party. We pulled an eminently successful surprise attack with stones that found several ice-cream-and-cake targets.

Most of the neighbors who lived around the street light were well disposed toward our gang. There was Mr. Lorenzo, who came from the same Sicilian town my mother did. Mr. Lorenzo grew the most beautiful flowers in Mount Allegro; he could make anything bloom. His wife worked in a tailor factory, and when she had saved a few hundred dollars she sent them to her brother Remo in Caltanissetta and invited him to come to America. Remo was a plump little man, who dressed like a dandy and never passed a pretty girl on the street without giving her a hopeful backward glance.

Remo lived with the Lorenzos for a few months; then he caught the Hollywood itch and decided that what this country needed most of all was a shorter and plumper

Valentino. As soon as he had earned enough money for the fare, he went to Los Angeles and enrolled in a dramatic school. About once a month he mailed his sister a new photograph of himself, dressed as a matador, a sheik, a cowboy, and finally an Indian. No pictures arrived after the Indian one, and the next thing we heard was that he had married an Assyrian girl and was working as a waiter in a Chinese restaurant.

A few doors away lived Mr. Bernstein, an Austrian Jew, who went mad the day Austria entered the war and paced his yard every day for more than a year ranting against the Emperor Franz Joseph.

Next to him lived some distant cousins of my father, Rosario Alfano and his wife Donna Rosalia. She was a morose woman who looked much older than her years, but Rosario was one of our favorite relatives. He liked to have us call him Rosario, and when we called him Don Rosario he would pretend to wince with pain. Donna Rosalia was always dressed in mourning for some relative or other and insisted that her husband wear black neckties and black hats. He did not object, but he wore his black hats at such a rakish angle that no one would ever have suspected he was mourning for anyone.

Donna Rosalia talked incessantly about the refined life she had led in Girgenti and about the horrors of living in America, where she had to associate with a lot of *cafoni*. She worked in a canning factory and Rosario in a shoe-repair shop. Like my Uncle Nino, they both dreamed of the day when they could go back to Sicily. Every week they set aside some money for their steamship fare and some to send to Girgenti, where it could be converted into lire and saved for them until they returned. The difficulty was that Donna Rosalia was always imagining she was afflicted with a horrible disease and spending most of their savings on doctors' bills.

The gang's best friends lived across the street. They were Mr. Michelangelo and Mr. Solomon, the oldest men on the street. Both of them had the admiration and respect of all the children in the block. They lived next door to each other. Mr. Michaelangelo may have been a little more popular because he owned a horse and wagon and was always glad to give us rides.

Mr. Solomon looked like a happy wizard. He was a giant of a man with a long white beard and he always wore the black skullcap of the Orthodox Jew. We were lucky he was orthodox because on Saturday mornings he would give one of the gentile kids (depending on whose turn it was) a nickel merely for lighting his gas jet. He could have had our unstinted admiration just for that, but in addition he was patient whenever we prattled to him. You could tell by the way he stooped down to listen that he was honestly interested in what we had to say. Mr. Solomon and Mr. Michelangelo were great friends and spent many hours together. None of us could ever understand this since Mr. Michelangelo spoke no English and Mr. Solomon no Italian. But they must have developed some means of conversation, for no two men could listen to one another as politely as they did without understanding each other.

On the other side of Mr. Michelangelo's house lived an old woman, the gang's worst enemy. Mr. Michelangelo, though he didn't know any English, often came to our rescue when we got into difficulties with her, which was almost every time we played a softball game. If we were playing anywhere near her yard, the Enemy watched us from a slit in her window shutters, which were kept closed winter and summer. The moment the ball fell over the fence into her yard, the old woman would dart out from the house with amazing speed, pick up the ball, and curse us. Mr. Michelangelo would appear, shaking his fist at her and demanding in eloquent Sicilian that the ball be returned to us. She would then beat a hasty retreat to her front room and continue the curses through the shutters.

She was obviously frightened of Mr. Michelangelo but she never gave up a single ball. Mr. Michelangelo called her *la Strega* (the Witch); influenced by the propaganda of the times, the gang referred to her as the Enemy or the German, even after we learned that she was a Canadian.

One afternoon we started a softball game in front of the street light. We were using a brand-new ball which represented all the pennies the gang had been able to hoard for a month. For this reason we were being cautious and hitting away from the direction of the old woman's house. In the very first inning Abe Rappaport foul-tipped the ball viciously and sent it into the middle of the Enemy's lawn. I was playing catch. As soon as I saw where the ball was going, I hurdled the Enemy's fence, picked up the ball, and was about to jump back into the street again when the blow of a leather strap over my shoulders sent me spinning backward.

It was the Enemy. She had seen me running toward

the fence and had come after me with a heavy black strap. Before I could stop her, she landed another blow across my face. Screaming with pain and anger, I grabbed the old woman by the wrists and twisted them so hard that the strap dropped from her fingers. By this time Mr. Solomon, who had witnessed the scene, and the gang came running to my rescue. The Enemy ran into the house, leaving the black strap behind.

Horrified by the deep welt across my face, my mother insisted on calling the police. By the time an officer arrived, Mr. Michelangelo had returned home from an errand and been told what had happened. While the policeman was trying to get into the Enemy's house, Mr. Michelangelo was in his back yard hurling Sicilian blasphemies into her kitchen window. After a long time the Enemy's spinster daughter responded to the policeman's knocking, and he disappeared into the house. When he came out a few minutes later, Mr. Michelangelo gave him a long harangue about the innumerable and insufferable sins of the old lady, quite oblivious of the fact that the policeman could not understand a word he said. He ended his speech with the supplication that she be taken away and electrocuted.

The policeman reported to my mother that he had reprimanded the old lady and also threatened to arrest her the next time she assaulted anyone. He added that if my mother wished, she could swear out a warrant for her arrest. But by this time the welt on my face showed signs of disappearing and my mother, peace-loving woman that she was, decided she did not want anyone arrested.

We had no trouble with the Enemy after that, but Mr.

Michelangelo's resentment against the old lady rapidly gained momentum. He finally announced that he could no longer bear the sight of the Witch, and one autumn morning began to erect a brick wall between his house and hers. Every day while the wall was going up, the old lady cursed Mr. Michelangelo and threatened him with the law. But apparently there was nothing the law could do about it, and the wall continued to grow with wonderful speed.

Some of the neighbors, including my father, tried to discourage Mr. Michelangelo, pointing out that he was shutting off one side of his house from the sunlight. 'I'll paint my side of the wall white and that will help some. I'll feel better when the wall is up,' he said grimly. 'I'm tired of the *Strega* and if I had to see her every day I might do something I'd regret later on. Do you know that every time I see her I lose my appetite?'

In two weeks' time the brick wall was up and painted, a strong, white monument to the old man's dislike for the old woman. The monument had the approval of all the kids in the block. Some of us took pride in the fact that we had helped Mr. Michelangelo mix the mortar.

Our street was no more than four hundred yards long. When we first moved into it, it was as beautiful and as restful as a country lane. Grass and tall comfortable trees softened the hardness of the cemented walk. Cherry and apple trees bloomed easily and in the spring the smell of lilacs was everywhere. There were fewer houses then and their wide yards stretched far back from the sidewalks.

We were as poor as the others, but my mother was a

better manager than most people and knew how to combine the expert advice of Mr. Lorenzo with the brute strength of her husband and her sons. In the back yard she grew tomatoes, from which she made *astrattu*. The front yard she filled with a sea of roses, which bloomed as early as May and as late as November — a triumph over Nature, considering the weather of Rochester. Although some of my relatives scoffed at the idea of wasting so much land and energy on a plant that could not be eaten, they made the garden their favorite meeting place in warm weather.

There were only three other flower gardens in the block that could compare. Mr. Lorenzo's was the most elaborate and would have won first prize in a contest. Not far from his house were the pansy and tulip beds of a merry Italian couple from Rome. Theirs was a small garden, but they owned a parrot which screeched '*Viva Garibaldi!*' at you as you passed by, and that helped draw your attention to the flowers.

The only other outstanding flower garden on the block belonged to an old man who was known to my relatives as *lu vecchio Americano*. He had lived on the street long before the Sicilians, the Poles, and the Jews moved in, and he obviously resented their intrusion. There was a high fence around his property and he seldom deigned to say hello to any of his neighbors. When we played games near his house, he stared at us and growled, though he was never as mean as the Enemy.

My relatives did not like him, chiefly because he made it so plain that he had no love for them. They found fault with the flowers he grew because they said they were like those that you plant over graves. When they heard that he was a factory boss who would never hire anyone with an Italian name, they were happy because they now had a good reason for disliking him.

As they sat in the garden, under the shade of our dying apple tree, they sometimes talked of their dislike. In time the old man grew into a symbol of the factory. When they had complaints about their working conditions or their foremen, they used the old man as a target for their jibes. 'My boss is as bad as *lu vecchio Americano*,' they would begin, and then they would tell you why. There were bosses who took advantage of your inability to speak English. There were bosses who made the days hell for you because they got to dislike you for reasons they never explained. In any case, a boss was a hard fellow to like because on him rested the decision as to whether or not you would be laid off during the slack season or told to find yourself another job.

Mr. Michelangelo, who liked my relatives almost as much as he did his own, was present at some of these discussions. One afternoon, when my relatives were talking about the old man, he said that 'All bosses are not alike.' Then he surprised everyone by revealing that for a short time he had been the boss of a Sicilian sulphur mine. He hastened to add that he had never permitted himself to forget that he had been an ordinary worker.

'I always tried to help my men, even at the risk of losing my job,' he said. 'Whenever a worker was killed in the mines — and that happened every week or so — I tried to make it appear that it had not been his fault, so that his family would receive the insurance money. It wasn't an easy thing to do, but it was the least that could be done for their poor families. After a while I became very unpopular with the mine-owners and they fired me because they said I didn't have their interests at heart. My wife told me I was a damn fool for worrying about others and not looking after my own skin. But you know the way women are.'

My Aunt Giovanna, who was one of the few of my Sicilian elders who ever went to church every Sunday, tried to defend *lu vecchio Americano* on the ground that he went to Mass regularly. But no one took that argument seriously because they considered themselves better Christians than the old man, even though they seldom went to church. Uncle Nino pointed out that the more guilt a man had on his conscience, the more often he was obliged to attend church. Mr. Michelangelo contributed the information that nearly all the bosses he had ever known went to church every Sunday.

One morning the old man died of a heart attack on his way to work. That put an end to my relatives' bitter discussions about him, though his widow continued his policy of snubbing them. My relatives hardly ever mentioned the old man after his funeral. And when they did, they used the expression *bonarma* after his name, to show their respect for the dead.

Talking American

MY FATHER COULD BE MORE SEVERE THAN MY
mother, but usually he was gentle with us and even con-
spired with us occasionally when we tried to avoid some
of the household rules my mother laid down. Probably
the most repugnant rule of all was that we eat everything
she cooked for us, regardless of whether or not we liked
the food or were hungry.

Unless my father protested, she persistently fed us
verdura, in the interests of health, usually dandelion or
escarole or some other bitter member of the vegetable
family. The more we complained about such dishes the
more convinced she became that they were good for us.
She was without mercy about such things. If one of us
dared protest while we were at the table, she would inflict
a second helping on him. In time, we learned the wisdom of pretending to look fairly enthusiastic about everything she cooked for us, regardless of how distasteful it
seemed.

Another unpopular rule she vigorously enforced was
that we speak no other language at home but that of our

parents. Outside the house she expected us to speak English, and often took pride in the fact that we spoke English so well that almost none of our relatives could understand it. Any English we spoke at home, however, was either by accident or on the sly. My sister Maria, who often talked in her sleep, conducted her monologues in English, but my mother forgave her on the ground that she could not be responsible for her subconscious thoughts.

My mother's insistence that we speak only Italian at home drew a sharp line between our existence there and our life in the world outside. We gradually acquired the notion that we were Italian at home and American (whatever that was) elsewhere. Instinctively, we all sensed the necessity of adapting ourselves to two different worlds. We began to notice that there were several marked differences between those worlds, differences that made Americans and my relatives each think of the other as foreigners.

The difference that pained me most was that of language, probably because I was aware of it most often. Child that I was, I would feel terribly embarrassed whenever my mother called to me in Italian while I was playing on the street, with all my playmates there to listen; or when she was buying clothes for me and would wrangle in broken English with the salesmen about the price.

My mother took no notice of such childish snobbery. As long as I remained under her jurisdiction, she continued to cling to her policy of restricting the family language to Italian. 'I might as well not have my children if I can't talk with them,' she argued. She considered it sinful for relatives to permit their children to speak a language which the entire family could not speak fluently, and claimed that if she were to cast aside Italian, the language of her forefathers, it would be like renouncing her own flesh and blood.

There was only one possible retort to these arguments but no one dared use it: the language we called Italian and spoke at home was not Italian. It was a Sicilian dialect which only Sicilians could understand. I seldom heard proper Italian spoken, except when my Uncle Nino made speeches or when one of my relatives would meet an Italian or another Sicilian for the first time. Proper Italian sounded like the melody of church bells and it was fresh and delicate compared to the earthy sounds of the dialect we spoke. Yet it was hard to understand how two persons could carry on an honest conversation in a language so fancy.

My Uncle Nino claimed that Italian was 'feminine' and Sicilian 'masculine.' He also said that the only reason Sicilians ever addressed each other in proper Italian was to show off their schooling and prove to each other that they were not peasants. He probably was right, for I noticed that the ostentation of speaking proper Italian was dropped as soon as two Sicilians had known each other for an evening and showed any desire to be friends. Anyone who persisted in speaking Italian after that was considered a prig or, at least, a socialist.

But if my relatives were under the impression that they were speaking the same dialect they brought with them from Sicily, they were mistaken. After a few years of hearing American, Yiddish, Polish, and Italian dialects other than their own, their language gathered words which no one in Sicily could possibly understand. The most amazing of these were garbled American words dressed up with Sicilian suffixes — strange concoctions which, in later years, that non-Sicilian pundit, H. L. Mencken, was to include in his book, *The American Language.*

Mr. Mencken's collection of Italian-American words is a good indication of what happened to the vocabulary of my relatives. Such words as *minuto* for minute, *ponte* for pound, *storo* for store, *barra* for bar, *giobba* for job were constantly used as Sicilian words.

One word that Mr. Mencken should include in the next edition of his book is *baccauso,* which has been in my relatives' vocabulary as far back as I can remember. My parents probaby picked it up from other American Sicilians when they first arrived in Rochester. Certainly, the word had no relation to their current mode of city life. It was used when referring to 'toilet' and was obviously derived from the American 'backhouse' that flourished in earlier and more rural America. Not until a few years ago when I first visited Italy, a nation without backhouses, and mystified Sicilians there by using the word, did I become aware of its Chic Sale derivation. Yet I had been using *baccauso* for a lifetime, always under the impression it was an authentic Sicilian word.

While the gradual effect of such bastard words was to break down the differences between the dialects my relatives spoke, there were enough differences of accent and vocabulary left to lend the various dialects their own peculiarities. Usually, the more distant the relative the greater was the difference between the dialect he spoke

and the one we used at home. The relatives who came
from towns on the sea (like my father) still talked as
though they were hurling words against the wind or
through the fog, in a piercing singing accent. Those from
towns far inland talked as though they had never heard
gay music, and their speech was heavy with mournful and
burly sounds.

I gathered that every Italian town left its individual
stamp on the language of its people. My Uncle Luigi
liked to tell the story of the American priest who spoke
perfect schoolroom Italian. When he went to Italy for the
first time, the priest decided that the best way of seeing
the country and meeting its people was to travel the whole
length of the nation, listening to confessions as he went
from town to town. He got along famously in northern
Italy. Although he found the confessions rather dull, he
had no trouble understanding the sins described to him.

Below Rome he began to have difficulties. The confessions were more interesting but the dialects he heard
were harder to understand, and on several occasions, he
suspected that the penance he imposed on sinners was
entirely out of proportion to the sins they had committed.
'It must have been very annoying when he got to Naples,'
my uncle said, 'for Neapolitans are some of the most
fascinating sinners in the world.'

When the priest reached Sicily, he was at a complete
loss. He could not understand a word of the dialects he
heard and was obliged to conduct all his confessions in
sign language.

When anyone who had not heard the story was gullible
enough to ask Uncle Luigi how that was possible, he would

gleefully grab the opportunity to show off his histrionic talents and act out a sin or two in pantomime. Invariably, of course, they were sins of the flesh.

There was never any effort made to keep any Sicilian words secret from us, no matter how heretical or bawdy. Yet my parents would be shocked whenever we repeated a word they did not consider proper. Once I horrified my parents with a word which my father often used in his speech. The experience taught me to regard every Sicilian idiom thereafter with a wary eye.

One evening my Aunt Giovanna gave a party for some of the women who worked with her at the tailor factory. She invited my family but, since my parents were expecting visitors that evening, they begged off and sent me, the oldest son, to represent them. Like so many women gathered together away from their husbands, my aunt's guests were inclined to be boisterous.

I was the only male present, but I was only eleven years old and did not inhibit them at all. They were all very attentive to me. My aunt let me drink a glass of wine, and when no one was looking, the buxom woman sitting next to me gave me more. After dinner, I pumped the player-piano while the women danced the schottische and the polka. By the time I was ready to leave, I felt quite stimulated by the gaiety of the evening.

I came into the house, my face radiant with the wine and the crisp wintry air. After introducing me to the guests, my mother asked about her sister's health.

'Aunt Giovanna is fine,' I said. 'Her *risotto* was good — and I had wine and nuts,' I rattled on enthusiastically.

'Did you drink much of the wine?' my father asked with a sly smile.

I avoided the question. 'There were lots of people there and I played the piano for them.' Without stopping to catch my breath I continued, 'The ladies danced and made a lot of noise and it all sounded like a *bordello*.'

My father's face suddenly went grim. My mother gasped, and one of the visitors giggled. My father said: 'Hold your tongue and go to bed at once. You've said enough.'

'But Papa,' I protested, 'it did sound like a *bordello*.'

'Stop using that word!' he thundered. 'Go to bed!'

I went upstairs and brooded. *Bordello* was a word I often heard my father use when he complained about noise. Why should he object to my using it? Downstairs I heard the visitors departing; one of them was telling my mother that boys will be boys and not to worry about me. There was an ominous silence after they left. I heard my mother puttering around the kitchen, and my father angrily creaking his rocking-chair.

It was all too much for me. I decided that I had probably committed some hideous and mysterious crime. My father had once told me the legend of a man who could destroy the world by uttering a single word, secret to everyone but himself. As I cried myself to sleep, I was sure that *bordello* was the word.

The next morning my mother said: 'You used a bad word last night. It is a word that only grownups are allowed to use.'

'But Papa uses it all the time.'

'Yes, but he's a grownup, my little squash.'

'What does the word mean?'

'The word wouldn't have any meaning for you now.

I'll tell you when you get older.   Now hurry to school or you'll be late.'

My mother would never explain adult words to me, though she saw no harm in exposing me to them.   Her theory seemed to be that if her children went to church regularly, they would surely develop an instinct that would teach them to tell the difference between good and bad.   So far as vocabulary was concerned, the theory worked out pretty well.   I had a secret vocabulary of dozens of words I would never dare use at home, even though I had heard many of them there originally.   Most of them were terrifying curses involving God, the Virgin Mary, and various kinds of barnyard animals.   They frightened me, so much so that I used them only when it seemed necessary to impress new playmates with my bravery.

Even my father felt inhibited by my mother's determination to keep English out of the house, and would only speak the language when it was absolutely necessary or when my mother was not present.   My father's English was like no one else's in the world.   Yet it could be understood more easily than the English spoken by most of my Sicilian relatives.   All that he knew of the language he managed to pick up during his first six months in America.   His first factory *bosso,* a noisy Irishman, provided the incentive.   My father wanted to learn enough English so that he could talk back to him.   He was most successful; the boss fired him the first time he understood what he was saying.

So elated was my father with the amount of English he absorbed in a half-year that he stopped learning the lan-

guage then and there and never made any further conscious effort to add to his vocabulary or improve his grammar.   But he made the most of what he knew, and in a
few years had developed a system of speaking English
which defied all philological laws but could be understood
by most Americans after about five minutes of orientation.
Probably the most astonishing aspect of his system was
that he used only one pronoun – 'she' – and only one
tense – the present.

The little English my mother knew she acquired from
my father.   But she spoke the language without any system, groping for nearly all the words she used, without
any of my father's wonderful sureness.   Although she had
been in America as long as he, she had never had
daily contact with persons who spoke only English.   The
tailor factories, where she worked when she arrived, were
nearly all filled with men and women who had recently
come from Italy and spoke only their native tongue.

The stores where she did her shopping every day were
operated by Italians whose customers were all Italians.
The Poles and the Jews who made up a large part
of Mount Allegro stuck to their native languages most
of the time.   My mother had little to do with them.   She
exchanged greetings with all of them, but you did not
need to know much English to keep on friendly terms with
a neighbor.   A smile or an occasional gift of cooked
spaghetti served the purpose just as effectively.

My Uncle Luigi, more than any other of my relatives,
had to depend on his smiles and charms to maintain good
relations with Americans.   His English was so rudiment-
ary that it could be understood only by Sicilians.   In
view of his burning ambition to marry a slim widow with

a fat bank account, his scant knowledge of the language proved something of a handicap. Most of the Italian widows he knew were fat and had very slim bank accounts. The few widows he met who qualified did not know a word of Italian.

It is possible that had he been able to speak English with any fluency, he might have married one of them, for he was six feet tall, and handsome in a gaunt and silvery way. He had been a widower for such a long time that his eyes had begun to dance again like those of a young bachelor. Yet despite all this and his most earnest efforts, he found that his sign language and his eye-rolling were not sufficient to establish communication with a rich widow's heart.

There was the time he fell in love with an Australian-born widow who lived on a five-hundred-acre farm on the outskirts of town and was said to own seven cows. People claimed she had so much money that every few years she imported a kangaroo from Australia and donated it to the city zoo. My uncle flirted with her in church for a month before she gave him a tumble. After that, she did most of the flirting and he decided it was time to carry matters a step further.

One evening he cornered me alone. 'My nephew,' he said gravely, 'I want you to do me a brotherly favor. I will pay you well for it. Do you think you could write a passionate love letter for me?'

At the mention of pay I became thoroughly interested and assured him I could write such a letter, if he told me what he wanted to say.

He became a little impatient. 'You, a young man with eleven years of life behind you, at least six of which have been squandered watching countless movies, have the gall to tell me that you don't know what to say in a love letter? Very well, I shall describe what I want said.' He paused to take a pinch of snuff.

'Her name is Belle. After I marry her I shall call her Bella. Tell Belle I love her, of course. It might be a good idea to repeat that in the letter a few times. Tell her, too, that I like the country and fresh vegetables and have a great fondness for cows — I detest milk, but don't mention that. You might reminisce a bit — women like nostalgic men — and let her know that I used to milk goats in my youth and probably would have no difficulty at all with cows. Have I made myself clear?'

I wrote the letter and promptly received my first fee as a ghost writer, twenty-five cents. But Uncle Luigi never received a reply to the letter, and when he saw the Australian widow at church the following Sunday she turned crimson and lifted her nose as high as it would go.

'What in God's name did you say in that letter, squash head?' he asked. 'Why, I could almost see the froth gathering at her lips when she caught sight of me!'

I mumbled that I had only written what he had asked me to. It was not until a few years later, when I was more qualified to think of the opposite sex as such, that I realized you could not woo a lady effectively by devoting most of your first letter to a discourse on your passion for milking cows.

Uncle Luigi was not discouraged. Within a short time he was campaigning for the heart and bank account of another widow. This one lived in Pennsylvania. For once she happened to be an Italian, an immigrant from Calabria, so that he was able to do his own letter-writing for a change. The correspondence progressed pretty well at first. They immediately struck a topic of mutual interest: their disapproval of their children. Each letter would be given to a thorough and heartless analysis of the faults of one of the children.

In their eagerness to show each other that they saw eye to eye, each one tried to outdo the other in stripping the children clean of any virtues they might have. They both had several sons and daughters, and the correspondence would probably have continued in this morbid vein indefinitely if my Uncle Nino had not stepped in with a piece of advice.

'You will never get anywhere that way,' he told Uncle Luigi. 'You must say more about love and less about your children. Children are the bane of all romance.'

Uncle Luigi, who had great respect for Uncle Nino's opinions on such matters, tried to follow his advice. The main difficulty with that was that the widow was well educated and he was not. This became more and more apparent as the correspondence grew more intimate. Uncle Luigi hesitated to mail her his crudely expressed declarations of love and had to consult frequently with Uncle Nino, who claimed to know more about love than Boccaccio. Uncle Nino would edit each letter, improving the phraseology considerably and adding two or three flowery paragraphs of his own, all of which Uncle Luigi laboriously copied.

The amorous sentiments of my Uncle Nino raised the correspondence to new romantic heights. One letter to which he contributed heavily had such a pronounced effect on the widow that she replied to it with a five-page poem. My Uncle Luigi was so enormously pleased with what he considered his own success that he gave readings of the poem whenever he found an audience.

But when the widow began to write all her letters in poetry, he became plainly disgusted. The correspondence was rapidly getting out of hand. Except for his handwriting and the postage, he was able to contribute nothing to it, for he was incapable of writing a couplet, let alone a letterful of rhymes, and was obliged to depend entirely on my Uncle Nino. When he threatened to go back to prose, my Uncle Nino pointed out that when a lady takes the trouble to address you in poetry, she expects to be answered in kind.

Uncle Luigi's only consolation was that up till that point he had managed to conceal the address of the widow from my Uncle Nino. 'You never can tell,' he confided in my father. 'Nino is an honorable man, but he might take it into his head to start a correspondence with her on his own. After all, he knows as well as I do that, in addition to being palatable, she is heavily insured and has a nice steady income. Frankly, I'm getting tired of this whole letter-writing business. Fancy phrases get you nowhere if they are not followed up with action. I must pay the lady a visit soon.'

But before he could save enough money for the train fare, he made the mistake of quarreling violently with Uncle Nino about the merits of their respective home towns. Uncle Nino, feeling bested, got back at him by refusing to write any more poems for him.

Uncle Luigi tried valiantly to maintain something of the poetic quality of the correspondence, but his literary style was too primitive and quite inappropriate for anything but the bluntest declarations. Having become a devout admirer of Uncle Nino's luxuriant phrases, the widow was repulsed by Uncle Luigi's sudden lack of literary grace and insisted on interpreting his bad grammar and crude sentences as signs of growing indifference.

The more my Uncle Luigi protested, the more ungrammatical he became. Finally, she could no longer tolerate the crudeness of his letters and gave up writing to him altogether.

In spite of his superior intellect, Uncle Nino never learned much English — chiefly because of an old grudge he bore against his wife. Whenever he quarreled with her he would shout that he had never intended to come to America in the first place and only did so because she so 'blinded' him that he could not distinguish between love and common sense. Even when he was not quarreling with her, you would have surmised from hearing him talk that he was through with America and was returning to Sicily the very next day.

Since he had ranted in much the same way for nearly twenty years, none of his relatives, least of all his wife, took him seriously. Yet the fact remained that during all that time Uncle Nino considered himself little more than a transient who would some day persuade his wife that it would be far more comfortable to return to Sicily and live on the fat of the land he owned there than to exist in a callow city like Rochester and slave all week for a few strands of spaghetti.

His arguments did not impress his wife, possibly because it was she and not he who slaved all week. My Aunt Giovanna sewed buttonholes in a tailor factory, while he ran a small jewelry trade from his living-room, an occupation that left him with considerable time and energy to play briscola and threaten to leave America.

It was quite true that if he had not met my Aunt Giovanna, he probably would never have set foot outside of Sicily. As a young man he was managing a prosperous importing business in Palermo — so prosperous, my mother said, that he could bribe judges to change their decisions. And then my Aunt Giovanna came along. She was in the throes of conspiring to secure admission into the United States after having failed twice before. Both times her application had been rejected in the belief that she had trachoma, the eye disease that was often contracted by Sicilians living in towns where the water was bad.

On her first attempt to get to America she actually got as far as Ellis Island. But American officials seemed less susceptible to her beauty than the Italian officials who had gallantly helped to smuggle her through the red tape in Palermo. Ellis Island was little more than a prison in those days. For eight days she spent her time looking through iron bars at the Statue of Liberty and the New York skyline, and weeping.

Every morning an Irish policewoman who spoke Italian tried to make her tell how she had got on the boat without a passport. But my aunt never told. Finally the immigration officials realized they were wasting their time and shipped Aunt Giovanna back to Palermo.

When my Uncle Nino proposed three days after he met her, she consented, but only on condition that he take her to America. He gave up his thriving business, married her, and took her on a honeymoon to France, where they thought she would stand a better chance of getting a passport. At Havre she was again turned down. Uncle

Nino got his passport without any trouble, but he saw little point in leaving his bride behind to go to a country that did not particularly attract him.

My Aunt Giovanna was never lacking in stubbornness. Against his better judgment, she persuaded him to sail alone, arguing that once he was in the United States it would be a simple matter for him to make arrangements to send for her. Was she not his wife? Surely, American officials could not be so heartless as to permit red tape to separate newlyweds. Uncle Nino loved his wife too much to argue with her.

Her reasoning proved to be faulty. Uncle Nino's presence in the United States did not stir up any sentiments American officials might have for young newlyweds. He spent a miserable year in New York filling out endless forms, pining for his bride, and cursing the moment he had given in to her arguments. He was about to return to Europe and take her back to Sicily, when word came that Aunt Giovanna had been able to persuade the French immigration officials that there was nothing wrong with her eyes that a less tearful existence could not remedy.

He had never forgiven her for those lonely months he spent in New York waiting for her. And after twenty years of America he was still angry with her for having wrenched him away from a successful career to a makeshift existence in a strange land where he had to depend largely on his wife's earnings.

If it had not been for this old grudge, Uncle Nino might have mastered English.

'He who knows the English language will go forward,' he was fond of saying. But he himself made not the slightest effort to learn it. 'Why should I try to master a language as difficult as English? By the time I learned to speak it properly, it would be time for me to die. If your demands are as simple as mine, it is not hard to get whatever you want without knowing the language.'

He liked to illustrate this point with a story he heard about the first Italians who came to Rochester.

'In the early days Italians were disliked far more than they are now,' he said. 'They could not speak a word of English; at least I can fool an American into believing that I know what he is talking about, but they didn't even know enough English to do that. Nor did they get much chance to associate with Americans.

'The men were good strong workers but the Americans regarded them as bandits and intruders, and their employers treated them as though they were nothing but workhorses. They all forgot that they had been foreigners once too, and they made life as miserable as possible for them.

'Although the Italians had money, the storekeepers would not sell them food and the landlords would not rent them homes. For many weeks they were forced to live in boxes and tents and depend on *cicoria* for their main food. Now, *cicoria* is one of the most nutritious foods God planted in this earth, but even *cicoria* can become boring as a steady diet.

'The men had tried praying to God, begging Him to remind the Americans that they were *Cristiani* like themselves. But that didn't help. They became desperate. What was the use of earning money if you could not buy the things you needed most? One afternoon they armed themselves with pickaxes and marched into one of the largest grocery stores in town. While they stood by with their pickaxes poised over their heads, their leader addressed himself to the chief clerk.

'The leader did not know a word of English. He made motions with his hands and his mouth to show that they were all very hungry. He also made it clear that unless the men were allowed to purchase food, they would tear up the store with their pickaxes. The clerk was a very understanding fellow and sold them all the food they wanted.

'Their success went to their heads. Now that they could buy food, they began to wish for real houses to eat it in. Even then Rochester was a miserably damp and rainy town, and a tent or a box was no way to keep snug. Once more the men got out their pickaxes and called on the grocery clerk. Again the clerk had no difficulty making out what they wanted. He begged them to calm down and indicated that he would try to help them.

'A few minutes later the police arrived. The clerk told them what the Italians wanted. The police told the Town Council, and the authorities told the landlords. In a few days the men were moved from their tents and shanties into real homes. These same Italians now have children who are some of the leading doctors, lawyers, and druggists in town. There's no doubt about it: you have to ask for whatever you want in this world, and prayer isn't always the way to ask.'

(F I V E)

God and the Sicilians

MY MOTHER AND FATHER WERE ON SUCH INTI-
mate terms with God that they never felt compelled to
attend church, except when a relative was baptized,
married, or died with enough money to have a Mass sung
over him. But every Sunday morning punctually and
with unshakable resolution my mother packed us off to
church, admonishing us, when she made her last-minute
inspection of ears and necks, to remember everything that
the priest said so that we could repeat it to her on our
return.

The only Catholic churches in Mount Allegro were
managed by Irish priests. Partly to soothe her conscience,
my mother often argued that there was little satisfaction
for her in sitting through sermons that were not delivered
in Italian. 'Who in the world has time to learn enough
American to understand what they say in those sermons?'
When Donna Rosalia surprised her once by pointing out
that a sermon could hardly be considered the most important part of the service, she abandoned the argument
and simply explained that God made special concessions

for mothers of four children who had all they could do on Sunday mornings to send their children to church.

My mother staunchly believed that God was nearly always willing to make concessions for Italian mothers. Wasn't the Pope an Italian, after all? And didn't God have his chief headquarters in the Italian city of Rome? My father never offered any explanations at all for not attending church, but we all agreed that he was too nervous a person to sit through an entire service.

Among my relatives my parents' attitude toward church attendance was hardly unique. Catholicism was so deeply ingrained in their bones that they could violate some of its strictest man-made rules without the slightest feeling of guilt. Unlike their Irish Catholic neighbors, they had almost no fear of God and felt as much at home with him as they did with each other.

Although they conceded that it was possible to offend him or make him angry, they were certain that God's divinity endowed him with an extraordinary capacity for benevolence and wisdom, and they fully expected him to exercise these qualities in their behalf. Children and old people, on the other hand, were not expected to take advantage of his benevolence. The young had yet to prove their devotion by going to church and following the other rules of the Catholic Church. As for the old, Death would soon catch up with them, so it was prudent for them to strengthen their peace with God before it was too late.

If God was not in a good mood (your conscience would tell you whether or not He was), my relatives would appeal to their guardian saint. A guardian saint was like a friend in court. He had special access to God's ear. If you took care to remember the saint with prayers and an occasional candle, you could usually count on him to remain loyal and carry out your wishes. Once in a blue moon it actually became necessary to make threats against a guardian saint in order to waken him to his responsibilities.

Rosario Alfano, who had once been a fisherman in Sicily, told that whenever he and his comrades failed to catch enough tuna they would appeal to the patron saint of the fishermen — San Francisco di Paolo. If their prayers did not produce a shoal of tuna within a reasonable time, they would take the statue from its niche, carry it to the beach where they were fishing, and set it down with its face toward the sea. The fishermen would then gather around the statue, shaking their fists at it and threatening, 'Either you get us more tuna or else we'll duck you.'

'He was a pretty good saint and usually helped us,' Rosario added.

Another such story my relatives told me was the one about the Sicilian in this country who had played the numbers for a long time without any luck. One day he decided to appeal to a saint for help. He went into the nearest Catholic church and prayed before the image of Saint Anthony. After praying every day for a week without any change in his luck, he lost his temper with the saint. 'You better see to it that I win tomorrow or else it will be an unlucky day for you,' he threatened.

The next day, having lost more money on the numbers, he became more specific. 'If I don't win tomorrow,' he

promised the saint, 'I'm coming in here to break you up in
a thousand pieces.' A priest passing by overheard the
threat, noted the seriousness of the man, and decided
Saint Anthony needed protection. When the gambler
came back the next day, the saint was gone. In his place
was a statue of the infant Jesus. The gambler looked
about the church; then failing to see Saint Anthony anywhere, he turned to the infant Jesus: 'Hey, boy,' he demanded, 'where's your father?'

Even though my parents did not go to church, none of
us ever had the slightest doubt about their devotion. It
was all around us. Their church was a corner in their
bedroom where a wine-red votive light burned steadily
before a crucifix thickly matted with artificial blood.
Over their bed was further testimony — a portrait of Jesus
and one of the Virgin Mary.

Next to them was a large picture of Jesus' bleeding
heart with a dozen angels hovering around it looking very
bewildered and unhappy. A copy of this picture hung
over the bed in my room, and many a night did the agony
of Jesus descend from the picture into my dreams. I was
so influenced by all this display that in the course of a
Sunday-school year I won three biographies of Christ (all
identical copies) for knowing my catechism better than
anyone else in the class.

My mother was determined to place us under the wing
of Catholicism at an early age. When we were old
enough to go to school, she tried to enroll Joe and me in
the near-by parochial school. That was a supreme gesture of devotion for her. A parochial school would have

meant a weekly fee for each of us, and she had barely enough money each week to feed the family.

She probably would have succeeded in making this sacrifice had not the Irish priest refused to enroll Joe along with me on the ground that he was not old enough to enter school. Not wishing to send us to separate schools, my mother gave the priest a noisy piece of her mind in English which only a Sicilian could understand, and marched us to the nearest public school, where she had no difficulty enrolling both of us.

Sometimes, on our return from church, we shocked her by reporting that the same priest had talked of nothing but the coal bills he wanted his congregation to pay. She did not like to hear anything that was derogatory about a representative of God, but gradually we were able to convince her that this particular priest was not all that a priest should be.

One of our complaints was that before the services started he would station himself in front of the main door with a collection plate, like a ticket-seller at a movie house, eyeing each entrant carefully and glaring at anyone who dared pass by the plate without dropping a coin into it.

We knew how blasphemous it was to disapprove of a man so near to God, but we made no bones about our dislike for him. He was too fat, even for a priest; he bullied the poor Italian women in his congregation who couldn't afford to donate to the collection plate at the door as well as the one he passed about after Communion. Moreover, we were among those at whom he glared.

I was inclined to blame the priest's bad manners on his

high blood pressure and let it go at that.   But my brother, whose ability to lose his temper was surpassed only by that of my father, took a different view.   He did not mind being bored by the priest's tedious pleas for more money, which often took the place of the sermon, but his blood boiled whenever the priest mistreated some helpless Italian woman who had not made her donation large enough to satisfy him.

One Sunday morning what I had been fearing for several weeks happened.   The priest had just finished delivering a long and scolding lecture on the current coal bill, and was passing the collection plate.   Two pews ahead of us sat one of my mother's friends, Donna Nunziata, who had been attending the same church regularly ever since her husband died.   She did not understand a word of English, but she had listened to the priest's lecture with rapt attention, as was her habit, no doubt believing that the priest's frequent losses of temper were part of his diatribes against the Devil.

When the priest reached Donna Nunziata, she dropped a nickel into the plate.   The priest became furious; he snatched the coin out of the plate and threw it back at her. I saw her bewilderment change to tears; then, before I could pull him down, my brother was on his feet shouting at the priest: 'You can't do that.   She is a poor woman. She can't afford any more!'

A murmur went through the congregation.   At that instant it sounded to me like a chord from an organ in hell.   Tony Pazienza, who was sleeping in a near-by pew, awoke with a start and began to clap, thinking for a moment he was in a theater.

The priest had turned as red as the flesh of a pomegranate. Joe was trembling, partly from rage and partly from fright over the sacrilege he had committed. I pulled him down to me, blushing furiously for both of us, and after a few minutes in which he had time to compose himself, I suggested we leave. We walked out of church in the most dignified manner we could command, feeling horribly self-conscious as eyes in every pew followed our exit down the aisle and through the door. On the street, Joe could no longer control himself and began to cry. I tried to console him as best I could, assuring him that I should have done the same had I had his courage.

Neither of us was brave enough to go home before the service was over. To kill time we nervously circled the block. Joe was afraid my father would punish him and spent some moments trying to figure out what form the punishment would take. Even when it was time for the service to end, we delayed going home; feeling reckless in our despair, we treated ourselves to ice-cream cones with the money we had been given to put in the collection plate.

As lunch-time approached, we became a little more courageous and began to walk in the direction of the house. When we arrived, it was an enormous relief to find Donna Nunziata in the kitchen telling my mother the story. At the sight of Joe, she ran to him with her arms outstretched, calling him a darling and kissing him noisily.

'Your son,' she said to my mother, 'is one in a million.'

'What is this Donna Nunziata has been telling me?' my mother asked. 'Anyone would think you were another Garibaldi from the things she has been saying about you.'

Since it was obvious that she had no intention of punishing Joe, we spared her none of the details, adding a few extra ones to make sure she would understand the incident as we did.

I reminded her that it was not the first time that the priest had thrown money back into people's faces. 'Yes, and he's always picking on Italian old ladies. He never bothers the Irish ones,' Joe added.

My mother carefully listened to all our testimony; then, with the seriousness of a judge, she announced her decision. 'This priest must be reported to the Bishop. He is behaving more like a moneylender than a man of God. Joe will have to confess the sin he committed this morning when he raised his voice during the service, but I am sure that the good Lord will understand how it happened and will forgive him. You,' she said, turning to me, 'must write the letter to the Bishop and give him all the particulars. But don't compare the priest with moneylenders, as I have. That would be sinful.'

I immediately composed a long and badly spelled letter to the Bishop, telling him what had happened to Donna Nunziata and describing similar incidents that had taken place in the past. I concluded by saying that priest was a good priest (this hurt, but my mother insisted I stress that point because she didn't believe there could be bad priests), but he talked more of money than he did of God.

There was no reply from the Bishop. My mother explained that he was too busy a personage to write poor folks like us; she was sure, though, that he would order the priest to improve his behavior. But for a long time nothing could persuade Joe to return to the same church. Every Sunday he walked an extra mile to attend another

Catholic church where he claimed the priest was more interested in God.

My Uncle Nino, who had more education than most of my relatives, was pleased when he heard the story. 'Do you know who the smartest people in the whole world are?' he asked.

'Our teachers,' I said promptly.

'The police,' Joe said.

He looked disgusted. 'No, you idiots; no one is as smart as the Catholic Church and the priests in it. A priest never goes hungry and he always knows the right answers.' To prove this he told us a story which he swore was true.

'There was a priest in Sicily who went from town to town as a missionary to bring strayed Catholics back into the fold. The leading officials of a certain town thought it would be amusing to embarrass him, and they invited the priest to spend a day in the country with them. He set out on horseback and after a few miles encountered a group of men who stopped him on the pretext of asking directions. They were his hosts disguised as peasants.

' "What is this!" they exclaimed. "Here is a priest riding a horse. Why do you ride a horse when Jesus Christ was content with riding an ass?"

' "Well, gentlemen," replied the missionary, "it is like this: inasmuch as all the asses seem to have become judges and civil workers, I just wasn't able to get one." '

It was hard to tell from this kind of talk whether Uncle Nino was a good Catholic or not. I never had any doubts, however, about our Uncle Luigi. He was a celebrity among the relatives because he had had the audacity to quit Catholicism and become a Baptist. When he first arrived from Italy in New York, he saw a church with a brightly-lit sign that read, 'The Italian Baptist Church.' He walked in and was greeted effusively by the minister.

'It was the first happy face I had ever seen on a cleric,' he explained, 'so I joined. We had a long talk first and he told me that you could go much further in this country if you weren't a Catholic. He said he had in his congregation some of the best-known Italian lawyers, doctors, and politicians in town. The minister told me the truth. Did you ever hear of a Catholic who ever became President of the United States? Of course, I can't say that being a Baptist has got me anywhere in particular; but it is better than fussing over a lot of saints. Why should a person worship anyone else but God?'

Uncle Luigi raised all his five children to be Baptists and they, in turn, converted their husbands and wives to the Baptist faith. But by the time that happened Uncle Luigi had embraced another religion. My relatives never seemed disturbed by the way he juggled religions. They merely considered him a bad Catholic who would eventually be drawn back to the arms of Mother Church. His children, having become passionate Baptists as a result of their father's zealous conversion campaign, made the best of the situation by remaining Baptists.

The only member of his family who turned her back on the Baptists was his American-born daughter Teresa, who was one of my favorite cousins because she was pretty and would reward me when I told her so by taking me to the movies. Teresa made her living working in one of the darkrooms of a film factory and seldom saw daylight. In the darkness of the factory, probably as an escape from it, she developed the idea of saving her money to go to Sicily and meet the many close relatives she had there, men and women she had never seen.

Her relatives laughed at this ambition. Since she hardly knew enough Sicilian to converse with her own father, they derived great amusement from speculating how she would communicate with her Sicilian relatives. Teresa, driven by some strong instinct to see the land of her parents, bore their amusement good-naturedly, and resolutely continued to save her money until she actually had enough for the trip. She set out for Sicily armed with a biography of Daniel Boone, an Italian-English dictionary, and a set of pink silk underwear for her father's sister Nina.

At the last moment my Aunt Giovanna tried her best to change Teresa's mind, pointing out at great length the hazards that faced a young pretty woman traveling alone. But all this only served to make the trip sound more alluring to Teresa, and she was positively gay when we took her to the station and put her on the train. Aunt Giovanna refused to see her off. She went to church instead and spent the whole day there praying for the safe journey of her Baptist niece.

The prayers may have been heard. Within a month after she arrived in her father's native village, Teresa, still speaking a brand of Sicilian that was little more than English with extra vowels, landed a handsome blue-eyed husband her own age. Not overenchanted with Sicily, Teresa married him on condition he would come to

America with her. He agreed on condition that she would become a Catholic.

From the first, Uncle Luigi was fascinated by the large number and variety of religious denominations he found in America, and he reacted to them in the manner of a lecherous male who, having led a monogamous existence all his life, is suddenly thrown into the midst of a harem. Following his experience with the Baptist Church, he became a veritable playboy of religions, and went to all the different churches he could find in Rochester. Whenever he went to Buffalo for a weekend, he spent most of his time attending the services of strange religious sects he could not find at home.

In a single Sunday he sometimes went to as many as three or four services in as many churches of different denominations. The only church he would not attend was the Catholic Church. Because he enjoyed good singing, he occasionally attended a High Mass of the Episcopalian Church, although he thoroughly disapproved of that church for its similarities to the Catholic Church. To offset the effects of attending an Episcopal service, he would go to a Methodist one.

On Fridays, after a meal which invariably included two courses of meat, he attended a synagogue with some of his Jewish friends. When he wanted drama and excitement, he went to the Holy Roller services. He claimed he was too old to participate in them (actually he was only fifty then) and that he sat in a back seat so that he could slip out easily when things became too hot.

None of us ever doubted that it was at that point that Uncle Luigi would be sure to move up closer to the front of the church, so that he might get a better view of what was going on. But we had been brought up far too carefully to give expression to such disrespectful suspicions about so close a relative.

If Uncle Luigi hoped to shock his relatives, he was disappointed. Whenever he ranted against Catholicism, my mother would smile patiently and tell him that he should certainly have become a priest instead of a mason. Uncle Luigi could be certain that his personal life would become a fertile subject for general gossip the moment it began to deviate from the conventional (as it often did), but his religious philandering was considered his own affair. The worst that was ever said about that was that he was a Turk and a Saracen and would probably serve a term in purgatory if he did not mend his ways.

He may have realized it, but he would never admit that Catholicism was so much a part of his relatives that it was futile to argue with them about it. You might as well have tried to persuade a confirmed teetotaler that strong drink was good for him.

Their Catholicism, like their lives, was enveloped in a heavy blanket of fatalism. In the last analysis, both were impervious to rational argument. Thinking was all right for professional persons, like doctors, lawyers, and teachers, but for laymen it was considered a superfluous and overestimated process.

If you wanted to keep your full senses, you accepted whatever happened to you in life with a full assurance that it was bound to happen. What was the use of thinking about it?

There might be a great deal of noisy emotionalism

among my relatives over a misfortune, like a death or the loss of a job, but eventually it was laid on the doorstep of Destiny. '*E u Destino.*' That single phrase explained everything. 'The good Lord has decided in advance what is going to happen to all of us. You can't fight Destiny,' my mother would often say to me.

All this hardly jibed with the philosophy of the Horatio Alger novels I devoured, nor did it fit in with what we heard in school. There we were taught in English, French, and Latin that every man is the architect of his own fortune, that anyone who works hard and has plenty of ambition can achieve anything he wants, that Abe Lincoln got to be President of the United States and so can you and you.

When I repeated some of this learning at home, my father smiled and said, 'Sure. Sure. America is a wonderful country,' but in his heart he found all this too much to swallow and, whenever he became angry with us, he complained that our school-teachers taught us fairy tales instead of manners.

His belief in Destiny could not be shed in his lifetime. For centuries his ancestors had been relying on the alibi of Destiny, for how else could they have become resigned to the obstacles that stood between them and a decent living? Their priests had talked about Destiny; so had their employers. They came to believe its power and to respect it. They heard nothing else.

Here in America, my father and his relatives, huddled together as they were in one neighborhood, heard the same thing, except from their children who brought home their school-learning. The only real connection they had with their new land was their children, but they had never heard of Sicilian parents learning from their children and they did not listen to them closely. They continued to talk about Destiny in the same vague but dogmatic way people have of talking about life or about depressions.

But life eventually ends and a depression is eventually conquered. Not so with Destiny. It had no beginning and no ending and no one could possibly cope with it. It was *Destino* that decreed my father should never earn enough money, never save any, and yet have a generous spirit that only a rich man could afford. It was *Destino* that kept sending my mother to hospitals for a series of operations that nearly killed her, and finally it was *Destino* that made it possible for her to survive.

To my parents *Destino* was the magic in the map drawn by God which charted the course of every human being. To us *Destino* never seemed to have any connection with God. Hell appeared like a more likely place for it. It hung over our thoughts like an unassailable dragon who somehow had become the final authority in determining the outcome of all important happenings in our lives, regardless of what our teachers and the Horatio Alger novels said to the contrary.

On Saturday afternoons my brother and I always marched off together (one to check on the other) to confess the sins we had committed during the course of the week. On Saturday mornings we helped my mother scrub the house, and before we went to bed we took our baths, but in the afternoons it was our souls that were cleansed.

I had a natural horror of anything that had to do with the cult of cleanliness, but I particularly dreaded the business of keeping my soul spick and span. For while it was possible to escape the wrath of my mother for overlooking ears and kitchen corners, there was no escaping the solemn, inquisitorial atmosphere of the confessional booth.

It was there that I first developed a tendency toward claustrophobia. As soon as the priest started asking me questions, the booth would seem to contract until I felt that no space remained between my conscience and the thin lattice that stood between it and my inquisitor. The purple drapes surrounding me became insinuating monsters, and I would blurt out sins which, in broad daylight, seemed trivial and hardly worth mentioning.

But the most frightening part of confession came whenever I admitted committing a mortal sin. The priest would scold me on such occasions in a loud voice that could be heard far beyond the thickness of the purple drapes. Although he was fairly quiet when I confessed such venial sins as losing my temper, calling people bad names, or telling lies, he became a holy terror whenever I admitted a mortal sin.

Mortal sins were not too difficult to commit. Not attending church on Sundays or breaking any of the Ten Commandments all came under the head of mortal sins. A single mortal sin might be sufficient to ruin a lifetime career of pure living, if it wasn't confessed, and send a departed soul to purgatory. Neither Joe nor I was old enough to break many of the Ten Commandments but, in spite of my mother, we did manage to miss church now and then.

For many months I accepted the noisy abuse of the priest as one of the annoyances Destiny had cut out for me. But one Saturday afternoon I rebelled. The stimulus (no doubt provided by a demon of Destiny who knew my susceptibilities too well) was in the form of a petite blonde girl with fat curls named Elvira who usually went to confession the same time I did.

I had fallen madly in love with her one week, and since she had already let me carry her books twice, I knew that she was not too displeased with me. Unluckily, it was the same week that I had committed the mortal sin of missing Mass. On Sunday Joe and I had been lured from the very doorsteps of the church by some Protestant and Jewish friends who were getting up a ball game.

It was humiliating to realize that Elvira would hear me chastized when I confessed the sin. I could hardly expect any mercy on the part of the priest. I was certain that if I tried to explain the circumstances, the priest's abuse would reach new vocal heights, and everyone in church would be bound to hear him, Elvira included.

After pondering over this problem for several days and almost concluding that there was no use struggling with my Destiny, a plan occurred to me that Machiavelli himself might have used if he had been in the same predicament. I was frankly surprised at having thought of it, for it involved arithmetic, a subject which exasperated me and, even more, the teachers who tried to teach it to me. Undoubtedly, it was inspired by that same demon who knew about Elvira and me. As a matter of fact, an apt title for the plan might have been 'How to Get Around God.'

I kept it to myself. Joe had no Elvira in his life and seemed to bear up better than I did under the priest's tirades. He was also much more devout than I and would undoubtedly oppose any scheming against the Church.

If I had any qualms about using my plan that Saturday afternoon when Joe and I arrived at church to confess, they were obliterated by the sight of Elvira's curls dangling over the pew in front of her as she bowed her head in prayer. I sat near the curls while waiting for my turn to enter the confessional, and as she looked up and smiled at me I knew it was my destiny to put the plan into action.

When I entered the confessional, the priest, in his usual manner, started the proceedings by asking if I had been attending church regularly. The lie came without any difficulty. The priest seemed entirely convinced and went on to query me about less important sins. When he asked me if I had told any lies during the course of the week, I played my trump card. Under ordinary circumstances, I should have confessed to five lies. But in accordance with the plan, I added to these the lie I had just told him and announced that I had lied six times. In the dark, the priest could not see my face flush as I said that, nor imagine that I expected a sudden bolt of lightning to strike me down. Nothing of the kind happened. After confessing a few more sins of a mundane nature, I was absolved with a light penance. The plan had worked perfectly.

When I came out of the booth, Elvira smiled at me sweetly and Joe looked puzzled. A few minutes later when it was his turn to confess, everyone in church heard the booming voice of the priest berating him vehemently for missing church. He came out of the confessional glowering from the scolding. It took him a long time to say his penance and, while I was waiting for him, I met Elvira in the lobby as she was leaving and made arrangements to walk home from school with her on Monday. Finally, Joe was finished with all the Hail Marys and Our Fathers he had been ordered to say.

'How come you didn't get bawled out?' he demanded as soon as we had left the church. I didn't know what to say. My demon had deserted me by that time. I suddenly felt ashamed of my trick. But I didn't want Joe to know about it for fear he would bully me into going back and confessing it.

'He bawled me out plenty,' I lied, 'but you couldn't hear him because he forgot to yell.' I made a mental note to confess this lie the following week.

'Are you telling the truth?' he asked.

'What do you think?' I replied indignantly, parrying the question that way so that I wouldn't have to chalk up another lie against myself. But I began to brood about the lie to the priest.

Technically I was in the right, I reasoned. I had told a lie, yes, but hadn't I confessed it? The trouble with that line of thought was that I knew God was everywhere and was probably aware of my deceit by now. My demon was nowhere and I became more and more despondent.

I wondered how soon God's wrath would descend on me, and when there was a thunderstorm that evening I was scared and convinced I was the cause of it. Each bolt of lightning seemed like a personal message from Him directed at me.   The blue flashes seemed to come nearer and nearer and, miserably, I thought of the way a cat plays with a mouse before the kill.   After every flash, I crossed myself and mumbled the words my mother had taught us to say during thunderstorms:

> Primo lampu,
> Doppo tronu,
> Jesu Cristo si fici omu
>
> (First the lightning,
> Then the thunder,
> Jesus Christ became a man.)

These magic words when spoken in Sicilian protected you from the fury of thunderstorms, provided you remembered to cross yourself as you said them.   You said them as soon as you saw the flash of lightning, and to make doubly sure you would be heard you repeated them during the ensuing thunder.   Being a monstrous sinner, I not only repeated them but genuflected as I crossed myself and, for extra measure, looked appealingly at the portrait of Christ hanging over my bed.

I survived the thunderstorm in that way but went to bed with the suspicion that I might never wake up again. And when I did awake the following morning, I was so surprised and grateful that I resolved thereafter to lead a pure and remorseful life.

In church that morning I listened attentively to the priest, despite Elvira's presence near-by, and this time found out exactly how much money was owing to the coal-dealer and the mason who had fixed the church steps.

I said more than my usual quota of prayers, and before I went to the altar to accept Communion I directed a personal appeal for forgiveness to God.

Figuring he might not hear me with so many services going on in the world on a Sunday, I also addressed a special prayer to my guardian saint, Saint Gerlando, and asked him to use his valuable influence, promising to light a couple of candles in his honor as soon as I got some spending money.

But my conscience was not appeased by such gestures. Another problem presented itself. Suppose God and Saint Gerlando had not forgiven me immediately, before I took Communion, didn't my acceptance of Communion double the crime? The purpose of confession, after all, was to cleanse your soul so that it would be in proper condition to receive Communion. The supreme blasphemy was to take Communion when your soul was still spotted with sinning. The thought plagued me, so much so that I blamed Elvira for all my troubles and even stopped flirting with her.

I felt the need to confide in someone, but there was no one who could be properly sympathetic. My parents were out of the question because they would surely feel that such high-powered sinning by their eldest son would be jeopardizing their own chances with God. My brother was not old enough. As for my uncles and cousins, they seemed either too devout or not devout enough to be helpful.

'What happens if somebody lies to a priest?' I asked at dinner.

'Stop asking silly questions,' my father said.

'That is a question for a priest to answer,' my mother said.

It was a silly question. I might as well have asked for the difference between right and wrong. Their attitudes on religion did not spring from learning, and it was futile to expect them to answer a question so theoretical. That was the kind of question one would ask of an American teacher, but not of Sicilian parents who were so immersed in their religion that they never felt obliged to think of its particulars.

I even thought of another plan to extricate me from the results of the first — a more elaborate one involving long division, this time, that would reduce my crimes nearly to zero. But finally I decided it would probably lead to a third plan and that the rest of my life might be spent in trying to wipe out what started out as an ordinary mortal sin. Scheming was out. I chose piety instead, probably in the knowledge that the worst-tasting medicines were the ones that were supposed to cure.

For the next twelve days — one for each of my years — I sneaked away from my playmates after school and, when no one I knew was looking, slunk into church. Each day I said an interminable number of Our Fathers and Hail Marys, prologuing each session of prayer with an explanation to God of why I was imposing such a stern penance on myself. Soon I began to be more at ease with my conscience and the world, and before the twelve days were up I had fallen in love again with Elvira.

In settling on a solution as tedious and lonely as prayer, I was undoubtedly influenced by the Irish priest, who, when he wasn't talking about the coal bill, insisted on depicting God as a harsh disciplinarian. My relatives were unhampered by such propaganda. Unable to follow the priest's English, they continued to believe, without any pains of doubt, that God, though somewhat eccentric, was essentially good-natured.

If I had taken as my cue the methods they used to develop friendly relations with God, I might have hit on a gayer and more interesting way of doing penance for my sin. I might have, for instance, made a deal with God like the one my mother's cousin Sarina made with Saint Joseph when it looked as though her husband Pietro were going to die.

Sarina had tried four doctors in quick succession, without any tangible results. Three of the doctors were licensed physicians. When she wouldn't permit the operation they recommended, they only shrugged their shoulders and sent her large bills.

The fourth doctor had no license. He came from the near-by town of Palmyra, where he was famous for his magic healing powers. He rubbed Pietro with hot oil and burnt salt, mumbled magic words over Pietro's back and chest, where the pains were, and used three leeches. His name was Jesu Santo but that didn't seem to help Pietro either.

Finally Sarina realized that her husband's fate was in the hands of God alone. One morning she emptied Pietro's medicines into the ashcan and addressed herself directly to Saint Joseph. She nearly always chose him to intercede for her when she wanted big favors from God.

Sarina told Saint Joseph about Pietro, what a good man

he was, and that he was dying, and how four doctors had been able to do nothing for him except make him poorer. Then she promised the saint that if he brought about Pietro's cure, she would go begging alms from house to house, and that on Saint Joseph's Day she would give a banquet in his honor with the money she collected.

Saint Joseph did not fail her. Despite the dire predictions of the three licensed physicians, Pietro survived his illness without an operation. Within a few weeks he was as good as new. Sarina, true to her word, tied a black shawl around her head and, looking very pious indeed, went begging for alms. It was considered lucky to give money to a cause like hers and, long before she had called on all her relatives, she had obtained the funds she needed for the banquet.

Although her begging was done among a select few, anyone who wished could attend the banquet. There were few Sicilians in Mount Allegro who did not attend. Fortunately for Sarina there were several banquets held on Saint Joseph's Day, so that everyone did not congregate at her house at the same time. Those who had any sense and good appetites — and most of them did — attended three or four banquets in the course of the day. After all, Saint Joseph's Day came only once a year — and what other saint could goad Sicilian women to the same culinary heights?

Sarina's long table of food stretched from one end of her living-room to the kitchen, and was piled high with a dazzling variety of meats, fruits, and pastries. Three Sicilian neighbors, who had a reputation for being always in need, sat at the head of the table supervising the feast. They represented Jesus, Joseph, and Mary.

The rules for participating in the banquet were so simple a child could follow them. Many of us did; in fact, so frequently that 'Jesus, Joseph, and Mary,' who were entitled to whatever food was left over, would glare at us with undisguised bitterness at our request for a third or fourth helping.

Each guest filed by the banquet table, cafeteria style, selecting the food he wished, and then went to the head of the table to have it blessed by Jesus, Joseph, or Mary. He then had the choice of either devouring the food right then and there, or tasting a little of it and taking the rest home in a paper bag. The children did both, but no one dared scold them because it was Saint Joseph's Day and everyone knew how much Saint Joseph loved little children.

My Aunt Giovanna, who could never resist the temptation to tell you how much better such things were done in Sicily, liked to describe a Sicilian Saint Joseph festival to anyone who would listen.

Her mother was named after the saint, and she prided herself on her ability to remember all the details connected with a Saint Joseph's Day in Girgenti. To celebrate the feast properly, she would point out, the three who played the rôles of Jesus, Joseph, and Mary would have to be beggars picked up at random from the streets, preferably from the steps of a church. She emphasized this so much that it always seemed a shame there weren't as many beggars in America as there were in Sicily. . . .

When you went to a Saint Joseph feast in Sicily it was like going to the opera. Everything that could be dramatized was dramatized. The three beggars selected for the rôles of Jesus, Joseph, and Mary actually re-enacted the thrilling episode in Joseph's life when he fled from Egypt in the middle of the night to save the infant Jesus from Herod's edict that all male infants be slain.

With 'Jesus' and 'Mary' seated on a donkey led by 'Saint Joseph,' the group entered the city dressed as ordinary peasants. Saint Joseph carried a shepherd's staff and wore sandals. When they came to the residential section of the city, Saint Joseph would rap at the door of the nearest home and beg shelter for himself and his family.

'He could usually expect to be turned away,' my Aunt Giovanna explained, 'for everyone knew it was Saint Joseph's Day and that they would be interfering with the drama if they took them in.' After being turned down at several homes, the trio finally arrived at the home where the feast was scheduled to take place.

When Saint Joseph begged shelter here, the head of the family would ask him to identify himself. At first Saint Joseph would merely say that he was a stranger in need of food and shelter for himself and his family, but at the host's insistence he would finally and reluctantly admit that they were 'Jesus, Joseph, and Mary.' Immediately there would be loud cheering and revelry among the assembled guests and the three would be taken to a room where a banquet table and an altar had been prepared in their honor.

The guests would then take their place around the table, with Jesus, Joseph, and Mary at the head. Joseph would say grace and the moment he was through the guests would yell 'Viva San Giuseppe!' and dig into the food. It was impossible, of course, to consume all the food that

was served. Parcels of it would be dispatched to neighbors and friends who hadn't been able to attend, and the
leftovers would be given to the beggars to take with them.

Even though he was not a Catholic, my Uncle Luigi
seldom missed a Saint Joseph banquet. But he always
was careful to explain his position:

'Why should anyone pass up good food when he can
get it for nothing? I can enjoy this food without sharing
your ideas about what it represents.

'For me it is excellent food, the kind I seldom get at
home because my daughters are too lazy to cook anything
but dull American dishes. For the rest of you this extravagance is part of the bribery you extend to your saints
and I don't approve of it. You try to get on their good
side because you are afraid of them, and so you spend
your hard-earned dollars in this fabulous way.

'In the old days, before anyone knew about dollars, they
used to kill people to make the gods happy. Now you
run out and buy a chicken and kill that. The principle
is really the same.'

He spaced each idea with enormous bites of food.

'Fear,' he added, 'is at the bottom of all this sacrificial
nonsense committed in the name of religion. Have I ever
told you about the rich, crazy family I knew in Sicily
when I was a young man?' It usually made no difference
whether he had or not; he would tell it to you anyway.

'The family was named Sacca. They were all fairly well
educated and they owned more land than they could see
from the top of their beautiful castle. Imagine a family
as rich as that being afraid of anything! They were most

afraid of the dead. They imagined that unless they were hospitable to the dead, the corpses of their relatives would rise from their graves and attack them.

'A mad family. One of the sisters lived by herself on the top floor and led the life of a martyr. As part of her penance, she had inserted a nut in the bones of her knee so that she could suffer intense pain whenever she walked. The woman naturally stank with pus. You could smell her fifty yards away. I used to do masonry work around the place and it would make me sick to see her muttering her prayers and creaking that knee around.

'Her brother Guido was an atheist. He had no use for her self-torture, and he never missed an opportunity to let her know his disgust for it. He cursed her roundly whenever she was within earshot. During the Christmas holidays, when the family ate together — the only times they ever did, by the way — he would make a long after-dinner speech to the relatives present on the theme that all Michela needed was a real husband to restore her sanity.

'He was a real devil, that man. Sometimes he would pay some little boy a few pennies to steal up behind Michela and yell out some horrible blasphemy. Poor Michela would turn around, terrified out of her wits, and start crossing herself as fast as she could.

'But what I started to tell you was this family's custom of feasting the dead. Once every year they would lay out an enormous banquet table with place cards bearing the names of close relatives who had died. The table would be loaded with food — a complete dinner with all courses, including a glass of fine brandy and my favorite dessert, *cannoli.* There were chairs placed around the table but no one ever sat in them.

'It used to make my blood boil to see all that wonderful food turning into swill. I once asked the gardener there, "Doesn't Don Paulo realize that ghosts don't care for food? If they ate food, they wouldn't be ghosts."

'The gardener told me to mind my own business, but I think he agreed with me. There were people in the town who didn't have a crust of bread, but Don Paulo went on feeding the dead. The food would stand on the table for three days. By that time everyone in the family pretended that the dead had eaten all they wanted. Of course the place smelled to high heaven. I never envied the servants who had to clean up the mess.

'Some people said that the reason Don Paulo celebrated the Feast of the Dead in that curious way was that he was atoning for his atheist brother Guido. Others, like myself, just thought he was a damn fool.'

I asked my uncle to tell me more about Guido.

'In his own perverse way Guido was a genius. He hated two things most, religion and the rich, and he did everything possible to show his contempt for them. He was so smart that he could pull tricks on both of them at the same time. His favorite trick was to make up a long and wonderfully detailed story about how he had seduced the wife of one of the town's most respected citizens and then go to confession with the story.

'The priests were fascinated by the details of Guido's confessions and listened to them with unpriestly eagerness. After he had worked up their interest to a great pitch, Guido would stop suddenly at the climax of an exciting confession and ask the priest how much he would pay him to hear the rest of it. After a while, they learned to recognize his voice and his tricks and would have nothing more to do with him.

'But the sins he actually committed were as imaginative as the ones he invented. He became notorious for making the daughters of rich men pregnant and then washing his hands of them. When they begged him to marry them, his reply was: "Go back to your rich father. He will take care of your illegitimate child. He takes care of a great many illegitimate things."

'Of course a man with that kind of genius was doomed from the start. When the war with the Turks came along, the Government wanted him in the army. His relatives, who were all generals and captains, wanted him to be an officer.

'He was a fine figure of a man and would have attracted many women in an officer's uniform (although he didn't do so badly without one, I must say), but Guido hated war and refused to have anything to do with the army. One night he disappeared. His family claimed they didn't know where he was. A few days later the *carabiniere* found him in a forest living on the bread and wine brought to him by a farmer's daughter. They stuck him in the army as an ordinary soldier. I heard from friends who served in the same regiment that he immediately began organizing a rebellion. But as is usually the case, some stool-pigeon gave him away a few days before the rebellion was to be sprung and Guido was arrested.

'Ordinarily, a soldier guilty of a crime like that would be court-martialed and shot as a traitor. And as a matter of fact, that is exactly what happened to the men who helped him plan the rebellion. But out of respect to his brother, who was an important general, the army decided to keep Guido in prison.

'One day his brother the general came to see him while he was in prison. Guido greeted him by saying, "As my brother, I embrace you, but as an officer of the Italian Army I spit on you." And that, in effect, is what he did.

'The family felt pretty much disgraced by the whole business, and I imagine they were relieved when Guido died of tuberculosis a few months later. I suppose they found a place for him at their banquet for the dead. I never found out because by that time I had left for America.'

The Feast of the Dead was celebrated by my relatives in the fall, at Hallowe'en time. Rich or poor, all of them, with the exception of my Uncle Luigi and a few heretics, observed the feast in the same way they had in Sicily. Unlike the Saccas, they regarded the event as a holiday rather than an opportunity for gloom. And, of course, no food ever went to waste.

The feast was intended primarily for children, but the grownups made much more of a fuss over it than we did. We were never very happy about it because the idea of paying homage to the dead always seemed unnatural, especially since none of our American playmates had such strange holidays in their homes. Our chief consolation was that we received colored candy gifts that were the envy of every kid in the block who didn't have Sicilian parents.

My Uncle Luigi had definite reasons for disliking the Feast of the Dead. For one thing, he did not care for the kind of candy the dead gave away. He also objected to the idea of the dead making gifts to children on the same ground that some people object to Santa Claus. The whole thing was a fraud, according to Uncle Luigi, a colossal lie that innocent children were bribed into believing. And what stupid bribes! Candy!

We heard him hold forth on this theme at least once a year but, like dutiful children, we had more faith in our parents than we had in him, and were convinced that one night a year some of the same corpses we had seen so carefully buried would push their way up through six feet of earth to bring us candy.

The idea frightened us, and my mother never had any trouble getting us to behave several days before the miracle actually took place. We were all afraid of offending the dead and, from a more practical point of view, we did not want to spoil our chances of getting our full share of presents.

After what seemed like an interminable stretch of perfect behavior, the eve of the holiday finally arrived, and we would go off to bed at sundown, trying desperately to fall into as deep a sleep as possible. There was an excellent reason for this. We had been fully warned that if the dead discovered any children with their eyes open on the night they delivered their gifts, they would be sure to pull out their eyeballs.

On such a night my sister Maria once woke up screaming that a corpse was tearing away her eyeballs. I had my share of bad dreams, but no matter how many times I woke during the night I made certain that my eyes stayed tightly shut. None of us had any curiosity as to what the dead looked like. We simply suspected the worst.

There was never a brighter morning than the morning afterward. The dead were definitely gone for another year, and there were presents for us hidden all over the house. For some malicious reason never made clear, the dead insisted on hiding their gifts in the most out-of-the-way corners. Sometimes it would take all morning to find them. My sister Giustina nearly always burst into tears in the middle of the hunt, insisting that the dead had forgotten all about her, and she would cry until we found the gifts for her, each one neatly labeled with her name.

Although we secretly disliked the dead for their threats and their bad manners, we had to admit that they had fine memories. None of us was ever left out. The gifts were trays of pastries (which tasted suspiciously like the kind my father made) and sugar-moulded saints, dogs, horses, and lambs, all of them decorated with red stripes.

The animals were usually eaten first; then the saints. In time, the soldiers fared no better.

(S I X)

Evil Eye

EVERY YEAR, ON THE SATURDAY BEFORE EASTER
while the saints in church were still draped with purple
mourning from head to foot, my mother armed us with
mops, sticks, and brooms and led us in a surprise and
violent attack on the Devil to drive him from our house.

None of us could see the Devil, but we had her solemn
word that he was lurking in some corner or under one of
the beds. While we covered the house from top to bottom, jabbing viciously in every corner and under every
bed, we yelled out the battle cry, '*Fuora Diavolo, trasi
Maria!*' This was an invitation for the Devil to leave and
the Virgin Mary to enter.

If you happened to jab in the right place and shout the
battle cry as you jabbed, the Devil was bound to slink
away with his tail between his legs. The moment that
happened, the Virgin Mary would enter in a blaze of
glory and spread enough peace and goodwill around to
last the Amoroso family another year.

My mother managed the battle like a general who cannot afford to lose. We were each assigned a specific

area to cover and ordered not to spend too much time on one corner, since the Devil might become accustomed to the blows you gave him and become your friend.

The attack was more difficult to stop than it was to start. Once we became aroused by my mother's lusty leadership, it was hard for us to realize when the Devil was licked, nor could we, above the din we made, distinguish between her commands to halt and her battle cry.

When the battle finally had died down, my mother carefully doused every corner of the house with holy water, on the theory that if our attack had not succeeded in driving out the Devil, the holy water would certainly do the trick.

Like most of my relatives, she firmly believed that evil forces had been in control of the world during Lent, and she deemed it essential to restore God and order by clearing out the Devil from her own little world. Only then would the Virgin Mary consent to enter her house — and, of course, anyone knew how impossible it was to raise a family of children decently without Mary's good influence, *i piccoli diavoli!*

But the Devil, like God, seemed to be everywhere. Mount Allegro was said to be populated with agents of the Devil whose destiny it was to carry out his evil wishes. These agents could cause disease or some other kind of bad luck by simply looking a person in the eye. Many a poor Sicilian had lost his job that way. If you were not quick to sense that *il mal'occhio* was directed at you, you were sunk.

The best way of protecting yourself from the Devil was

to carry a pointed amulet, preferably a horn, so that you could grasp it when someone with the evil eye looked at you. If you did not have the amulet, then the next best thing you could do was to form your hand in the shape of two horns. Making the sign of the cross would give you the same protection, but the trouble with that was that it was too obvious. It might offend the person with the *mal'occhio*.

Those conveyers of ill fortune were not always willing agents of the Devil. They had to be treated with all the civility accorded an ordinary human being. It was bad manners to cause them embarrassment. Often, they were persons who had every desire to lead a quiet and respectable life but, having been selected at birth by the Devil to do his dirty work, there was nothing they could do about it.

Persons who had the *mal'occhio* were said to be marked with certain physical features that distinguished them from ordinary human beings. They usually had a cadaverous and olive-skinned face, and their eyebrows came together in an unbroken line.

For a while I was worried because my face was cadaverous and olive-skinned, and I was afraid of looking people I liked straight in the eye for fear of causing them some disaster. But when I confessed my worries to Mr. Michelangelo, who was an expert in such matters, he assured me that my soul belonged to God and that I was quite incapable of causing anyone evil because my eyebrows did not come together in a straight line.

It was impossible to get any real information on subjects of this kind from my parents or uncles. When I asked

them about such things as *mal'occhio* and *iettatura*
(curse), they laughed at my seriousness and claimed that
those were fantastic notions that grew in the minds of
ignorant Sicilians who didn't know the difference between
fact and fancy.

My Uncle Nino, who never missed a chance to expound
his theories, added that notions of that sort were the
natural result of primitive thinking. 'The Sicilians who
believe in that kind of thing were probably *cafoni* in the
old country who never went to school. If such a thing
as a *iettatura* were possible, my little turnip, do you think
we could have as many wicked people in the world today?'

Uncle Nino liked to answer his own questions. 'No, of
course not,' he said. 'All you would have to do would be
to pay someone with a particularly powerful *mal'occhio* to
give the wicked a sickness from which they would never
recover. Ninety per cent of the world's ills could be
wiped out by getting rid of the top men at the bottom of
them.'

Despite such learned enlightenment, a pair of locked
horns to drive away the evil spirits hung over the doorway
of Uncle Nino's home, as well as our own. And when my
mother or aunt dropped anything, she chanted:

> San Gerlando,
> Senza dannu.

If it was a fork, she was positive someone was gossiping
about her or some other member of her family, and if it
was a knife that fell, it was a sign that someone was about
to call.

Whoever the caller was, he could not enter the house

without passing underneath the locked horns over the doorway, thereby losing whatever evil he might be trying to smuggle in.

My mother believed implicitly in the power of the horns and dusted them as regularly as she dusted the crucifix in her bedroom. Uncle Nino and Aunt Giovanna, on the other hand, each disclaimed responsibility for the horns over their doorway. In spite of my aunt's zeal for cleanliness, they were never dusted. My uncle claimed that the horns were placed over the doorway on my aunt's insistence, while my aunt swore by the memory of her saintly mother that it was he who had ordered them placed there. Whoever it was, they remained there through the years, grimy symbols of a past that still clung to them.

When my cousin Rosina went crazy, there was so much grief among my relatives that some of them forgot their disdain for superstitions and began to say that Rosina's madness was undoubtedly brought about by a *fattura*. How else, they argued, could so healthy and normal a human being become insane?

A *fattura* was far more deliberate and insidious than the evil eye, for it presupposed the services of a witch with a professional knowledge of black magic. Rosina was more loved and admired than any other Sicilian woman in the neighborhood; she was as generous and kind as she was beautiful. 'How could anyone dislike her so much as to hire a witch to put a curse on her?' my mother asked, the tears gathering in her eyes.

Rosina's mother and Mr. Michelangelo had a ready

answer to questions like that. The person they blamed for the tragedy was the middle-aged spinster who lived next door to Rosina. They explained that this jaded virgin had become so envious of Rosina's beauty and her three young sons that she had gone to a witch and asked her to place a *fattura* on her. Envy, they pointed out, was at the root of most evil.

As a matter of fact, it was known that the spinster had gone to the authorities and told them that Rosina was not taking proper care of her children. The spinster was the sister of an alderman and the authorities took her word without investigating. They warned Rosina that unless she took better care of her children, they would be taken away from her.

Rosina was pregnant when this happened, and the threat from the authorities must have unnerved her. She began to see ugly faces peering in through the windows; she heard voices outside the kitchen door telling each other what a bad mother she was, and when she found window rods and chairs in her home mysteriously broken, she was sure that someone was plotting against her.

Her husband Vincenzo tried to dispel her fears by telling her she had read too many fairy tales in her youth, and by promising he would stay home with her in the evenings more often. But like other promises of this kind he had made in the past, he soon broke this one too. Vincenzo, unlike my other relatives, had an insatiable passion for heavy drinking which his Sicilian friends attributed to his association with Irishmen. Wherever he acquired it, it played havoc with his family life. The few evenings he stayed at home were nearly all devoted to drunken parties for the men who worked with him at the factory.

When Rosina began to tell her relatives that she was going mad, no one took her seriously at first, least of all her husband. But soon it became apparent that the spinster's complaints to the authorities were now justified, even though they may not have been at first. She began to neglect the children entirely, and spent most of her time visiting friends in Mount Allegro.

She often came to our house and sat for hours, staring into space without saying a word, then suddenly bursting into loud peals of laughter. Sometimes her children came while she was there, ragged and hungry, the tears streaming down their faces at the relief of finding her.

When they greeted her, she would push them away. 'Why do you come to me?' she would ask. 'Don't you know I'm a bad mother?'

A few minutes later she would start crying and fondle them, begging each one to forgive her. 'I'm all right now,' she would announce to my mother, and take the children home.

But she wasn't right for long, even after she gave birth to her fourth child, a girl. The doctors advised placing her in an institution. Some of my relatives, who were certain by this time that Rosina was the victim of a *fattura*, convinced Vincenzo that the only remedy was to take her to someone who knew how to treat the bewitched.

One of them knew a man in Buffalo named Cristo who had a wide reputation in upstate New York for fighting the Devil successfully. He claimed to be the reincarnation of Christ, and there were many in Buffalo who believed him. Unlike Christ, he demanded a fee for his services either in the form of money or food, on the ground that he was preparing for a great holy campaign that would take the world by storm.

Vincenzo planned to pay him with food because he considered food more holy than money. In preparation for the expedition he filled five gallon jugs with wine and three large baskets with food. From his closest relatives he borrowed train fare and invited them to accompany him on the expedition. They all accepted.

Rosina, aware of the purpose of the trip, was the only one who was at all skeptical. She advised Vincenzo to fill the gallon jugs with water instead of wine. 'Since we are going to visit Christ,' she said, 'it will be a simple matter for this great holy man to repeat the miracle at the marriage of Cana.' Then, remembering other details of Christ's life, she also suggested that they leave the baskets of food behind and take Cristo a fish and a loaf of bread instead.

Her attitude did not improve when they were ushered into the inner sanctum of Cristo. Rosina took one look at him and said playfully, 'Why, Cristo, you have changed the color of your beard!'

Her husband hastily took Cristo aside and explained the purpose of their visit. When Cristo began to mutter incantations over her and pour oil down her back she giggled and, looking him straight in the eyes, said, 'You know, I really think that it is you and not I who is crazy.'

Her giggling infected Rosario Alfano, her godfather.

He tried to suppress the sounds in his throat but it was no use. Soon everyone, except Cristo, was smiling, at first gently, then broadly. Someone started to snicker. Flabbergasted by all this irreverence, Cristo spilled his holy oil all over the front of his trousers. Then he lost his temper, and cursed them all in a vocabulary that was amazing for a man of such holy repute. By this time they were roaring with laughter. Cristo could tolerate them no longer. He ordered them out of his house, ranting that he could do nothing for skeptics and heathens.

They took the wine and food with them and spent the rest of the day picnicking in a park near the station. The experience had a healthy effect on Rosina for a while, so much so that Vincenzo began to believe that perhaps Cristo had actually succeeded in curing Rosina, in spite of herself.

But shortly afterward Rosina had her worst attack and, a few days later, she was confined to a psychiatric ward. At first, the authorities allowed Rosina to visit her family every few days and, during such times, she would let her relatives take her to holy magicians who tried to drive the evil spirits from her, but her condition did not improve. After a few months, she became so unmanageable that she was not allowed to leave the institution for any reason.

My father was among the few who neither believed in superstitions nor made fun of those who did. The only time he had been guilty of consorting with the supernatural was when he first came to Rochester as a young bachelor.

He was homesick and lonely during those first few months in America. As he so gallantly put it, 'I felt alone in America up till the moment I met your mother.' He yearned for the sea and the long beaches of Porto Empedocle, for the pastry shops, where he had so recently served his apprenticeship as a *pasticceri*, and even for the smell of the coffee-urns.

Whenever he had time, no matter how raw the weather was, he rode out on the streetcar to Lake Ontario to pace its sandy beaches and look out across the lake. The waters of the lake were not as blue as those of the Mediterranean, but they too seemed to stretch out endlessly and meet the falling sky. And although he was not a regular churchgoer, he went to Mass every Sunday in those days, so that he could look at the familiar idols of the saints and hear the same Latin incantations he had heard in Porto Empedocle.

It was during this particularly susceptible period of his life that he was approached by an Armenian, who worked in the same candy factory. In broken Italian the Armenian asked him if he wanted to talk with his father and mother.

'But my parents have been dead for a long time,' my father said.

'Exactly. That is precisely why I can help you,' the Armenian said. 'I am on the most intimate terms with the spirit world and can summon the spirit of any dead person dear to your heart. For only two dollars I will arrange for you a five-minute conversation with either your father or mother. Both would cost you three dollars. Your money back if you aren't entirely satisfied.'

'I should have known from all this talk that something was wrong,' my father told me, 'but when a man gets down to specific cases, tells you how much a head he is going to charge you, and even offers you a bargain, you're liable to believe him. Besides, I was pretty young and simple in those days. My nose had not grown to its full length.'

The Armenian was a good salesman — he had once been a rug peddler — and he also persuaded Tano Cipudda and Rosario Alfano, who worked on the same floor with my father, to interview the spirits of their deceased parents. Like my father, both of them had been in the United States only a few weeks and were homesick.

It was agreed that they were all to meet at the entrance of the Catholic cemetery at midnight Saturday. Tano and Rosario each paid the Armenian two dollars in advance; my father, being almost broke, told the Armenian he would pay him on the following payday.

The three friends agreed to spend the evening together before taking the long streetcar ride to the cemetery. None of them had ever had any experience with the spirit world; they were not sure what preparations should be made. When they met after dinner, Tano suggested going to confession, but they were relieved to learn that there were no confessionals open at that hour. They decided that it probably would not be considered sacrilegious to while away their time at a game of billiards, if they kept their bets small.

On their way uptown they passed an auditorium with a huge sign bearing the word 'Temple.' It was the only word in the sign they could read. In front of the place there was a ticket booth and a girl with blinking eyes and a luscious bosom sitting in it. There were also several photographs about of girls with impressively rich natural resources wearing little more than mesh stockings and black garters. Unanimously, they agreed it would be instructive to find out what kind of worship went on in this temple.

And so it was that my father and his two *paesani* saw their first burlesque show. It did not put them in an ideal frame of mind for communicating with a higher astral plane but, at least, it gave them something to muse about on the long and tedious streetcar ride to the cemetery.

The Armenian had not yet arrived when they got there. As they hovered near the entrance of the cemetery, trying to look casual whenever the guard glared in their direction, they wondered what they would say to the spirits of their parents.

'You just can't talk about the weather,' my father pointed out, 'and it certainly would not be tactful to inquire about their health.'

'Suppose my father should ask me what I'm doing in America, instead of staying in Girgenti and supporting my sisters there?' asked Rosario.

'Speak the truth,' advised Tano. 'Tell him there was more money to be made here. Tell him you make five dollars a week in the candy factory just putting pieces of candy from a tray into a box. Remind him of all the sulphur one would have to shake out of the earth to earn that same amount in Sicily.'

After a pause Tano said: 'I'm in worse straits. You re-

member Peppina Scallone? My father always intended I
should marry her. If he had lived, *bonarma,* I probably
should have been her husband now. But what happened
was that after he died, Peppina became so sympathetic at
my being left an orphan that I had no difficulty seducing
her. When she became pregnant, I took a boat to
America. I heard later that she joined a nunnery.

'I can't very well tell my father these things because
Peppina's father was his best friend and *compare.* Perhaps I should talk with my mother instead. She has been
dead a longer time and does not know as much about my
affairs.'

The Armenian was on the next streetcar. He wore
plaid golf knickers and a bright yellow sport cap. His
manner had the offensive eagerness of an aggressive salesman.

'Hullo, gentlemen!' he shouted. 'Wonderful weather
we're having. A wonderful night to communicate with
the world of the spirits. No moon and no stars. Shall
we start? But before we start, do any of you gentlemen
want to change your mind and talk to both of your parents? Tonight, on such a fine night as this, my price is
no longer three dollars for both parents but two dollars
and a half. A real bargain for you, gentlemen, which I
am extending only because you are my fellow-workers.
How about it?'

They all said No. One spirit at a time would be enough
for one night, my father explained.

'All right, gentlemen,' the Armenian said. 'But you are
missing a real opportunity. Of course, if you don't love
your parents enough to spend a half-dollar on one of them,

it is hardly my fault.' He repeated this last remark to make certain they understood him.

The Armenian's Italian was poor, but Rosario understood enough of it to become insulted and want to beat him up. 'God's blood!' he shouted. 'Let me at him. He is carrying broken Italian too far.'

My father and Tano managed to restrain him. Tano gradually quieted him by reminding him that they had already paid the Armenian two dollars and they might as well get their money's worth.

Subdued by Rosario's angry outburst, the Armenian, without another word, led them to a side entrance of the cemetery where they could not be seen by the guard. Before they entered, he gave them some simple instructions, and a brief solemn lecture on the gravity of the occasion, emphasizing the importance of approaching the experience with complete faith.

'And now, gentlemen,' he concluded, 'I will say *addio* to you for a little while. I must go confer with my friends in the spirit world and make certain everything is in good order. Remember, don't talk too long with your parents. Spirits get tired very easily. They simply don't have the same resistance we mortals have.' With a jaunty farewell salute, he disappeared among the gravestones.

Tano lost his composure the moment the Armenian was out of sight. 'Suppose the guard thinks we're vandals and shoots us down,' he said.

'In that case, they wouldn't have to take us very far to bury us,' my father pointed out.

'Something is tugging at my ankles,' hissed Tano a few seconds later.

'Probably a spirit,' my father said, calmly removing a bramble that had entwined itself around Tano's foot.

When they had advanced a hundred yards into the cemetery, as the Armenian had instructed them, they stopped and conferred as to who should be the first to speak with his parent. The choice was an easy one to make. Tano was shaking visibly by this time, and the color of Rosario's complexion had undergone a radical change.

Following the instructions, my father took ten steps forward. 'Where art thou, Mother?' he bellowed. He had intended to talk with his father but in the excitement he forgot.

The reply came almost instantly. 'Who is calling me?'

The voice was very high-pitched, and the words were spoken in broken Italian. Could it be that spirits stopped speaking their native tongue once they left their bodies?

'This is thy son, Peppino!' he yelled as politely as possible. 'How is it with thee, Mother?'

'What is it you want of me? Speak to me, my son!' the voice demanded screechingly.

My father could not believe that his mother, whom he remembered as soft-spoken, would have the rudeness to be shrieking at him. His faith in the whole undertaking suddenly collapsed.

'*Veni ca, cani!*' he thundered. 'The dog. I'm going to tear him apart,' he said to his companions. 'I'll make a real spirit of him.'

'Come here, you dog,' he repeated, expecting somehow in his anger that this order would be obeyed. 'If you don't come here, I'll come and get you,' he threatened.

But no one came and Tano, becoming more and more frightened, wanted to go home. He was certain that my father was mistaken about his suspicions and that his defiance of the spirits would mean their doom.

Tano's fright was so real that it emanated from his body like steam, giving forth a strong, unpleasant odor. In the darkness his face was phosphorescent with yellows and greens. My father and Rosario decided it was time to leave. But Tano could not move. He insisted that two spirits were holding him down by his feet. My father and Rosario had to carry him to the entrance. Once he opened his eyes and saw there were no more gravestones around him, he was able to stand on his own feet.

At the front gate of the cemetery Rosario spotted the Armenian near the car stop, trying to conceal his rotund body behind a telegraph pole. When he realized he had been seen, he exposed himself full view and came toward them. His face was scratched in several places and his knickers had tears in them, but his manner was as bright as ever.

'Did you talk to them all right, gentlemen?' he asked cheerfully.

He paused when he saw the storm signs in my father's face, and tried to cover his agitation with talk. 'I had a strenuous time wrestling with a bad spirit who would not follow orders,' he continued nervously, 'but I guess we made out all right.'

'You're going to have a strenuous time with me right now,' my father said, advancing on him. The Armenian suddenly stopped his chatter, and with marvelous agility started sprinting toward the city.

My father, remembering it was at least six miles to the city limits, soon gave up the chase.   He also remembered he had not paid the Armenian his two dollars and that gave him some satisfaction.

The three friends kept their cemetery adventure a deep secret, knowing they would be laughed at if the story that they had been tricked by an Armenian rug peddler got around the factory.   The Armenian took care not to be left alone in a room with any of them after that but, apart from this simple precaution, he behaved as though nothing had ever happened.

The Unholy Three

MY AUNT GIOVANNA, WHO LOVED CALAMITIES almost as much as she loved her nephews and nieces, thought nothing of frightening us with startling statements if that was the only way she could command our attention.

Unable to have children of her own, our interest in anything she said or did seemed to be essential to her happiness. In her zeal to win us over, she baited us with gifts and endearments and did her best to offset my mother's Spartan influence. She might have succeeded had it not been for my father, who was openly scornful of her tactics. My father never hesitated to express his scorn to her face, so that we were made constantly suspicious of her attentions.

'If Saint Joseph had not interceded,' she told us, 'I don't know who you would have as a father — or mother.' Obviously enjoying the awe these words inspired in us, she continued: 'I don't know whether or not your father ever told you, but it was never his intention to come to North America. He planned to go to Argentina, and would be there today if he had not missed the boat at Palermo by a matter of ten minutes. It is lucky for all of you that your father has never been a patient man. Rather than wait two weeks for the next sailing to Argentina, he took the very next boat that left Italy. And that's how he happened to land in Boston instead of Buenos Aires.'

She didn't stop at that but went on to explain that when my father met my mother in Rochester and proposed marriage, she and my Uncle Luigi did their best to discourage my mother. Both were convinced that because Peppino Amoroso was underweight and nervous he would never survive the harsh climate of Rochester, and would soon become an invalid or make their sister a widow long before her time.

I was glad to hear that my mother, taking courage from my grandfather's neutral attitude, married him anyway. He proved to be one of the healthiest males who had ever married into my mother's clan and, aside from occasional attacks of melancholia and an understandable tendency to feel antagonistic toward my Aunt Giovanna, he made a fairly good husband.

Terrified though I was by the thoughts of what would have happened to all of us if my mother and father had never met, my aunt's speculations intrigued me and I caught some of her love for playing with the word 'if.' I wondered what would have happened if my mother and father had met in Sicily instead of Rochester. That was not a very big 'if.' My father might easily have met my mother there since they had been brought up in towns less than five miles apart. The possibilities fascinated me and I spent many a day-dream in my father's home town, rowboating on the Mediterranean or fishing from the window of the living-room.

Some of my 'ifs' led to dead-end streets. It was inconceivable, for instance, that my father and my uncles Luigi and Nino might have gone through life without knowing each other. Yet I knew from what my aunt told me that this would have happened if my Uncle Nino and my father had not married into the same family.

My aunt liked to attribute all good products of Fate to the foresight of Saint Joseph, her favorite saint, but from what I knew of Saint Joseph it was hard to believe that he would have had the originality and daring to bring together three cronies so noisily compatible and so blasphemous that many of my relatives called them 'The Unholy Three.' Later it seemed to me that there must have been a more obscure saint in heaven, with a slightly ribald sense of humor, who thought out that combination — probably the same saint who caused my father to miss his boat to Buenos Aires by ten minutes.

When the three came together over a bottle of wine, there was no telling whether they would spend the evening exchanging extravagant compliments or curses. When they quarreled, they did so with a relish and ferocity that only men genuinely fond of each other can bring to a quarrel. And every quarrel, no matter how violent, inevitably led to a reconciliation that only surpassed the quarrel in intensity.

Any one of the three had no trouble precipitating a quarrel: Uncle Luigi because he was given to bragging too much; Uncle Nino because he had the largest vocabulary of maledictions; my father because he could lose his temper most quickly.

Because he was the biggest and had the loudest voice, Uncle Luigi could win almost any argument by the simple expedient of roaring down his opponents. The only things he would never dare argue about were my father's cooking skill, which had the admiration of all my relatives, and Uncle Nino's great talents as a storyteller and letter-writer.

In matters of love and religion Uncle Luigi was in his fullest glory. As a widower, he could afford to talk about his past and present exploits with women, whereas my long-married father and Uncle Nino had to depend on their book-learning or what little of their past their wives already knew. Religious arguments were easy for Uncle Luigi because he could speak as an ex-ardent Catholic who had become converted to the Baptist religion, while his cronies had never been anything more than half-hearted Catholics.

The trio usually assembled at our house because my father made the best wine. As an excuse for drinking and talking together, they played cards — *tri sette* if they were alone, briscola if there was a fourth. Their favorite topics of conversation were Girgenti, Porto Empedocle, wars, and my Great-Uncle Minicuzzu.

If my Great-Uncle Minicuzzu had been younger, he might have been a regular member of the group. But he had reached the age when he considered it necessary to make his peace with God. He spent most of his spare time attending various Italian church functions and planning campaigns for extracting contributions from Italians to finance the huge fireworks celebrations that were held every year for Saint Anthony and other favorite saints.

In fact, he was one of the four men who, in recognition of his devotion to the cause, was permitted to hold one corner of the American flag in the annual Saint Anthony procession, while spectators threw their nickels and dimes into the Stars and Stripes.

Occasionally some particularly devout fan of Saint Anthony's would drop a dollar into the flag and the whole procession would come to a standstill, statue and all, while my Great-Uncle Minicuzzu or one of the other flag-bearers carefully pinned the bill into the flag so that everyone could see how generous some Catholics could be and would be shamed into giving more.

In spite of his attachment to the church, Great-Uncle Minicuzzu enjoyed all the vices of the Unholy Three: talking, eating, card-playing, and especially drinking. He had an enormous respect and capacity for wine, and he liked to attribute his excellent health to the fact that he never touched water. A blacksmith by trade, he contended that it was not safe for a man who worked as hard as he did to drink water because it would cool off his body too rapidly and bring on pneumonia. He was also sure that water would ruin any stomach and, when taken with meals, would turn food into lumps of mud.

'Look at what water does to iron pipes. Look how rusty they become!' he argued. 'Do you imagine your stomach can withstand the ravages of water more easily than an iron pipe?' If anyone had the effrontery to look unconvinced, he tied up the argument with the line that 'If water were any earthly good, it would not be free.'

He commanded a good deal of respect among my relatives — because, unlike most of them, he went to church regularly. That impressed them, of course, but more impressive was the knowledge that he had fought under Garibaldi as a youth and later covered himself with more glory by siring twelve children. It was hard to tell which achievement they admired most. Yet as much as they praised his virility, they disapproved of his rôle as a father.

They told how his excessive drinking in Sicily lost him some fine jobs; how he was constantly going from town to town looking for employers who had not heard he was a drunkard. Most of his children were girls. Their father's habit of spending almost everything he earned on wine made it impossible for them to be provided with dowries, so that when they reached the marriageable age, they were faced with the choice of either marrying someone outside their class or migrating to the United States. Most of them chose the United States.

In time, Great-Uncle Minicuzzu found himself alone in Sicily, with most of his children either married or gone to America. By that time no one within an area of a hundred miles would hire him as a blacksmith, so he decided he and his wife might as well come to America too.

The colder weather of Rochester had a sobering effect on him. He gave up blaspheming and reduced his drinking to one bottle of wine a day. He began to go to church regularly, and set up a blacksmith shop in his back yard. At first he enjoyed the respect his children paid him and the frequent visits they made to his home, but that soon began to wear off. He began to complain that, with the exception of his youngest son, who owned a pool room and eventually achieved local fame as a prizefighter, his children bored him because they insisted on reminding him of his age. When he was seventy, they came as a delegation to ask that he give up his blacksmith shop and allow them to support him and their mother in their old age. His answer was to chase them out of the house with an empty wine jug, threatening to break it over their collective heads.

He enjoyed the company of my father and uncles because they showed him little deference, beyond addressing him with the respectful pronouns due a producer of twelve children. They, in turn, liked him so much that they did not hesitate to play jokes on him or give imitations of the expressive way he snuffed tobacco while he ranted about his children.

My Uncle Nino was very proud of one of the jokes he played on him. One day he had the good luck to meet the coaldealer who had been supplying Great-Uncle Minicuzzu with fuel all winter long. The two men shook hands cordially, the coaldealer because Uncle Nino still owed him a bill and my uncle because he hoped to order more coal from the coaldealer on credit.

'I was just on my way to your Uncle Minicuzzu,' the coaldealer said conversationally. 'He owes me a pretty big bill and I thought maybe I could collect a little on it.'

My Uncle Nino sighed lugubriously. 'Ah, *bonarma Ziu Minicuzzu,*' he said, shaking his head and rolling his eyes heavenward.

The coaldealer became worried. 'Has anything happened to him?'

'My friend,' Uncle Nino said gravely, 'I'm afraid you will never be able to collect your bill from him. It hap-

pened only a few weeks ago.' He reached for his handkerchief to wipe away some imaginary tears. 'He was an
old man, you know, and we all have to go sometime. God
has willed it so.'

The coaldealer also reached for his handkerchief and
blew his nose, but it was hard to tell whether it was in
sympathy for Great-Uncle Minicuzzu or because of the
bill he had not collected.

The next day Uncle Nino called on Great-Uncle Minicuzzu. A heavy snow had just fallen and he had no
trouble steering the talk around to the subject of coal.

'That reminds me,' my great-uncle said. 'I wonder
why Mr. Spavento, the coaldealer hasn't been around. I
owe him a lot of money. Only God and the Virgin Mary
know how I am ever going to pay it all, but I wish he
would visit me so that, at least, I could give him a little
on the bill.'

Uncle Nino sighed heavily and said: 'You can forget
the bill. Mr. Spavento, *bonarma*, passed away a week
ago from scarlet fever.'

'What a shame!' my great-uncle said pleasantly.

Uncle Nino sighed. 'Well, we all have to go sometime.
God has willed it so.'

'What God has willed no man can change,' Great-Uncle
Minicuzzu observed. He paused to fill their glasses.
'That explains, of course, why Mr. Spavento hasn't been
here lately to collect. Well, he was a good coaldealer.
Let us drink to Mr. Spavento's soul.' They clinked
glasses.

'Tell me, Nino,' he said as if to change the subject, 'does
Dante make any mention of coal in his description of
hell?'

When Great-Uncle Minicuzzu reached his eightieth birthday, his relatives marveled because he still had full control of his faculties and could argue as vehemently as ever with any member of the Unholy Three. Although most of my relatives lived fairly long lives, they regarded old age as something of a miracle, especially if sound health went with it. Usually they began to think of themselves as 'old' when they reached the age of fifty; every year of good health after that was regarded as a special favor from God.

In spite of his years, Great-Uncle Minicuzzu still put in a long day's work hammering out iron fences with lacy patterns and pretty curlycues, and shaping enormous locks and keys for Sicilian customers who had no faith in the efficacy of those tiny and delicate American contrivances that were supposed to protect you from intruders.

His main recreations were his church activities and his favorite friends. If my father or uncles failed to show up at his home at frequent intervals, he would complain bitterly and speak eloquently about the ingratitude of friends who only visited him regularly in the months of January, February, and March, when his wine was most plentiful.

Once my Uncle Luigi made the mistake of not visiting the old man for several weeks. When he finally got around to calling on him, he found Great-Uncle Minicuzzu huddled in a chair gazing vacantly out of the window. There was no reply to Uncle Luigi's greeting. In fact, the old man showed no sign that he was aware of his presence. Uncle Luigi became alarmed.

'*Ziu Minicuzzu, Ziu Minicuzzu!*' he shouted, shaking him by the shoulder.   ' 'Tis I, Luigi, your nephew.'

There was almost no reaction.   The old man's mouth opened a little, like an idiot's, and he grunted 'Uh.'

'Your nephew Luigi who loves you so much is trying to talk with you,' Uncle Luigi said desperately.   'Can't you say something to me?   One little word.'

'Uh.'   It was the only sound he seemed capable of making.

'Can you hear me, *caru Ziu?*' he pleaded.   'Your beloved nephew, Luigi, wants to know.   Can you hear me? Just nod your head if you can.'

It was no use.   Again there was only an 'Uh' for a reply, and his eyes still had the same vacant stare.

Thoroughly discouraged, Uncle Luigi patted the old man on the head affectionately and went home.   When he had recovered from the shock of the experience, he lost no time spreading the news among the relatives.

'Ah, I've just made a horrible discovery,' he announced. 'Old age has finally caught up with *Ziu Minicuzzu.*   I have just come from seeing him.   He could neither talk to me or hear me, *poveru vecchio.*   All I could get out of him was "Uh." '

When my father heard this, he paid his Uncle Minicuzzu a hasty visit.   He had no sooner entered the door when he heard the old man's booming voice greeting him: '*Ah, buon giorno, caru Peppino.*   It is good to see you. How about a glass of wine with me?'

My father was dumbfounded.   'Are you all right, *Ziu Minicuzzu?*'

'Sure I'm all right.   I used to be able to drink more

wine when I was a younger man, but I don't do so badly now.'

'Can you hear me speak?' my father shouted.

'For goodness' sake stop your yelling. Why shouldn't I be able to hear you speak?'

'But Luigi said — '

'Oh, my beloved nephew Luigi.' The old man grinned mischievously. 'Has he been telling stories about me?'

'Why, he told me that you had lost most of your faculties and that he came to see you and you couldn't talk to him or hear what he was saying.'

'And, pray tell me, why should I bother listening to him or talking with him?' he asked. 'He comes to see me about once every new moon and then expects me to receive him cordially. Why should I? He can go on thinking I've lost my faculties for all I care.' As he took a pinch of snuff he said 'Uh' and chuckled.

'What do you say to a spot of wine to quiet your nerves, caru Peppino? You seem to be on edge today.'

Great-Uncle Minicuzzu and my Uncles Luigi and Nino were avid guests at nearly every banquet my father gave. They flanked him on both sides at the table, like the disciples of Christ at the Last Supper, and they partook of his wine and cooking as though each meal were their last one.

There was a banquet for as many occasions as my father could imagine, and his imagination was fertile. He once gave a banquet for some relatives who were moving to California and, when they were suddenly obliged to change their plans, he gave another banquet to celebrate their staying. He no sooner had finished with one banquet than he began to talk about the next one. He had the pride of an artist in his cooking, particularly his pastrymaking, and he never denied the story that when the Baron Michele, the richest man in the province of Girgenti, went on his honeymoon to Palermo, he took my father along to prepare his favorite desserts.

He was especially noted for a Sicilian delicacy called *cannolo*, which was unsurpassed by any of the other pastrycooks in Rochester and seldom equaled even in New York and Palermo. As a boy he had been apprenticed to a famous Sicilian pastrycook and he learned his trade well. He might have become a celebrated pastrymaker had he remained in Sicily, but here in America, the land of ice-cream and pie, there was not enough of a market for his products and he became another factory worker, expressing his real talents on holidays and other occasions when he could give banquets for his friends and relatives.

Although his *cannoli* were masterpieces, his recipe for making them was no secret and he willingly itemized it for anyone who wanted to attempt it. Needless to say, no one ever approached his results, though several of his more determined imitators came to his kitchen to watch every move and measurement he made. The ingredients were simple: cottage cheese refined to a smooth paste; tiny bits of chocolate mixed into the paste, and a few drops of a magical spirit known as *cannela* (a liquid cinnamon), whose sharp odor recurs to me with fully as many memories as a cup of tea ever gave Proust. The trick, my father claimed, was not so much in concocting the cream as in preparing the crisp, cylindrical shells that held it.

Like most good art, the *cannoli* looked simple but entailed much more work than would seem necessary to a layman. So that he would have no distractions, my father often started making his *cannoli* at three in the morning. Until dawn, he hovered over the shells like an anxious mother, nursing them to their proper crispness. After the shells were done, there were almonds to be roasted and crushed into golden crumbs that would be sprinkled over the ends of the *cannoli* once they were filled with cream. And always there had to be perfect timing. Judging from the amount of patience *cannoli* required and the small amount my father usually showed, he must have saved a little patience every day so that he would have enough to make his *cannoli* once or twice a year.

The more enthusiasts his *cannoli* bred, the less inclined he was to make them. His explanation was that since he did not have time to make *cannoli* for all his friends and relatives, he would make them for no one but his immediate family. When occasionally he broke this rule, our house would take on the atmosphere of a secret underground society.

My father would solemnly warn us not to tell anyone he was making *cannoli* and, when they were finished, he would count them out carefully into empty shoe-boxes he hoarded for such occasions and sneak them to favored relatives and friends, the right number for each family, begging them not to say a word about the gift to anyone lest someone take offense at being left out.

He never took money for his *cannoli* and would be hurt

if anyone tried to pay him. Once he opened a pastry shop and featured *cannoli* as his specialty. For a few months business seemed good; many Sicilians bought many *cannoli*. Yet my father made no money. It was not until he closed the shop that he realized he had failed to charge enough to cover the cost of the ingredients.

In those few months he was in business scores of new *cannoli* addicts were born and, ever afterward, they telephoned hopefully a week before an important holiday like Christmas or Easter to ask if Don Peppino would make a few dozen *cannoli* for them. He enjoyed answering the telephone at such times, even though his answer was usually No, for like any good artist it heartened him to know that his product was still appreciated and in demand.

As temperamental as he was, my father could be relied on to assume responsibility for cooking all Sunday dinners. This sometimes involved preparing at least a half-dozen courses for as many as twenty persons. To show her gratitude, my mother gladly took charge of such details as serving and dishwashing and, when she was certain there were enough guests listening, she complimented him extravagantly not only on his abilities as a cook but also as a carpenter and a paperhanger.

We were all aware of the strategy behind her flattery, yet we realized that she sincerely believed him to be the best cook on earth. When they teased each other, my mother would declare that it was only because of his cooking skill that she had married him, whereupon my father would retort that she could be sure that was not the reason he had married her.

On Sunday mornings he rose earlier than the rest of us and took complete charge of the kitchen, using my mother and one of the children for the menial jobs of peeling, grating, and slicing. His meals had an extravagance about them that was far out of proportion to his salary. To finance them he often had to borrow money. But for him that was less important than sharing the joy and warmth that good food and gay company created.

Like the rest of my relatives, he believed implicitly in the goodness of food and liked to repeat the motto: 'Food is the only thing you can take with you when you die.' This was not said in any morbid sense, but as encouragement for more eating. If a guest had the temerity to turn down another helping of food, the motto was sprung on him with great gusto if it was obvious that the guest's eating capacity had not yet reached its limits (the guest, of course, was never permitted to decide for himself what those limits might be), and as a polite rebuke if it was clear to the host that his guest could not eat another morsel of food without bursting. My relatives' passionate faith in food as a soul and body builder was, in the last analysis, an expression of their philosophy: If you ate well, you felt well. And if you felt well, all was well with the world.

For weekday suppers a soup course, some spaghetti and meat, followed by a salad, was an ample meal. But on Sundays and holidays it was assumed that your appetite became gargantuan and, besides soup and salad, you were expected to stow away at least three different courses of meat, four or five vegetables, along with celery and fennel, all topped off with pastry, fruits, and nuts.

One of my father's meat courses was usually *brusciuluna*, a combination of Roman cheese, salami, and moon-shaped slivers of hard-boiled egg encased in rolls of beef that had been pounded into tenderness. All this was held together by an engineering feat involving many strings and toothpicks. The other meats served were chicken (two kinds usually — boiled chicken, from which the soup had been made — and roast chicken), lamb, and veal. I daresay that if deer meat, pheasant, and rabbit had been more easily available, they would have been served too.

The accompaniment to all this eating was bread and wine. They went with every meal, as inevitably as a theme runs through a song. You drank wine with everything except the soup — though there were those like my Great-Uncle Minicuzzu and Rosario Alfano who liked to drink wine even with their soup, and were fond of repeating the ancient Sicilian boast that they could drink wine even while riding in a cart bumping over a country road.

Bread was eaten with every course, except with such other flour products as spaghetti and pastry. It would have been considered redundant eating bread with them. My relatives, like all Sicilians, had a deep-seated reverence for bread, and they transferred it to their children to such an extent that none of us, even to this day, can eat food without bread and not feel guilty. It was considered sinful to waste bread, or to permit a loaf of bread to sit upside down, or to eat meat without eating bread. One of the most hospitable gestures a host could make during his campaign to gorge a guest with food was to give his guest permission to eat his meat without bread. Once that permission was granted, no risk of sinning was incurred.

Aside from its traditional association with the body of Christ, bread to my relatives was a daily reminder of the hardships they and their ancestors had endured to survive, a symbol of man's humbleness. They regarded bread as some God-bequeathed friend who would keep their bodies and souls together when nothing else would. And when times were bad, they said to each other, 'As long as God grants us a piece of bread, we shall get along.'

Possibly because Sicilians, more than any other group of Italians, have suffered greatly in their struggle for existence, their attachment to bread and what it symbolized was stronger and they put their best efforts into making it. They made it finer and tastier than any other Italian bread. They sprinkled sesame seeds over it and wrought it into a dozen different designs expressing their love of life and fear of the Devil. They made loaves with replicas of flowers on them, loaves formed like a woman's braided tresses, loaves to look like giant amulets, and loaves shaped the way you would shape your hand if you met up with the evil eye. The most common kind was the loaf with three gashes cut into its top – a warning to the Devil of what might happen to him if he tried to interfere with the goodness of God.

The only bread that had a finer texture was the bread that was prepared in honor of Saint Joseph on his birthday. It was firmer and sweeter than everyday bread and as fancy as bread could be without being pastry. My relatives knew of no greater culinary tribute to pay a saint. So closely was this bread associated with Saint Joseph that eating it made me feel a little like a cannibal; as much as I liked its taste, I was always careful not to bite into the bread too hard.

Next to bread and wine, *pasta* was the most cherished of foods. My relatives agreed that no matter how much food a man ate, he could not satisfy his appetite if his main meal did not include some form of *pasta*. This might be in the form of noodles or spaghetti served with sauces of butter, or oil and garlic, or *suco* made from meat and tomatoes. If you got bored with noodles or spaghetti, you had the choice of a score of different shapes of macaroni with as many different names, including butterflies, angels' hair, stars, little worms, sparrows' tongues, and big cannons.

If my father knew in advance that his guests were to include a couple who were expected to announce their engagement, he would advertise the situation by serving a tubular macaroni about three inches long known as *mezzo-zittu*, which means half-engaged. And if the couple were already engaged and about to be married, the macaroni he served was *zittu* (engaged), almost twice the size of *mezzo-zittu*. This was about as far as a Sicilian's sense of delicacy would permit him to go. Once they were married, such suggestive symbols were considered superfluous and any kind of macaroni would do.

My father was a powerhouse of charm. No matter how engrossed his guests might be in his cookery or how loudly they might be babbling to each other, when he rose from his chair he had their complete attention. His opening words at the table were part of his own ritual.

'It is terribly dark,' he would say, even though the sun might be streaming into the room. 'We must light the candles.' Thereupon he would pour red wine into the tumbler of each guest.

With each successive 'lighting of the candles' the room would glow more and more with the good cheer of the guests.   The meal would continue for at least two hours, getting noisier with talk and laughter as the appetites of the guests diminished.   By the time the last course was served, the conversation was so loud that it was difficult to be heard unless you had a strong voice.   The climax of the meal would be reached with the serving of the vermouth and whatever pastries my father had baked for the occasion.

At that point my father would rise, stand on a chair to make himself taller and wave a bottle to command attention; then, by some miracle which I have never understood, proceed to toast each guest seated at the table in rhyming double-entendres.   With each toast, he poured out a drink of the vermouth in a special glass which was shared by all, and handed it to the guest he had toasted. While he waited for the glass to be emptied, he composed the next toast.

Regardless of how many guests there were at the table, my father never seemed to become exhausted or repetitious.   Many of the guests he had toasted on other occasions, but he had a different toast for them each time.   If the guest was a recent acquaintance, my father's toast was likely to be in the nature of a compliment.   For older friends he made up toasts that lampooned their favorite weakness without causing any offense.   The older the friend, the franker the toast.

Some of the toasts were in the nature of congratulations for newly acquired jobs, triumphs over recent illnesses, and blessed events.   Only the suckling infants, who were

considered too young to be of drinking age, did not receive individual toasts. When my father was through
toasting the adults, he toasted the infants collectively and
then poured out a drink for himself.

The dinner usually closed with my Uncle Nino making
a speech in pure Italian. He used the longest and most
sonorous words he knew and, although only a few of the
guests had gone to school long enough to understand
everything he said, everyone listened attentively. His
speeches either eulogized the occasion and the company
present or dealt with some scholastic honor that one of the
children had achieved.

Uncle Nino had surprising ideas about what constituted
a scholastic honor. If one of us passed a grade or brought
home a report card that wasn't littered with failing marks,
or happened to mention that his teacher had singled him
out to erase the blackboards or to take charge of opening
or closing the classroom windows, that was sufficient incentive to launch Uncle Nino into an oration on 'scholastic
honor' that was never less than a half-hour long.

However trivial his subject might be, nothing he ever
praised sounded trivial. He had a natural talent for en-
riching the slightest theme with a rain of melodious
phrases. As if his own embellishments were not enough,
he wound up every speech, regardless of its theme, with
a quotation from Dante, his favorite author. Carried
away by his own oratory, he would sometimes forget his
original subject and talk about the glories of Italy or the
wonders of New York City, but always he remembered
to finish up with Dante.

On patriotic holidays, he seemed to forget his anxiety to return to Sicily and spoke about the United States with religious fervor. At such times he sounded like an old-school Fourth of July orator. The only difference was in the foreign language he used and in the fact that instead of quoting Lincoln, he quoted Dante.

It was difficult for the children to take Uncle Nino seriously on such occasions, for we all knew him as an incurable tease who kept us in a state of laughter or tears. He was one of the few relatives we ever dared address familiarly, without saying 'Uncle.' We treated him as one of us, letting him join in our games and calling him the same devastating names we used among ourselves whenever he cheated or tried to make rules of his own.

When he got up to make a speech, it was hard for us to suppress our giggling. But gradually the awe and respect we saw in the faces of the adults around the table silenced us and we would listen to what he was saying, trying to look as enraptured as the grownups but understanding only occasional words, even when he happened to be talking about one of us.

In a sense, Uncle Nino's speeches were the only kind of sermons my relatives heard, and, though they did not deal with the glories of God, they dealt with glories they understood and cherished. His words carried them away from their mundane factory existences back to a past which by now had been prettified beyond recognition by the tricks that memory can play on human beings who are not in complete harmony with their present. And although they could not understand all his allusions, they preferred him to the Irish priests who spoke a language

which they understood less and which did not do as much
for their souls.

After one of my father's banquets the Unholy Three
would sit around the table with Great-Uncle Minicuzzu
and settle the most pressing problems of the world.   My
father and great-uncle did most of the talking since they
were considered experts on war and politics — my great-
uncle because he was the oldest and had the longest memory, my father because he could read the American newspapers.   My great-uncle usually won all political discussions by insisting that no one who had not fought under
Garibaldi could know anything about the true nature of
political history.   Since he was an old man, no one dared
contradict him on this point.

The men talked in glib generalities about the causes and
effects of war, about the way the rich stuck together to
keep the poor down, and they said many harsh things
about kings and rulers who were more interested in power
than they were in the welfare of their people.

American politics were seldom discussed, except in
terms of particular candidates who were promising to
make conditions better 'after the election.'   Election was
a magic word for them.   If things were not going right,
they comforted each other by saying: 'Conditions are
never good before an election.   They will get better as
soon as the new candidates are in office.'   They seldom
knew what the 'new candidates' represented, but they persisted in believing that any change might be for the better,
even though the miracle election that would make everything right never seemed to come.

Political discussions were bound to have a sobering effect on all of us, no matter how colorfully my father described the time he saw Kaiser Wilhelm in a Palermo parade or how many anecdotes Great-Uncle Minicuzzu told about his life with Garibaldi, and it was a decided relief to everyone when the men turned to storytelling, an art they found more compatible than politics. Although the men repeated the same stories, they sneaked new situations and characters into each retelling, so that eventually they could hardly be recognized as the same stories. As in everything else, my uncles vied with each other as they spun their yarns, each one trying to make his sound more involved and more imaginative than the others'.

All that my Uncle Nino needed was the suggestion of a story; he would fill in the details, the sequences, the climaxes, and might even give it a title of his own. He had once read an Italian translation of Shakespeare (he pronounced it 'Shakispiro') and had developed his own versions of the playwright's best-known classics, though he insisted they were Shakespeare's.

When he told the story of *Romeo and Juliet*, for example, he barely made any mention of Shakespeare's love theme, but concentrated his attention on the pharmacist who had broken the law by selling Romeo the poison for his suicide. The climax of my uncle's version was not in the vault with Romeo and Juliet, but in a courtroom with the pharmacist on trial for his life.

My Uncle Nino ended his version of the play more cheerfully than Shakespeare. He had the pharmacist's brilliant lawyer convince the court that although it was contrary to law for the pharmacist to have sold Romeo the poison, it would have been inhuman and immoral for him to have refused the large sum of money Romeo offered for the poison.

Having had more education than the rest, my Uncle Nino had theories about storytelling. 'No one except a dimwit can possibly find pleasure in stories made up mainly of facts,' he said. He cited Dante's writings to uphold this belief, and that was final proof, of course, for no one in his right senses would have dared imply that anyone ever approached Dante in literary genius. The greatest stories in the world, he insisted, grew out of the writer's imagination and illustrated universal truths and proverbs. He had profound faith in the ability of proverbs to guide human minds along the wisest channels. 'If you knew all the Sicilian proverbs,' he claimed, 'you could act wisely in any situation that presented itself.'

If the truth were known, Uncle Nino was a writer himself. No one had ever read anything he wrote and he never talked of it. My Aunt Giovanna, who liked to discuss her husband when he was not present, said that he wrote late at night when she was trying to sleep. She said he kept his writings locked in his safe along with his stock of jewelry.

Like many respectable people, my relatives considered writing some kind of secret vice and never became openly curious about my uncle's literary life. No one ever discovered what his writings were about; certainly not my Aunt Giovanna, whose reading ability did not extend beyond cooking recipes. She once showed me a ledger with pages and pages of his beautiful script, but what was written in it I did not know, for I could not read any Italian then.

In spite of his theories and his scholastic turn, Uncle Nino could dramatize a set of facts more effectively than any of my relatives. He had a flair for making the most ordinary situations absorbing and if he was sometimes suspected of stretching a narrative into the realm of fancy, he was forgiven on the grounds that he was only doing what Dante might have done. On the whole he was faithful to the main facts of a story, for he had a profound respect for truth; when he touched it up now and then, it was only to make truth more attractive than it generally seemed.

His most effective trick was to introduce a climax every few minutes, piling one on top of the other, and giving the impression all the while he told his story that each climax was the final one. He punctuated his stories with long, tantalizing pauses and a versatile set of facial expressions, which included a diabolically suggestive leer and the raising of either his left or right redhaired eyebrow.

He was at his best when he dealt with stories of his home town, Caltanissetta. His favorite one concerned the daughter of a peasant widow who married the richest baron in the province. My uncle had been secretary to the baron's nephew as a young man. That was many years after the events described in the story took place, but he had picked up a number of facts from his employer that were not generally known.

Although the theme of the story was a noble one, there were many ignoble details in it which I was not able to grasp until I was older. It would be futile to try to tell it

as my Uncle Nino did but here, at least, is the gist of it —
without the benefit of his tantalizing pauses, his eyebrows,
and his magnificent leer.

Baron Albertini was rich and handsome and was be-
sieged by women of his own class but, except for purposes
of casual love-making, he showed no interest in any of
them.   One day while riding through the fields on a hunt,
he saw a girl about fifteen years old spinning in the sunlight.   Her raven-black hair fell over her shoulders like
a dark cascade and, when she turned her face toward him,
he fell in love with her and resolved right then and there
to make her his wife.

The girl's mother was a peasant widow who made her
living by weaving, and it was difficult at first for her to
believe that a man of his education and wealth could have
honorable intentions toward her daughter.   'I think I
have a good idea of what a person of your class means by
"marriage," ' she told him bluntly.   The Baron begged her
to believe that he wanted, more than anything else in the
world, to make her daughter Annichia his legal wife.

'Very well,' the widow said.   'I'll give you my daughter
in marriage, but first you must prove your good intentions.
You must first provide her with the means of an education.
Although she is fifteen years old, she has never been to
school.   The only things she can do are cook and weave
and, as your wife, such knowledge would be useless.   No
matter how much you loved Annichia, you would soon
become bored with so uneducated a wife.'

The Baron complimented the widow on her great wisdom and agreed to follow her suggestion.   And so it was

that Annichia, the poor weaver's daughter, was sent to the best schools in Italy. She did remarkably well, and within five years she had lost all traces of her peasant upbringing and could read and write as well as anyone who had been born of a rich family. Although she now combed her hair on top of her head, she was still as appetizing as ever to the Baron and he promptly married her.

When the Baron's rich friends heard of the marriage, they were frankly cynical about it and made all kinds of dire predictions. 'A weaver's daughter, mind you,' they said to each other. 'Imagine our Baron making such a foolish marriage, when he had the pick of any number of well-bred girls. A woman from such a lowly background is bound to do him in.'

A drinking-friend of the Baron's named Benito was one of the most vociferous prophets and didn't hesitate to tell the Baron to his face that a girl of such background was incapable of being a faithful wife. 'Her inferior blood,' he explained, 'naturally gives her base instincts which she can't possibly escape, no matter how much education you have pumped into her.'

The Baron was only amused by such talk and offered to wager Benito that his wife would always remain faithful to him. Benito, a man of convictions, took up his offer at once. The two men agreed that if Benito ever presented the Baron with evidence of Annichia's unfaithfulness, the Baron would give him a quarter of all his lands, which were considerable. If, on the other hand, Benito was proven to be wrong, he would present the Baron with an equivalent amount of his land. When Benito told a few of his most intimate friends about the wager, none of them doubted that Benito, being handsome and cunning, would win out.

Not long afterward Benito heard that his friend the Baron had gone to Palermo on business. He saw this as his golden opportunity, and hurried to present himself at the front door of the Baron's home. When the butler announced his name to Annichia, she recognized it at once as that of a friend of her husband. She greeted him with great courtesy and warmth and, to honor him properly, ordered the servants to bring pastries and wine. Benito, interpreting all this show of hospitality in terms of his good looks and charm, felt he would have no trouble in carrying out his plan.

As he drank more wine, his conversation became less formal, his manner more intimate and, in a few hours, confident that he had succeeded in arousing Annichia's baser instincts, he boldly suggested that they continue their conversation in her bedroom. Annichia, blushing and agitated, said No at first. But when a few minutes passed and she still had not shown him the door, Benito resumed his advances.

Within a short time, he had progressed to the point where she was coyly protesting, 'But supposing my husband finds out.' Benito reassured her eloquently on that score. No one would ever know. As for the servants, he could persuade them to keep their mouths shut with gifts of money. Nothing must stand in their way to happiness.

Finally Annichia said: 'Very well. But not now. I prefer that we wait until after dark. Most of the servants will have retired by then. Come in by the side entrance.

I shall leave it unlocked for you.'

Benito tried to seal the agreement with a kiss but An-nichia put him off, saying, 'Not now. Later. Tonight you will have everything.'

When Benito left her he was in the seventh heaven. He would not only acquire a large piece of land by this pleasant escapade but he would also be enjoying the favors of a beautiful woman. Moreover, he reasoned with himself, he would be teaching her husband a valuable lesson about the lower classes.

When the appointed hour came, Benito was waiting for Annichia at the side entrance. Annichia appeared in a low-cut loosely flowing gown, which Benito sensed could be slipped off quickly. In one hand she carried a candle; with the other she motioned him to follow her upstairs, beseeching him with her eyes to be as quiet as possible. So seductive did she seem to Benito that he was strongly tempted to leap on her as they climbed the stairway. But his upper-class breeding prevailed and he summoned enough patience to wait until they reached her bedroom.

Annichia led the way through a number of winding passages, with the passionate Benito close at her heels. 'She must have a secret bedroom which she uses only for love-making,' he mused happily. At last they came to a huge bronze door which gleamed in the semi-darkness of the hallway.

'Here we are,' announced Annichia. 'You go in first. I have a little errand to attend to but I'll be back in a minute.'

Fairly quivering with anticipation, Benito entered the room. In the darkness he could make out nothing.

When he lit a match to find the lamp, there was no lamp. There was nothing. The room was perfectly empty. In his astonishment, he burned his fingers. He lit another match and discovered that the room was like a huge vault, with no windows and with walls of solid bronze. The ceiling was of boards but it was at least twelve feet high. He ran to the door but now there was no door, only a huge block of bronze which could only be opened from the outside. Benito began to yell and scream in a manner that was entirely out of keeping with his upper-class breeding. He might as well have saved his breath. He yelled all night but no one came.

The next morning when Benito was still screaming, Annichia's maid lifted one of the loose boards in the ceiling of Benito's prison and listened to what he had to say. When Benito saw the servant's face through the aperture in the ceiling, he had a great deal to say. He was hungry. He was thirsty. He must get out at once. And although he was talking to a servant he was humble, though a trifle noisy.

'Please bring me something to eat,' he begged.

The maid left, and reappeared a few minutes later.

'Do you have any food for me?' Benito asked hopefully.

'No,' said the maid. 'My mistress instructed me to tell you that if you wish to eat you must earn your food. Here is the spindle her mother used in her poorer days,' she said, lowering it on a piece of string. She also threw him a package of fiber. 'And there is your material,' she added brightly. 'You will be paid according to the work you turn out. Now remember, *Signorino,* if you want to eat, you must spin.'

'But I don't know how to spin,' Benito groaned.

'A man of your intelligence — and hunger — will soon learn,' she assured him, and left him alone with the spindle and fiber.

When she returned five hours later, Benito had produced only a few feet of yarn. 'Now for God's sake,' he implored, 'please bring me something to eat.'

The maid examined his work contemptuously and took it to Annichia. She came back a few minutes later and threw him two *centesimi*, an amount barely equivalent to an American penny.

'That is all your work is worth so far,' the maid told Benito, 'and I can assure you that my mistress is being generous. I myself would not give that much for it.'

'But I want to eat. What good is the money to me?' wailed Benito. 'Please take this money back and get me some food.'

'Well, two *centesimi* won't buy very much, but I'll do the best I can,' the maid said.

She came back with a crust of bread and some water. 'That is all I could buy with the money. Your spinning will have to improve if you want to eat better meals,' she said.

In the days that followed, Benito's spinning did improve considerably. Before long, he was earning enough to have a bit of fruit with a slice of bread and water. His living conditions, on the other hand, became worse. There was no receptacle in the room for Benito to use when he had to relieve himself. Consequently, it smelled horribly, so much so that the maid barely said anything to him any more, not being able to tolerate the stench of the place when she removed the floor board in the ceiling.

She would hastily draw up whatever thread he had spun during the day and, after Annichia had judged its monetary value, return with whatever food his earnings would purchase. His appearance, of course, changed drastically. It would have been difficult for anyone to imagine that this haggard, unkempt, unshaved creature desperately bent over a spindle, was the gay and handsome blue-blood who only a few days before had dined with a baron's wife and engaged her in intimate conversation.

After a week had passed, Antonio Luppo, a close friend of Benito's who knew of his rendezvous with the Baron's wife, became envious. 'Benito must be having the time of his life with that wench,' he told his crony the Notary. 'Imagine a whole week of uninterrupted love-making with that luscious piece. What bliss! I think I should share in some of that bliss. After all, if she is willing to go to such lengths with our friend Benito, she will probably be glad to extend her favors to me.'

The Notary confirmed the soundness of his logic, and Antonio presented himself at the castle. Annichia was all smiles when she greeted him.

'I take it that you have come to inquire after your friend Benito,' she said.

'Yes, I have,' replied Antonio. 'But, dear lady, I might as well confess at once that I am more interested in you than I am in Benito. My interest in him only extends to the point where I should like to emulate his activities of this past week.'

Annichia did not blink an eyelash. 'You shall certainly have your wish,' she said. 'Would you like to come along with me now?'

Antonio palpitated at the boldness of this lovely creature and assured her he would like nothing better. Avidly
he followed her upstairs, through the winding corridors.
And when she told him to precede her through the bronze
door because she 'wanted to do a small errand first,' he
could hardly restrain himself.

The door closed behind him as he entered. His head
began to whirl when the odors of the room struck his nos-
trils. Under a ray of light that came from a slit in the
ceiling he saw his friend Benito, his hairy profile pointed
at a spindle.

'What is this?' cried Antonio.

'So she has trapped you, too,' Benito said placidly.

'What in hell are you doing?' asked Antonio, pointing to
the package of fiber and the spindle.

'I'm spinning for my next meal, and I want to warn you
now that I am barely able to spin enough to keep myself
alive. You may be a dear friend of mine but don't expect
me to spin for you. If you want to eat, you'll have to
spin.'

Antonio held out until the next morning, when the
gnawings of hunger overcame his pride. He asked the
maid to bring him some fiber and a spindle and then he
begged Benito to give him instructions. Before long he,
too, was spinning thread for his food. In a few days he
was able to earn as much as Benito and, from one point
of view, that was unfortunate, for the more often the two
of them ate, the more frequently did Nature take its usual
course, and the more unbearable the room became.

Antonio's friend, the Notary, knew nothing, of course,
of the fate of his two friends. He imagined, with a wealth
of erotic detail, that they were having a gay and lively

time with Annichia. Being a man who was still ade-
quately equipped for bedroom frivolity, though no longer
in his prime, he reasoned that he would be doing a great
injustice to himself if he passed up this ideal opportunity
for pleasure.

'After all,' he told himself, 'if the wench can entertain
my two friends so well she can surely find room for me
too. Without a doubt, she must be the sort of low-class
woman who finds it agreeable to be ravished by a variety
of men. No reason why I should not add to the variety.'

With these pleasant thoughts radiating through him,
the Notary hastened to the Baron's house. Annichia received him with the same cordiality and provocative manner she had received Antonio. In a few minutes, like a
hound eager for his bone, the Notary was following her
up the stairs and through the winding corridors, his very
being watering with keen anticipation.

You can easily imagine the scene that ensued when the
Notary came in through the bronze door and came face
to face with his cronies. He soon joined them in spinning
for food and I regret to report that, because of his advanced age and the growing numbness in his fingers, he
had a more difficult time learning to spin than either of
his colleagues. In fact, he would probably have starved
to death had not the Baron returned from his trip when
he did.

Annichia greeted her husband with great affection and,
after he had refreshed himself with some wine and her
gentle caresses, she announced that she had a tremendous
surprise in store for him. Leading him to the room above
the prison she lifted the board and pointed down to his

friends. They sat on their haunches, huddled together like beggars on a church stair, their diamond-studded fingers desperately working over their spindles. The fumes from the room were so suffocating that the Baron was forced to replace the board after a few seconds. Before he did, the three of them were begging him for mercy.

'Please get me out of here,' pleaded Benito. 'I'll pay you the bet the moment I'm free. I'll do anything, but get me out of here quick.'

But Annichia was not done with them yet. Through the servant they were informed that if they wanted their freedom, they were to scrub and clean the room first and then send for their personal physicians to disinfect it. 'In that way,' Annichia explained to the Baron, 'we shall be certain that the whole town will know of their disgrace.'

And that is exactly what happened. The physicians could hardly be expected to keep the details of such a rich story to themselves. The Baron himself was not at all reluctant to tell the story to his friends, for it proved he had a wise and virtuous wife. In less than a week's time, the story had spread through the entire province and the only ones who had not heard it were the stone deaf. So ridiculed were the three would-be seducers that they were compelled to move many miles away. Benito, of course, paid off his debt to the Baron before he left. The Baron and Annichia, as far as my Uncle Nino knew, remained happy and faithful to each other to the end of their days.

(E I G H T)

Sicilian Virgin

STRAFALARIA MIGHT SOUND LIKE A PECULIAR disease, but among my relatives it was a powerful invective — more powerful than 'hussy' or 'slut' — used against any woman who either flaunted her sex brazenly or was suspected of misbehavior with men. The women liked to use the word more than men because, like most other women, they were more inclined to be severe judges of members of their own sex.

Yet *strafalaria* had such an ugly connotation that it was seldom applied to Sicilian women, almost never to relatives. Behind her lovely back my second cousin Annina was called the Merry Widow — despite the existence of a husband — simply because she was endowed with the kind of vivacity that made men envy her husband, but I never heard her called *strafalaria,* even by the women who were obviously jealous of her.

Most women who rated the word were *Americani.* They, more than anyone else, seemed to know precisely how to violate the Sicilian's strict code of female etiquette. Their manners were considered too free and easy. They made no bones about flirting with any man who was not too feeble, regardless of whether he was married or unmarried. And they smoked as though they were prostitutes, and did not wear enough clothing.

The most serious charge was that American women were, by nature, promiscuous. When a relative was known to be on friendly terms with an American woman, it was immediately assumed that their intentions toward each other were strictly dishonorable. He was encouraged to keep them on that basis, for it was a foregone conclusion that an American wife — that is, a wife who was not Italian — could not possibly be faithful to her husband for long.

Marriages with Americans were so rare that whenever a relative married one he was henceforth known as 'the-one-who-married-the-American.' Apart from the prejudices they had about Americans, one of their strongest objections to marriage with them was that they believed in divorce. That horrified my relatives. Marriage, they argued, was something willed by God. To break up a marriage was to go against the will of God.

Alfonso Barrone, a godson of Rosario Alfano, shocked my relatives by marrying an American girl and then divorcing her a few months later. The fact that he was mainly to blame for the divorce did not arouse any sympathy for the girl. What mattered to my relatives was that the marriage vow had been broken. None of them doubted that if Alfonso had married a Sicilian girl, such a catastrophe would never have occurred.

The first girl I ever heard called *strafalaria* was Maureen Daniels, who lived on the next street. Maureen was no more than seventeen years old. Without knowing as much about her as the boys in Mount Allegro knew, my relatives were certain that she would come to no good end. She smoked in public like a truck driver, with a cigarette drooping from a corner of her mouth. Her skirts barely covered her thighs, and her large breasts could be seen bulging above her low-cut dresses, unhampered by a brassière. I once overheard my Uncle Luigi confiding to my father that when he saw Maureen he never knew where to look first.

What my relatives did not know was that almost any boy who was old enough could easily persuade her to spend a few minutes with him in the garage back of her house. There was an old automobile seat on the floor of the garage just long enough and wide enough to hold Maureen's outstretched body. That much we kids could see through a crack in the back wall. None of us could make out the details, because the two small windows of the garage did not let in enough light; we could only hear her whimpering and sometimes crying out dirty words, and somehow we knew she enjoyed doing both.

Before any of the boys in my gang were old enough to interest her, Maureen came to the end my relatives had prophesied for her. It all came out of a Marathon dance in which Maureen was one of the contestants. Her partner was a Sicilian who looked like Rudolph Valentino and turned out to be a distant relative of mine. The Marathon lasted four days and five nights.

The Sicilian and Maureen won the second prize of fifty dollars, and all the boys in my gang were proud of Maureen because she came from Mount Allegro. But a few weeks later the story got around that Maureen was pregnant. Everyone was certain it was the Sicilian. According to the most authoritative gossips, Maureen ran away to New York when the Sicilian refused to marry her. We never saw her again.

No one blamed the Sicilian for what had happened, least of all my relatives, who interpreted Maureen's fate as just punishment from God. After her disappearance, they no longer referred to her as 'Maureen' but always as *strafalaria*. And because they held her mother partly responsible for permitting Maureen too much freedom, she was occasionally called *strafalaria* too.

My relatives always expected God to punish *strafalarii*, but they never failed to be impressed whenever he did. Examples like that of Maureen Daniels were cited over and over again, particularly in the presence of unmarried girls, to show that God would not stand for that kind of thing. But the most popular example concerned a Sicilian *strafalaria* who had worked with my Aunt Giovanna in a tailor factory. My aunt loved to repeat the story, partly because she never liked Angelina Tosta and partly because it proved how wise God was in his workings.

Angelina Tosta was imported to the United States by her uncles, two brothers, who assumed responsibility for her when her parents died. One of the uncles felt the weight of his responsibility so much that he seduced the girl after she had been here less than a month. Although the uncle was twice her age, there was nothing to do but marry her when it became obvious to everyone that she had become pregnant. They had three children, but their married life was an unhappy one, filled with quarrels and beatings.

Aunt Giovanna insisted that the chief trouble was that Angelina fancied herself a beauty, while Mr. Pizzano was neither handsome nor young. After they had lived together for nearly five years, Angelina fell in love with a young mason, a *paesano* of my relatives.

'*La strafalaria* made no bones of her affair with him,' my aunt said, 'and of course Pizzano soon found out what was going on.

'Pizzano carried on like a madman and said he would cut both of their throats if he ever caught them together. On the advice of her lover — I don't think she was smart enough to think up the idea herself — Angelina took advantage of his rages to have him declared insane and locked up in the City Hospital.'

While insisting he was sane, Pizzano declared he would rather be in the institution than have anything further to do with his wife. Moreover, he was certain that if left to his own devices he would eventually carry out his threat and murder Angelina and her lover. In the hospital Pizzano got along famously. The Superintendent, who liked to play cards with him, came to like him so much that he put him in charge of the candy and cigarette commissary.

Pizzano proved to be an excellent manager. Before long he was entrusted with all the purchasing of goods for the commissary and treated like a respected employee rather than an inmate. Pizzano was unscrupulous enough to take advantage of the situation. He developed a scheme for cheating on the profits and was hiding away a few dollars every week.

In the meantime, Angelina's lover jilted her for a young Sicilian virgin, whom he married without delay. Angelina mended her broken heart with the help of other lovers. From them she got money for a few clothes and incidentals. Because of her three children, the local authorities provided her and the children with money for food and shelter. This situation continued for nearly ten years — until Pizzano became seriously ill.

When the authorities informed her that her husband was dying, Angelina refused to see him, nor would she permit the children to visit him. When he died, she scandalized her relatives all the more by not attending his funeral.

A few weeks after Mr. Pizzano was buried, his brother found among his few possessions a huge roll of bills totaling fifteen hundred dollars. The news produced a miraculous change of heart in Angelina. Whenever she had an audience, she moaned about the loss of her 'dear husband, *bonarma*,' weeping noisily and copiously. She put on heavy mourning, with veils that completely hid her face, and even borrowed five dollars from one of her lovers to have a Mass sung for her husband's departed soul.

It was a beautiful show, all in all, but her relatives were not convinced. They refused to part with any of the money and told her that it would be placed in a trust fund for the children. When she threatened to have them arrested for embezzlement, one of them spat at her.

Angelina hired a lawyer, but by the time the case came before the Probate Court the hospital where Pizzano had been confined discovered that the old man had been cheating the commissary for years. The Judge did not hesitate to award the entire sum of money to the hospital. The only thing Angelina got out of it was a bill from her lawyer and some severe comments from the Judge on her late husband's dishonesty.

The whole affair embittered Angelina so much that she moved to Buffalo, where my Aunt Giovanna was certain she continued to play the part of the *strafalaria*.

None of my relatives expressed any sympathy for Angelina. In their eyes, she had broken their most sacred rules of conduct. The women said that the unhappiness she suffered was only a fraction of what she deserved. In Sicily, a woman who carried on like that would have been driven to a nunnery or a brothel. Here in America, where virtue did not seem as highly prized, she could wipe out her past and start a fresh series of sins simply by going to another town.

As usual, the man was not blamed — neither the uncle who seduced her nor the lover who had given her bad advice and then jilted her — for it was generally acknowledged that, given an opportunity with a woman, a man was bound to make the most of it. God had made him that way, and it was entirely up to the woman to resist him if she wanted to preserve her virtue.

American morals bewildered my relatives. In Sicily their rules of conduct were well defined and though strict, fairly simple to follow, because the same rules had been used for many centuries and were known to everyone in the community, even to those who broke them. Here there were many different kinds of people and, as far as they could make out, no rules that were taken seriously. In fact, everything seemed to conspire toward the breakdown of the rules they had brought with them.

In America their women could work in the factories without being considered *strafalarii*. Men and women, who were neither married, engaged, nor related in any way, could walk down the street together in broad daylight without anyone's thinking anything of it. Here their children picked up strange American ideas about courtship and marriage. They could become engaged without using their parents as intermediaries. They could marry without even consulting their parents, let alone getting their permission. A crazy land. A father was no longer master in his own house. At eighteen his children could do as they pleased; they could even leave home. And there was not a blessed thing he could do about it except swear and growl '*Managgia l'America.*'

In my time my relatives accepted some of these strange customs without too much swearing. They consoled themselves with the thought that their children were not really responsible for such gross disrespect. They blamed America, and they said it was a land where money was put above respect and family honor. Even so, they could not accept everything. A line had to be drawn somewhere, and they usually drew it around their daughters.

My father's cousin, Antonio Ricotta, had five sons and one daughter, but his main worry was his daughter. Don Antonio was a born tyrant and was able to inspire fear both in his children and his wife. Apart from their tendency to marry young, his sons treated him with the respect he demanded, even to the extent of bringing him

their weekly wages in a sealed envelope, just as they
would have done in Sicily.

It was not surprising that Don Antonio had an attack
of indigestion whenever one of his sons broke the news
that he was going to marry. They were all fine brick-
layers and earned handsome salaries, especially the oldest
son, Pasquale. When Pasquale left home to be married,
his father had an especially bad indigestion attack. By
the time the third son had married and Don Antonio had
suffered his third attack, the relatives knew, without being told, when another Ricotta boy was about to marry.

But it was Cicca, his youngest, who caused him the
most pain. Don Antonio was worried about her from the
time she was fourteen. That year her breasts began to
ripen with disconcerting promise and her eyes became
illuminated with a soft glow that attracted men as though
they were moths. The more beautiful she grew, the
more concerned did her father become. He watched her
like a jealous husband, and few men could feel comfortable near Cicca when he was about.

When Cicca was fifteen, a college boy in the neighborhood wrote a poem about her beauty, which was printed
in a literary magazine and dedicated to her. Almost
every day two or three boys would trail her from school,
greedy for any crumbs of attention she might throw to
them. As they neared her home, the boys would fall
back at a respectful distance. Don Antonio's furious
temper was well known to them.

With such a father and five older brothers, no one, except a few relatives who were skeptical about everything,
doubted that Cicca's virtue would remain intact until she

was married. But it followed that one of her admirers would eventually be dissatisfied with crumbs and that she, in turn, would want something more substantial than the flattery of being trailed home from school.

One evening when Don Antonio had gone out to play cards, Cicca told her mother she had an appointment with her girl friend Tina to study for an algebra examination. Mrs. Ricotta, who was nothing like her husband, believed her and gave her permission to spend the evening at Tina's house, with the understanding she would come home early, before her father did.

Unfortunately, Don Antonio returned sooner than expected. When his wife told him Cicca was studying with Tina, he was immediately suspicious and telephoned Tina's house. No one answered. He began to bellow at his wife for being gullible. Mrs. Ricotta, who had little love for her husband, said later that he probably would have beaten her if it had not been for neighbors who were sitting on a near-by porch and could look into the house.

When Cicca had not appeared at eleven o'clock, Don Antonio went out to look for her. Mrs. Ricotta, fearing the worst, went to her room and began praying before her statue of the Virgin Mary. In the meantime, Don Antonio stationed himself at the street corner near the trolley stop, hiding himself in the darkness of a doorway from which he could look in several directions.

About eleven-thirty he spotted Cicca with a boy getting out of a streetcar. He waited until they rounded the corner into a more dimly lit street, and, as they hovered in the shadow of a tree kissing each other good night, he pounced on them. Holding Cicca fast with one hand, he got a stranglehold on the boy's head and bit off a piece of his ear. Then releasing the screaming boy, he dragged Cicca off. Frightened and trembling, she blubbered all the way home: 'Honest, Pa! We didn't do anything. We only went to the movies. . . .'

The gory detail of the bitten ear came to light two days later when the boy's father had Don Antonio arrested on a charge of assault and battery. The Judge fined Don Antonio one hundred dollars and ordered him to pay the boy's doctors' bills. The only reason he did not send him to jail was because of Don Antonio's advanced age and the indigestion attack he had while he was in the court. But, what was more shameful, to my relatives, all the newspapers in town carried sardonic accounts of the episode under such headlines as 'Man Bites Ear.'

About a month later we heard that Don Antonio tried to marry Cicca off to a *paesano* who was more than twice her age. But Cicca would have nothing of him and threatened to commit suicide if her father insisted on the marriage. He ranted against her 'American' ideas and reminded Cicca that her mother had not had such ridiculous notions when she followed the instructions of her parents and married him. Cicca held her ground, and in the end he took her threat seriously enough to make no more mention of the *paesano*.

For the next three years, until she was eighteen, Cicca led the exemplary life of a Sicilian daughter. In keeping with my relatives' idea that there was no use wasting much education on a girl, she left school as soon as the law would allow her and got a job clerking in a department store. Every payday she dutifully handed Don Antonio her weekly wages in a sealed envelope, seldom complaining about the small allowance he gave her in exchange. She was home early every evening, either helping her mother with the housework or sewing; the only times she went anywhere, to a movie or a party, she was chaperoned by her mother or Don Antonio.

A less attractive girl might have settled down to this dull existence, but Cicca was more beautiful than ever, and, working every day among girls who were not handicapped by Sicilian fathers and who did little else than talk about the men they had dated the night before, she could hardly be expected to conform to Don Antonio's Sicilian rules indefinitely.

Not long after her eighteenth birthday, the rumor got around that a blond American boy named Lee Wallace, the son of a doctor, had fallen madly in love with Cicca and was seeing her at lunch-time every day. We wondered how soon her father would find out and what he would do about it.

My Aunt Giovanna and my mother conceded that if the boy's intentions were honorable, it might not be a bad idea at all for Cicca to marry the son of a *dottore*, even though he was not an Italian. But this meeting the boy secretly, behind her father's back, was bad, not only because no one ever knew what might happen when a boy and girl crazy about each other are alone together — but also there was Don Antonio's terrible temper to take into account. Of course, Cicca could only see him during her lunch hour; so it wasn't likely they would be getting into trouble, but you never knew. . . .

When Don Antonio finally learned what was going on, he first had one of his indigestion attacks — this one lasted longer than any of the others — then he asked Cicca to bring the young man to supper. Cicca, thinking that by some great miracle her father had changed his notions, was overjoyed and invited Lee to dinner the next day. Knowing nothing more about Don Antonio than that he would not allow his daughter to have dates with boys, young Wallace had no hesitation in accepting the invitation.

As soon as the meal was over, Don Antonio lost no time coming down to cases. His English was muddled, but there was no mistaking what was on his mind.

'Mr. Wallace, you like Cicca, yes? You go out with her sometimes, yes?'

'Yes, sir,' Lee replied nervously, not knowing what the old man was leading up to.

'Mr. Wallace, I am the father of Cicca. I no want you do that. My daughter Cicca, she good girl. You two make engagemento, yes? You do that — then everything o.k. You come to house, you eat here. Then maybe we make wedding, yes?'

'I love Cicca very much, Mr. Antonio,' Lee stuttered, 'but I don't think I could get engaged to her just now. You see, I'm still in school, and my parents think I'm too young to be engaged.'

'If you too young, you too young,' Don Antonio said philosophically. 'But you no see Cicca without engagemento. You understand, yes? I no want you to see her at store, or I make trouble. Maybe you know I bite ear of boy who make trouble for me with Cicca?'

There was nothing left for Lee to say. He left in a great hurry, without shaking hands with the old man and only nodding quickly at Mrs. Ricotta and at Cicca, who sat in a corner of the room quietly sobbing.

Cicca cried a good deal after that, but Don Antonio gave no sign of changing his attitude. This time he had the wholehearted support of his wife and most of the relatives. They agreed that if the young man did not love Cicca enough to become engaged to her, then it was pointless and dangerous for her to continue seeing him.

For nearly a month afterward Lee made no effort to see Cicca. But apparently the strain of trying to forget her was too great, and he appeared at the store one day and begged her to elope with him.

In his anxiety to persuade her, Lee told her that his mother would surely forgive him once he was married to Cicca and would probably invite them to live with her. But Cicca's fear of defying her father was more powerful than her love for Lee.

'I don't think your mother would ever forgive me if we eloped,' she said. 'Let's wait until you're out of school.' It was her way of telling him that it was no use.

The following Saturday, while the family was eating supper, the telephone rang. A long distance call for Miss Cicca Ricotta from Newark, New Jersey, the operator said. It was Lee, and he sounded as though he had been drinking. He just wanted her to know he had eloped with another girl, a girl he didn't care about. His voice suddenly broke and, blurting out that it was her fault that he had married someone he didn't love, he hung up.

'You should be glad you never married him, Cicca,' her relatives told her. 'A boy who would do a crazy thing like that would never make a good husband.'

It was poor consolation for a girl in love, but in time Cicca came to believe it herself.

A Man and His Vice

AS LONG AS WE DID NOT INTERRUPT, WE WERE permitted to listen to all family discussions. There was no effort made to 'protect' us from the Facts of Life or the scandals of our relatives; nor were there any of those spelling bouts some parents conduct to guard their young from ideas they consider taboo.

Probably in the belief that the more we heard the sooner we would blossom into adults, my parents allowed us to observe the skeletons in the closets of our relatives through transparent doors, long before any of us were old enough to understand why family skeletons were kept in closets.

One scandal I remember especially because it concerned my father's favorite *compare*, Calogero Boccanova, and also because it gave me my first inkling that Sicilian marriages were not always what God ordained them to be.

Mr. Boccanova was not actually a relative, but he might as well have been one. His devotion to our family dated back to the day when he chose my father to be his son's godfather. Thereafter, the men always called each other *compare,* and their wives called each other *comare,* and they became as inseparable as any of my relatives.

A *compare* occupies a special place in the hierarchy of Sicilian friends. No firmer relationship can exist between two men who are not related by blood than that of *compare.* Sometimes a relative would choose another relative to be his *compare,* but more often the honor was reserved for unrelated friends. It was a simple way of making them almost related.

What Compare Calogero and my father lacked in blood ties they made up for in the quantity of red wine they drank in each other's company. Compare Calogero was an eloquent talker and my father a willing listener, even when his *compare* bragged, which was often. Mostly Compare Calogero liked to brag about the numerous organizations he belonged to and show off their emblems and buttons on his coat-lapel. He also bragged of the important people who came to drink at his saloon; and of his acquaintance with policemen, firemen, streetcar conductors, and anyone else, in fact, who wore a uniform. The only thing he did not brag about was the thing he had a right to brag about: his way with women.

He was a man in his fifties, but his talents for charming women were widely reputed to be those of a younger and more handsome man. That was hard for me to believe because he was short and round and almost bald. Whenever he smiled, he revealed a glaring array of gold teeth and inlays. At the time I imagined that maybe that accounted for his popularity with women.

My brother, who was always wiser about such matters, would smile at me annoyingly and tell me flatly that teeth had nothing to do with it. Whatever it was, Compare Calogero's wiles and adventures distinguished him as a man who knew how to exercise his sex appeal in a period of life when most men are afraid of losing it completely.

Although my father would never admit it, he was amused by his *compare* and by stories he heard about his conquests. My mother heard these stories, too, and she liked to tease my father by comparing his exploits when a bachelor with those of Compare Calogero as a married man. But she wore a frown when Compare Calogero was around. She liked him but thoroughly disapproved of him. She was afraid of any influence he might have on my father (who occasionally enjoyed being influenced) but, more than that, she was a close friend of his wife, Comare Alfreda, and had a deep sympathy for her 'Cross,' as Compare Calogero was often called.

Comare Alfreda was even shorter and rounder than her husband, but she had a beautiful mouth and dancing eyes; unless you kept reminding yourself, you were apt to forget that she was having an unhappy married life. She was always gay with us, and though she had children and grandchildren of her own, she brought us candy whenever she came. It was shocking to realize that anyone would dare mistreat her.

My mother was her chief confidante, and, by listening to their talk, I learned a great deal about Compare Calogero's philandering. According to my father, his *compare's* exploits were not to be taken too seriously since the women probably were not respectable. But adultery of any kind was a serious sin in the eyes of my mother, and she berated my father for any comments he made which might be construed as a defense of Compare Calogero.

In spite of her criticism of her *compare,* my mother had lapses when she would philosophically remark, 'Man is a creature of bad habits.' If my father was about, she would look significantly in his direction and add, 'We all have our different Crosses to bear.' And if she felt especially resigned about the 'bad habits' of men, she would repeat the ancient adage her father taught her: 'Every man has his special vice. He is either a gambler, a drunkard, or a philanderer.'

The reason I approved of Compare Calogero was that he owned a beautiful saloon and always gave me pretzels or peanuts whenever I went there with my father. In the summertime, we usually drank beer with our meals, and, while my sisters were setting the table, my father would go to the saloon for a fresh pail of beer. I liked to go along on account of the pretzels and the peanuts and because it was pleasant watching the foam of the beer oozing out of the pail as Compare Calogero filled it.

What fascinated me most about the saloon was the art work on the huge mirror behind the bar. There I got my first glimpse of the Bay of Naples and Mount Vesuvius. The volcano was in scarlet red and the bay in dazzling blue, and the whole scene was set in a tremendous gold frame on which were glued wooden roses. On the bay were a large number of sailboats, with their sails bent in opposite directions, so that it appeared as though the wind were blowing from two directions at the same time. A purple ribbon was draped over the top of the frame, and on it was printed in Italian, 'See Naples and Die.'

Above the whole thing an Italian flag was entwined with an American one, between a calendar reproduction of 'September Morn' and a sign with rhinestone letters which read, 'Home Sweet Home.' The Italians who frequented the saloon admired all this art work, particularly the bay and the volcano, and some of them would bring their wives to see it. My father, who knew a great deal about boats because he grew up on the waterfront, made fun of the sails blowing in different directions but conceded that the painting was a fine work of art.

I never saw any Sicilian women in the saloon, but sometimes, when we went for beer, we found Compare Calogero seated at a table with one or two other Sicilians and two heavily painted women with yellow hair. They were as exciting to look at as the bay and the volcano, and the air around them smelled like some of the cordial my father made. The women called me pet names and asked me some of the silly questions adults ask young boys, but my father held my hand firmly and muttered something under his breath which meant, 'Pay no attention to them.'

After a while, the women would lose interest in me and go back to their drinking and talking. They knew a few obscene Sicilian words, and whenever they used one, everyone would shriek with laughter and the women would slap the men on the knee. In private my father would always warn me that they were 'bad women' and never to say anything about them at home.

But somehow the news that two American *butani* were regular visitors at Compare Calogero's saloon got back to his wife. According to her information, the women left the place each time with different men and, sometimes, with Compare Calogero.

No one could explain how it happened, Comare Alfreda least of all, but for the first time in her life she lost her meekness and became a tornado of wifely indignation. The story of how she practically blew her husband from his saloon into a piano factory became one of the sagas that my relatives loved to repeat again and again.

Comare Alfreda wisely chose a Saturday evening for her *Blitzkrieg,* figuring that the women would surely be there on payday.   Compare Calogero was behind the bar, helping his bartender, when Comare Alfreda came hurtling through the swinging doors, brandishing a long black umbrella in the air, as though she were an officer leading a regiment.   Her first victim was the yellow-haired woman she saw drinking at the bar.   No one tried to stop her as she advanced, holding the pointed umbrella in front of her like a bayonet.

The woman tried to run away but was blocked by the general stampede of customers toward the exit.   Comare Alfreda tripped her neatly with the crook of the umbrella and started beating her across the shoulders, while the woman protected her head with her hands.   Not satisfied with his punishment, Comare Alfreda made a sudden lunge for the yellow hair.   This time the woman managed to squirm away and dash through the exit in time to escape any further damage.

Compare Calogero, protected by the bar, shouted soothing remarks to his wife while she tried to reach him with the umbrella, but he might as well have tried to quiet a storm.   Comare Alfreda suddenly remembered that there had been two women.

'Where is the other?' she demanded.

Getting no satisfaction from him, she began to explore the back room.　In the ladies' room she found the second girl seated.　Comare Alfreda made the most of her advantage.　Lifting the woman from her sitting posture by the roots of her bleached hair, Comare Alfreda, according to her own accounts, dragged her out of the ladies' room and chased her to the exit, all the while jabbing the pointed end of the umbrella into her buttocks.

That night she announced to her husband that he was no longer in the saloon business.

It had been a profitable business, even without the women, and he had no trouble disposing of it.　I regretted the passing of Compare Calogero's saloon, for the Irishman who bought it immediately painted out the Neapolitan scene and substituted a huge flag of Erin in its place.

For a while it appeared as though Compare Calogero had settled down to the life of a respectable married man. He got a job in a piano factory and was home for dinner every night.　He was even seen in church several Sundays.　When he drank wine with my father, he talked like a man who had learned his lesson.　But as it developed he was only gathering strength for another extramarital campaign.　It wasn't long before his church-going ceased and his wife's complaints were heard again.　This time Compare Calogero was guilty of committing the supreme indiscretion of his married life.

At first only his daughters suspected he was carrying on with the blonde German-American woman next door, but it wasn't long before Comare Alfreda knew what was going on.　What made the affair particularly sinister was that the woman was married to an earnest young factory worker who seemed completely unaware of his wife's unfaithfulness. All the relatives, including my father this time, were enraged. It was one thing to be a philanderer, who played around with *strafalarii* unknown to your wife and children, and quite another to have an affair that was almost public with a married woman who lived next door.

Secretly, my relatives marveled that a young buxom woman should be attracted to a potbellied old man who was the grandfather of two youngsters, but they concluded that American women were all crazy. Contrary to popular expectation, Comare Alfreda took no action this time. Humiliated because her children knew what was going on, she became morose and cried a good deal in her talks with my mother. The affair was a severe blow to her pride. In pathetic detail she told how *l'Americana* sat on the porch facing her kitchen night after night and how Compare Calogero, sitting at the head of the supper table, would stare at her through the windows when he thought Comare Alfreda was not looking.

She was positive they had a signal system contrived between them for exchanging endearments and arranging for meetings. The window shade in one of the upstairs rooms, facing the woman's apartment, would be drawn differently from the way she had left it, she noticed. Also, when her husband was home, the window shade in the *strafalaria's* apartment went up and down, for apparently no good reason. It was obvious to her that the two were using the shades to communicate with each other.

Comare Alfreda knew the woman well. In her backyard talks with neighbors she had often conversed with Anna Schmitt. They both did their wash on Mondays, and, as they draped their wet clothes over the lines on wash day, their chats became warmer and more confidential. Gradually, Anna Schmitt came to learn of Compare Calogero's Don Juan leanings. On the surface, she pretended to be horrified and sympathetic, but, at heart, she must have been charmed by the episodes Comare Alfreda recounted, and often pressed her for details. Comare Alfreda was only too happy to tell her troubles to a sympathetic neighbor, and before long, Anna Schmitt knew as much about Compare Calogero's adulterous adventures as she herself did.

In the course of their friendship Comare Alfreda learned that Anna Schmitt was employed as a part-time waitress in a restaurant near the factory where her husband worked. Comare Alfreda saw an opportunity to do her sympathetic neighbor a service and suggested that Compare Calogero drop Anna off on his way to work in the mornings. Compare Calogero had often admired his blonde neighbor from a distance, and nothing suited him better than the prospect of seeing her alone every day. But he was a wise man and he took care to grumble a little when his wife suggested the arrangement. When he finally agreed to it, he gave a perfect imitation of a man grudgingly giving his consent.

'I might as well have made their bed for them,' Comare Alfreda wailed afterward. 'But how in God's name was I to know that a young and pretty woman with a husband would pay any attention to an old fool like Calogero?'

It soon became obvious to everyone that Compare Calo-

gero's relationship with Anna Schmitt was more than that
of a chauffeur, and Comare Alfreda was so tormented by
her suspicions that she lost five pounds in a single week.
It improved her figure, but my mother became alarmed
and advised her *comare* to have a showdown with her
husband before she lost any more weight.

'But I have no real proof,' she said. 'He will only deny
the whole thing and then make life more unbearable for
me than it is.' Comare Alfreda's morale seemed shat-
tered; it was hard to imagine that this was the same
woman who had raided her husband's saloon a few months
before.

'You don't need proof,' my mother insisted. 'Just tell
him your suspicions and make them sound like facts.
Don't be afraid of him.'

My mother's advice had some effect on her. She decided to do some detective work on her own. Compare
Calogero rose at six to be at work at eight-thirty. The
next morning when he got out of bed, Comare Alfreda
pretended to be sound asleep.

As was his habit, he made his own breakfast in the
kitchen downstairs and was ready to leave around seven-
fifteen. As soon as Comare Alfreda heard the back door
slam, she went to the window of her bedroom, which
overlooked the garage and the back yard, and peeked
through a slit in the curtains. She saw the Ford back out
of the garage a few feet and draw up directly beneath
the window.

Compare Calogero emerged from the car and waited,
smoking a cigarette. A few minutes passed, and then she
saw his lips part in a grin. He threw away the cigarette,
and then Anna Schmitt appeared, swinging a handbag.

The next minute gave Comare Alfreda the most dreadful moment of her life. With one sweep, her husband picked up the giggling Anna in his arms and carried her toward the car. It was too much for Comare Alfreda. She felt as though she had been mortally wounded, and she wanted her husband to know. But her pride held out and her tongue kept still. She did the best she could under the circumstances. Lifting the lower window as far up as it would go, she slammed it down with all her strength. Compare Calogero had just deposited Anna in the front seat when he heard the crash. He stuck his head out of the car window and looked up, just in time to see his wife's white face slide out of sight.

Compare Calogero immediately started up the motor, backed the car out of the driveway, and drove away as though all the demons of hell were after him.

The two daughters heard the crash of the window and came running into their mother's room. There was not enough light for them to see the pallor of her face or the agonized expression in her eyes. As calmly as she could she explained that she had tried to close the window and it had accidentally slammed. Her humiliation was so complete that she felt incapable of confiding in anyone at the moment.

Her morning chores helped ease her anguish somewhat, and by noon her thoughts were almost crystallized to the point where she was ready to announce an important decision. She came to tell my mother of the morning's episode and ask her advice. Actually it was only a chance to think aloud that she wanted. My mother, noting her extreme agitation, advised her to wait another day before she took any drastic action. But it was plain that Comare Alfreda had made up her mind as to what she was going to do.

'I can't stand it a moment longer,' she wept. 'I have had enough of him and that *strafalaria*. I'm going to have it out with him tonight.'

Supper that night was a sullen affair for the entire family. The children knew that something was up by their mother's nervous manner and their father's obvious embarrassment. Not a word of the morning's incident was mentioned at the table, but while the dishes were being washed and Compare Calogero was about to settle down to his evening paper, his wife drew a deep breath and asked him to accompany her on a short walk. He blinked with surprise at this unusual request but didn't refuse.

As soon as they were a few yards away from the house, Comare Alfreda, looking straight ahead, began in a low monotone, 'I want to tell you that unless you stop seeing that woman at once I'm going to leave you or ask you to leave.'

Compare Calogero stopped dead in his tracks. 'What in God's name are you talking about?' he asked excitedly.

'It is no use taking God's name in vain,' his wife said quietly. 'And it won't do you any good raising your voice. You know very well what I'm talking about. I saw you pick her up in your arms this morning and carry her into the automobile. Do you think I'm blind?'

'You're crazy. That's what you are,' he shouted angrily. 'You saw nothing of the kind because nothing like that happened.'

She began to cry. 'I'm sick and tired of your lies,' she sobbed. He looked hurt and lonely and for the fraction of a moment, Comare Alfreda said, she wanted to draw him close to her — 'as though *I* was one who needed to be forgiven!' His wife's tears made him realize the futility of any further denial. Without another word, he walked away from her.

When she got home, she found her daughters sitting quietly around the living-room table.

'Where is Pa?' Fortunata asked.

Comare Alfreda shook her head, afraid to let them hear the sound of her voice, and went up to her room. The girls waited downstairs, talking in hushed whispers, and then slowly went up to bed. Comare Alfreda worked on her embroidery, while her mind shuttled from one worry to another. What was keeping him? What would she say to him when he did come home?

At last she heard his step on the front porch and his key in the lock. Should she go down and talk to him, or should she go straight to bed and let him be? There was really nothing else she wanted to say to him, but it seemed wrong to her going to bed before he did. Downstairs she heard a chair fall and, after a few moments, another piece of furniture. The noise worried her. She wondered if he had been drinking. On tiptoe she began to make her way down the stairs.

His back was toward her as she reached the living-room. He was bending over the desk groping for something. In a flash she realized what it was. When he turned around with his fingers encircling a shiny revolver, she was not surprised.

'Go away, Alfreda,' he said.   'I'm going to shoot myself.
I've caused enough unhappiness around here.'

She tried to keep her voice firm.   'Don't be crazy, Calogero.   Put away that gun.'

'Please go upstairs,' he said.   His hand was shaking so
violently Comare Alfreda was afraid the gun would go off.
He suddenly darted toward the trapdoor in the kitchen
that led to the cellar.

Shrieking at the top of her lungs, she threw herself on
him from behind and tried to pinion his arms behind his
back.   Her cries aroused the two daughters, and they
came dashing down the stairway.   The sight of their
parents grappling horrified them.   Josephine, thinking
her mother was defending herself from a beating, yelled:
'Let her alone, Pa.   For God's sake let her alone!'

'Help me!' shouted their mother.   'He wants to kill
himself!'

With tears streaming down their faces, the two girls
joined their mother in trying to pull him down to the
floor.   He was too heavy and much too strong for them.
But during the scuffle he lost his balance and banged his
head hard against the wall.   The blow took all the fight
out of him.   He offered no resistance when they sat him
on a chair; his fingers over the gun relaxed and Comare
Alfreda gently took it away from him.

With the revolver out of the way, Comare Alfreda and
her daughters experienced such a deep sense of relief that
they all sat down and cried.   They cried for some time,
while Compare Calogero kept repeating: 'You should have
let me kill myself.   I've been a bad father.'

Out of the sobs and protestations gradually came quiet

and then sentiment. 'We all felt,' said Josephine, talking
about it later, 'as though somebody had died and we had
to be good to each other from then on.'

'Father — and you too — Mother,' Josephine began, 'let's
be sensible about what has happened.   Let's move away
from this neighborhood.   With the rent we could get
from this house we could easily afford to live in another
section of town.   We need more room anyway,' she added
brightly.

Compare Calogero said nothing, but he offered his
handkerchief, and they each took turns wiping away their
tears.   Then Comare Alfreda sent them all to bed.   After
she had hidden the revolver where her husband would
not find it, she shut the windows and the doors and joined
Compare Calogero upstairs.   The next morning she took
a streetcar ride into a faraway neighborhood and began
looking for another house.

The details of the story soon got around to my relatives
Some of them, like my Uncle Luigi, were amused by it.
He expressed the hope that Comare Alfreda would find
a house 'between the insane asylum and the Old People's
Home, so that her husband would have fewer temptations.'   But most of them were genuinely relieved to know
that Compare Calogero had escaped the clutches of the
strafalaria next door, even though it meant moving out of
Mount Allegro where he and his family had lived for
fifteen years.

Uncle Nino and the Underworld

IN THE SPHERE OF CRIME, MY RELATIVES WERE a distinct disappointment. From the newspapers one gathered that Sicilians in general had a passion for murder and blackmail, but my relatives did little to uphold that reputation. Considering their large numbers — there were several hundred in Rochester alone — the crimes they committed were few and hardly the kind to enhance my prestige with my playmates. Except for mundane misdemeanors like playing the numbers and occasionally bootlegging, they led such respectable lives that they might as well have been Polish, Irish, German, or even Northern Italian, for all the glory I got out of them.

Unless I perverted the facts, there was no point in bragging about the only murder in our family, for it concerned an uncle who might still be alive if he had not had a strong sense of responsibility. My Uncle Cicco was my mother's favorite brother and the father of two children. He was killed at a wedding party when he tried to stop a fight between two drunken guests. Uncle Cicco was the *compare* of the newly wedded couple and felt obliged to keep the party going smoothly, even though he realized that one of the men was carrying a revolver. The killer was sentenced to the chair after the jury had been convinced that Uncle Cicco was a gentle and kindly soul who hated strife of any kind. All this was just, but it did not lessen the tragedy. My relatives mourned him for twenty years and kept talking about his murder as though it had happened only a week before.

Another relative who got into trouble was Uncle Nino. But since he, too, was the victim of a crime rather than the criminal himself, there was nothing for me to brag about. I could not honestly brag about his courage, for the incident revealed that my uncle was a man of greater discretion than courage. It also showed that when a man as sensitive and learned as my Uncle Nino has a revolver shoved in his face, he is liable to suffer more than most people.

When the robbery took place, my uncle was earning some money by selling jewelry to Sicilians in Rochester. He kept his stock in the living-room of his home. Most of his clients were men who were about to be engaged or married. They came to his living-room with their betrothed or with pictures of them. They knew of my uncle's reputation as a wise and honest man and they had full confidence in his taste and judgment, so much so that some of the men came to ask his advice on matters of etiquette and love.

If their problems dealt with love, my uncle would be careful to give them the kind of advice they obviously wanted to hear. He charged nothing for doing that and achieved a wide reputation as the Redheaded Solomon.

Whether his customers came to purchase jewelry or to ask
for advice, he treated them as guests.   Before permitting
them to discuss business, he would entertain them with
conversation and drink a little wine with them.   He encouraged his customers to take their time about making
their selections, and he would cheerfully drag out tray
after tray of jewelry long after a sale was clinched, like
a boy showing off his playthings.   When he finally permitted the customer to make his purchase, he would bring
out the wine again and propose a toast to the customer's
marriage.

One morning, a few minutes after Aunt Giovanna had
gone to work, my Uncle Nino heard a loud knocking on
the kitchen door.   He got out of bed and put on his robe.
Without unlatching the door, he shouted, 'Who is it?'

' 'Tis a friend.   *Ce permisso?*'   The voice was familiar;
the accents were Sicilian.   Uncle Nino unlocked the door
and opened it.   As he did so, two men pushed their way
through, drawing revolvers out of their coat pockets.
They had white handkerchiefs tied over their faces.   One
of them locked the door, while the other, who seemed to
be the leader, ordered Uncle Nino to keep quiet.   He did
all the talking.

'Sit in that chair and don't make a move,' he commanded, pointing to a chair in the living-room.   As Uncle
Nino followed his instructions, the second man put his
gun back in his pocket and drew out some rope with
which he bound my uncle's ankles to the legs of the chair.
The leader stood over him all the time with his gun
pointed into Uncle Nino's face.

'We want you to tell us the combination of your safe.

If you don't tell us, you will never be able to talk again.'
My uncle was sure from the voice that he knew who the
leader was, but he didn't dare show any sign of recognition.   Furthermore, he was trembling with fright and
had obviously lost his faculty of speech.   The gunman
handed him some paper and a pencil and, holding my
uncle's wrist to steady it, ordered him to write out the
combination.

They opened the safe and emptied all the jewel trays
into a burlap bag.   The only items they left behind were
two ledgers, one of which my uncle used to keep a record
of his accounts; the other was the one filled with the
beautiful script.   Before they left, the gunmen bound his
wrists to the arms of the chair; then they stuffed a gag in
his mouth and tied a handkerchief around it.

Nearly ten minutes passed before my Uncle Nino was
sufficiently recovered from his fright to start working on
his bindings.   By putting his head down to the arm of
the chair he was able to loosen the handkerchief around
his mouth until it slipped down over his chin.   Once he
got rid of the gag, he started calling for help.   At first his
shouting was weak but soon he had full control of his
vocal cords, and he used them so effectively that four
neighbors came running from several directions.   Except
for Mr. Kaplan, the neighbors were all Sicilians.   While
one of them undid the cords that held my uncle to the
chair, Mr. Kaplan took it upon himself to call the police.

Uncle Nino was aghast when he learned that the police
had been summoned.   Like many of my relatives, he had
no confidence in the law and he felt certain that once
the police entered the picture, his chances for recovering

the jewelry would disappear. When the officers arrived, he gave them a general description of the robbery in his best broken English. He accompanied them to the station house, where there was an official interpreter, but beyond repeating his story and giving them a list of the stolen goods, he was vague, and unwilling to guess at the identity of the robbers.

The police immediately reached the wrong conclusions and, when the newspapers broke the story that evening, they broadly hinted that Uncle Nino himself had plotted the robbery in order to collect insurance money. Neither the police nor the newspapers had bothered to study my Uncle Nino's statements carefully, nor check the facts; if they had, they would have learned he had no insurance at all. The robbery wiped him out completely.

Uncle Nino's lack of faith in the law was by no means uncommon among my Sicilian relatives, nor was it confined to American law. The incident of the robbery only served to justify their attitude, particularly when my Uncle Nino revealed the aftermath of the story. After his interview with the police, Uncle Nino called on a *paesano* reputed to be powerful in the Rochester underworld and gave him the full details of the robbery, including the name of the gunman who had done the talking and a full description of his accomplice. The *paesano*, like my relatives, was shocked to hear the name of the thief, knowing that he had been a frequent guest at my Uncle Nino's table.

The *paesano* promised to investigate the case among his colleagues and salvage as much of the jewelry as he could. 'They had no business robbing you,' the *paesano* said.

'Everyone knows you are a man deserving of the highest respect. You have befriended many a *paesano* who comes from a lower station of life. No reason at all for the robbery, particularly since your goods were not insured. Give me three days to see what I can do.'

But the *paesano* could do nothing, as powerful as he was. The police and the newspaper publicity had ruined everything, he said. 'When the men who stole your goods saw the newspaper story, they became frightened and left for Sicily. Their original plan had been to pull off a number of robberies and then leave the country. But yours was the only robbery they had time to commit.'

The *paesano* spent the next ten minutes heaping abuse and curses on the heads of the two men, and calling them all kinds of vile names for having stolen from my Uncle Nino without first consulting him or any of his partners. 'They probably knew that any of us would have discouraged the robbery,' he said when he had calmed down a little. 'But what can you do with *cafoni* who have no manners and don't know the meaning of respect?'

My Uncle Nino's interview with the underworld *paesano* surprised no one but myself. My relatives agreed that he had done the wise thing and that if the police and the newspapers had not meddled with the case, he would undoubtedly have retrieved all the stolen goods. My Uncle Luigi told of several instances where Sicilians 'as deserving of respect' as Uncle Nino had not only recovered stolen goods but also enjoyed the satisfaction of knowing that the robbers had been punished for the crime by their own underworld colleagues. In none of these instances, of course, had the police been summoned.

I gathered that this had been a fairly common practice in Sicily. As long as a Sicilian enjoyed the 'respect' of his community and was not offensively rich, he could be fairly certain of being left alone by any local gang of law-breakers. If they annoyed him in any manner, he could feel free to call on their leader and insist on his right to be 'respected.' In the event the leader agreed that he merited 'respect,' all possible redress would be made. If it happened that the crime had been committed by one of his own men with his approval, he washed his hands of the matter by blaming it on some out-of-town-gang. In any case, the leader was usually courteous and sympathetic since he too wanted to be 'respected.'

It was several months before Uncle Nino could bear to talk about the robbery or any crime without quivering and turning pale. By that time there were wide gray streaks in his red hair. He never quite survived the shock of having had his life threatened by a man who had eaten at his table, and the memory of the gun in his face stayed with him long after he had become accustomed to the idea of being penniless and having to depend almost entirely on Aunt Giovanna's small earnings.

Even when he reached the point where he could discuss the robbery outside the immediate family circle, he spoke about it in cold, clipped sentences, without his usual eloquence and fire. My father and Uncle Luigi became eloquent for him whenever the subject was mentioned, while Great-Uncle Minicuzzu, as an expert on the past, provided the historical details about crime and Sicilians.

'Where there is poverty you will find the vulture of crime,' he said. 'Sicily was filled with criminals because it was the poorest section of Italy. The political gentry in Rome didn't do much to maintain law and order. They were not averse to collecting heavy taxes from the people and making friends with the sulphur-mine owners but, aside from that, they didn't think it was worth bothering about an island that could barely support itself. Of course, there were always enough policemen around to squelch any uprising, but there was little done about protecting Sicilians from those who had turned to crime for a living.'

'You mean the blackmailers and the crooks who belonged to the Mafia,' my Uncle Luigi said.

'You don't know the first thing about the Mafia,' Great-Uncle Minicuzzu said. 'My grandfather, *bonarma*, claimed that the Mafia was nothing but a means some honest Sicilians used to get justice. They could not get it through the Government, so they formed secret societies to get justice for them. For a long time the Mafia gave Sicilians the only kind of real law and order they had known.'

'Ah, but the Mafia degenerated and did harm to a lot of innocent people,' my father said.

'All good things degenerate with time,' Great-Uncle Minicuzzu replied. 'As long as Italy has a government that isn't interested in the people of Sicily, you will find Sicilians stealing and depending on each other for justice. What poor Sicilian has not stolen? There were times in Sicily when you had to steal in order to eat. As long as you stole from those who had plenty, it wasn't so bad. It was when we began to steal from each other that I thought we offended the Good Lord.'

'I don't remember any Mafia in my home town,' my Aunt Giovanna said, 'but I remember how the population took matters in their own hands when the law did nothing to stop the crimes of the three Castagna brothers. They had everyone in town frightened. They would disguise themselves as peddlers and approach you in public. While they pretended to be selling you goods, they would whisper that unless you delivered a certain amount of money at a certain spot by a certain time they would kill you or some member of your family.

'They were men of their word and murdered several of my *paesani* who did not take their threats seriously. They liked to pick on old men and women who had sons in America from whom they were getting a regular allowance; they threatened them as often as the money came.

'One night they entered the grocery store run by Donna Nella and her sister Lucia. Both of them were old women. They had owned the shop as long as I could remember and everybody respected them. They tied the old women, as those cursed ones tied Nino, and used a knife to scare them into telling where they kept their savings. Donna Nella went insane from the shock and Lucia died of grief when they put her sister in an institution.

'This terrible crime infuriated the townspeople. Some of the men got together and decided that if the law wasn't going to do anything about the Castagna brothers, they would.

'Sure enough, a few days later one of the brothers was found strangled at the bottom of an abandoned well. The other two brothers left town right after the funeral and spent several weeks visiting relatives in Siculianna. When they came back everyone realized that they would soon be up to their old tricks but decided to do nothing as long as they behaved.

'The day after they threatened Don Pasquale with his life — Don Pasquale had a mason son in Brooklyn who sent him a little money once a month — Pietro Castagna was shot through the heart while he was sitting in front of his house. There were a number of people around when it happened, but when the police arrived and asked questions, no one knew anything.

'With two of his brothers gone, you can imagine how nervous Cosimo Castagna became. In the middle of the night he went to the home of my cousin Rafaelle, who was a tailor, and, at the point of a gun, forced him to pad his jacket and sew him a bulletproof vest. It wasn't very bullet-proof, of course, because Rafaelle was a tailor and not a blacksmith.

'The very first day Cosimo Castagna wore the vest, someone shot at him from behind but, thanks to the vest and the padding, he wasn't seriously hurt. Incidentally, his wife took the vest back to Rafaelle after the shooting and demanded that he repair it free so that her husband could wear it again. Imagine the gall of some people!

'Anyway, Cosimo Castagna began to realize that, vest or no vest, he was a marked man. So he decided to come to America. He had two sisters in New York and he wrote them a letter saying he would arrive on the next boat from Palermo. His sisters were at the port to greet their brother but he didn't seem to be among the passengers. The sisters began to think he had missed the boat

until they learned that the body of an unidentified stow-
away had just been found in the hold of the ship.   It was
Cosimo Castagna, all right.   He had hidden himself in a
coalbin and, while he was asleep, the ship had lurched to
one side and smothered him under a heap of coal.   When
we heard what had happened, we knew it was the hand
of God reaching out to punish Cosimo Castagna for his
evil life.'

'There is more to that story,' Rosario Alfano said.
'After the Castagna sisters had buried their brother, they
wrote Cosimo Castagna's wife in Sicily to find out who had
arranged for her husband's passage to New York.   They
learned it was a racketeer called Ignazio Agnello who
had made a fortune promising innocent Sicilians voyage
to America and then stowing them in such dangerous
places as coalbins.   The sisters decided to avenge their
brother's death.   They got busy with the Italian Consul
in New York, and before long Ignazio Agnello was arrested by the Italian police and sentenced to seven years
at hard labor.   So, you see, the law does have its uses
sometimes.'

It was obvious that my relatives did not always believe
that justice and law meant the same thing.   Ahead of
written laws, they placed the unwritten laws that had
been passed down to them for centuries.   In Sicily they
saw little reason for scrapping their unwritten laws in
favor of the written ones.   The lawbooks there had been
filled with fine-sounding distinctions between right and
wrong, but this fact had not stopped men from stealing
when they were hungry, nor had it prevented brigands

from plundering when the law was not interested enough to enforce its own rules.

Some of my relatives' unwritten laws stemmed from the Church, but most of them were inherited from ancestors who placed honor and respect above all written law. These legacies from the past were as real to them as health and disease, yet far more important, for while it was possible to regain health, the man who lost his honor could never get it back again.

My father told how in Sicily his friend Carmelo Primavera became a hero for killing a man who had dealt lightly with his sister's honor. Carmelo Primavera, who ran a small grocery store, had an unmarried sister named Santa. Although she was not pretty, a number of men fell in love with her and proposed marriage. None of the suitors met with her parents' approval and they were all turned down, including Angelo Piazza, whom Santa did not like anyway.

But Angelo Piazza was a stubborn young man and he spread the word among his friends that Santa would be sure to change her mind and marry him. Why or how he never explained. His friends asked each other: was he going to use some sleight-of-hand trick to persuade her, or perhaps a *fattura*? Or did Angelo Piazza believe that if he broadcast the possibility of marrying Santa widely enough, Santa herself might come to believe it?

Whatever his theory was, his optimism grew and he became bolder about it every day. A man so stricken with love would naturally have turned to drink or to other women, but not Angelo Piazza. He intensified his propaganda campaign and even took to calling on Santa's brother at his grocery store.

In spite of the cool receptions he got from Carmelo Primavera, Angelo Piazza insisted on treating him as though he were already in the family. Before long he began addressing Santa's brother as 'my brother-in-law.' Carmelo Primavera's temper blazed at this, for this form of address was nothing less than a slur on his sister's honor. One day he warned Angelo Piazza that the next time he called him 'brother-in-law' would be the last time.

Possibly because he was badly blinded with his love for Santa, Angelo Piazza failed to take him seriously. A few days later when he stepped into the grocery store and jovially addressed Carmelo as 'brother-in-law,' Carmelo reached for the revolver he kept near his money box and shot Angelo Piazza dead with one bullet. Then, calmly pushing the body out of his way with his foot, Carmelo walked out of his grocery store and surrendered himself to the authorities.

Within an hour the news had spread through the town that Carmelo Primavera had killed Angelo Piazza for insulting his sister's honor. When it reached one of the town gossips who had long before predicted the tragedy, she fainted away with delight. Nearly everyone in town who could walk went to the jail and clamored for Carmelo's release.

After a few hours of shouting, the Mayor and the Warden could no longer bear the noise, and it was graciously announced that 'after due and serious consideration' the Mayor had decided to set Carmelo Primavera free. The noise was even worse after that. Carmelo Primavera was fêted like a conquering general for more than a week, and his business increased to such an extent that he was obliged to move into larger quarters.

If Uncle Nino could be said to have any hero other than Dante it was probably Clarence Darrow — or 'Darro' as he deliberately called him, being certain that a barrister with so much eloquence in him must have had an Italian relative somewhere on his family tree. Uncle Nino would pore over the newspaper quotations from Darrow's court speeches with the fierce concentration of a child reading a fairy tale. When his English failed him, as it often did, he would let out a long stream of blasphemies against the complications of the English language and, when he had cooled down, order one of us to translate for him.

More than Darrow's eloquence, my uncle admired his talent for snatching people away from the law when it seemed most likely of winning. The law has its uses, sure, Uncle Nino would argue, but unless there are lawyers smart enough to cope with its tricks 'true justice' is liable to be frustrated. 'Darro,' he once explained to the other members of the Unholy Three, 'is the kind of lawyer who ranks with the great Sicilian lawyers I knew in my youth. They understood the meaning of true justice, and when the law got in their way, they knew exactly how to get around it.'

One of these great Sicilian lawyers was Giuseppe Scalla, who had often been a guest of my Uncle Nino's father at Caltanissetta. My uncle regarded him as the Sicilian counterpart of Darrow because he had the same genius for beating the law at its own game. He enjoyed telling us about some of the Sicilian's astonishing cases. One of them was particularly dear to him not only because it was impressive evidence of Scalla's genius but also because it illustrated what he meant by 'true justice.'

The story began with a young married couple who found employment as caretakers of an estate owned by Don Alfonso Cavallo, a rich middle-aged landowner. Although their relatives envied Salvatore and Grazia Cataldo for their jobs, Grazia was secretly perturbed by the lecherous attentions of her employer. Hardly a day passed that Don Alfonso would not try to put his arms around her, or pass bawdy remarks when she was making his bed.

Grazia warned Don Alfonso that if her husband ever found out he was trying to make love to her, he would surely kill him. Don Alfonso probably realized that was true and was most discreet when Salvatore was about, but the moment he left the house he would renew his campaign. Grazia managed to keep her virtue intact but, with her employer becoming bolder every day, the situation became increasingly impossible for her. When she could no longer tolerate it, she told her husband she was feeling ill and wanted to live among her relatives in Caltanissetta for a change. She had not been looking well for some time, and Salvatore readily gave her permission to stay with her aunt until her health was better.

Grazia's absence from the estate only increased Don Alfonso's ardor, and he made frequent trips to the city to see her. Now she became more worried than ever for fear her aunt or some of the neighbors might become suspicious of Don Alfonso's intentions and tell her husband. Needless to say, in spite of his pleas and offers, Don Alfonso got nowhere with Grazia.

In the meantime, Grazia had become pregnant, and her husband happily spread the news. When their son Giovanni was born, Salvatore was the most jubilant of fathers, and when Don Alfonso proposed that he become the boy's sponsor, Salvatore didn't know how to express thanks to God for his good fortune. Only Grazia knew that Don Alfonso's gesture was simply a trick to see her more often, for as a *compare* of the young couple he could come and go without arousing anyone's suspicions, least of all Salvatore's.

But Don Alfonso's trickery was futile. Although Grazia tried to respect him as her son's godfather, she found it difficult to be civil to him and, when they were alone, she would often show her contempt. By this time she had become an obsession with the rich landowner and he was more determined than ever to seduce her. In desperation, he decided to play his trump card and get rid of Salvatore. As long as Salvatore was alive, there seemed to be nothing he could do to persuade Grazia to change her mind. Perhaps she would become more sensible once Salvatore was out of the way. With this thought in mind, Don Alfonso invited him to the tavern for a bottle of wine.

He had no trouble getting Salvatore drunk. The caretaker was flattered to have so rich a friend, the godfather of his first-born, sit down with him for an evening of conviviality. When Don Alfonso was certain that Salvatore was too drunk to think clearly, he picked an argument with him about the last wheat crop. In the heat of the debate, he suddenly drew a gun from his pocket and shot Salvatore dead.

He told the police he had killed Salvatore in self-defense and, despite ample testimony to the contrary, the landowner was acquitted. 'In Sicily the police have always been the guardians of the rich,' my uncle explained. The people of Caltanissetta were angered by the court's decision, but no one dared lift a hand against a man as powerful as Don Alfonso. After a while they said the whole thing was Destiny and their anger died down a little. Taking no chances, Don Alfonso left the province for a couple of months. When he came back, he took up his old life, as though nothing had ever happened, and even had the audacity to try to see Grazia.

'Naturally,' my uncle said, 'she would have nothing to do with the beast. He pestered her for a few months while she was still in deep mourning but finally gave her up when Grazia met him at the door once with a cocked pistol and threatened to pull the trigger if he didn't stop bothering her.'

When Giovanni Cataldo was a young man, his mother sold everything she had to send him to medical school. She had never told him of the murder. Giovanni believed that his father had died a natural death during a cholera epidemic. One summer day, while he was on vacation, an acquaintance pointed to a handsome old man seated on a large chestnut mare and said, 'There goes the man who killed your father.' He refused to give Giovanni any further information and advised him to ask his mother about his father's death.

Grazia would say nothing at first. 'It was an epidemic, my son. You were too young to remember. It killed many people and took your father in three days' time,' she told him.

'Mother,' he said deliberately, 'I know that is not true. Unless you tell me the truth I shall kill the man who murdered my father this very night.'

Bursting into tears, Grazia told him exactly what had happened. When she was through, she begged him not to do anything foolish. 'The matter is closed now,' she said. 'There is no use stirring up old troubles. I've had enough unhappiness. Please don't add to it.'

If Giovanni heard her plea, he ignored it. He set about becoming familiar with Don Alfonso's habits and learned that he spent his evenings in a certain wine tavern. One night, when his mother was asleep, he slipped a bread knife under his cloak and went to the tavern. He hid himself in a near-by doorway and waited for Don Alfonso. About one o'clock in the morning the old man came out of the tavern. Giovanni confronted him a few steps beyond.

'Are you Don Alfonso Cavallo?' he asked.

'I am. What do you want?' Don Alfonso said.

'I am Salvatore Cataldo's son and I want your life.' With these words, he plunged the bread knife into the old man's breast. As Don Alfonso fell screaming, Giovanni ran in the direction of his home, confident that no one had seen him. But, unluckily for him, an old woman named Brigita Puzza was sitting on her balcony directly across from the scene of the murder and saw everything. When the police came, she told them that she had come out on her balcony for some air when the stabbing took place. She was certain that the murderer was Grazia Cataldo's son Giovanni.

'My son has been in bed all night,' Grazia told the police. 'I swear it by the Virgin Mary and Jesus. I should have heard him if he had left the house any time. Why, I sleep like a cat.'

'Please call him and don't waste our time,' they told her. 'He must have left the house because Signora Puzza with her very own eyes saw your son stab Don Alfonso.'

'Signora Puzza is a decrepit old woman,' Grazia protested. 'Her eyes are like dried seeds. If you had any conscience, you would not accept her statement as gospel truth.'

The police lost patience with her and went after Giovanni themselves. They found him sitting in bed in his nightshirt, rubbing his eyes as though he had just been awakened. They ordered him to dress and searched the room. Giovanni denied having left the house and kept insisting he knew nothing of the stabbing, even after the police found his blood-stained cloak. Giovanni claimed the blood was from a cut he had received sharpening his razor.

'Are you in the habit of sharpening your razor with your cloak on?' one of the policemen asked. The officer in charge was more polite but no less skeptical. He told Giovanni that although he could easily understand his motive for killing Don Alfonso, he had no other choice than to arrest him for murder.

Grazia wept bitterly at this new misfortune. She had lost her husband and now she was going to lose Giovanni. It was little consolation to her that nearly everyone in Caltanissetta sympathized with Giovanni. In their estimation, Giovanni had done the honorable thing in avenging the murder of his father. Law or no law, they declared that any Sicilian son worth his salt would have done the same under the circumstances. Many of her *pacsani* called on Grazia and asked what they could do to help, but they were all poor people like herself and knew they could do nothing. In the face of Signora Puzza's testimony, there seemed to be little hope that Giovanni would escape the penalty for murder.

Among the people of Caltanissetta who sympathized with Giovanni Cataldo's plight was a retired old judge named Ugo Valente. The old man had carefully analyzed the history of the case and decided that, guilty or not, Giovanni should be given every possible opportunity to escape the maximum penalty of life-imprisonment. Not wishing to embarrass the authorities by supporting Giovanni publicly, he disguised himself as a monk one night and went to Grazia's house. Grazia was preparing to go to bed when she heard his knock on the door.

'Who is it?' she asked.

'An old monk begging for a cup of water,' he replied.

She let him in and, noticing that he looked tired, suggested he rest a bit while he drank the water.

'God bless you for your kindness,' he said.

'Thank you, Father. I am badly in need of God's blessings these days,' she replied.

'You seem bitter, *figlia mia*. Do you have reason to be unhappy?'

Prodding her with his sympathy, the old man heard the detailed story of Grazia's troubles, dating back to the days when she and Salvatore went to work for Don Alfonso.

When she was finished, he said: 'Except for a miracle of God, there is only one man I know in Sicily who might be able to save Giovanni from prison. He is a lawyer named Giuseppe Scalla and he lives in Girgenti. You should see him as soon as possible and tell him the same

story you have told me.   If he agrees to take the case, I
think there will be some chance of saving Giovanni.
Otherwise, I'm afraid you will have to give up all hope
of seeing your son free again, for no ordinary lawyer can
do anything for him under the circumstances.'

Grazia kissed the old man's hands in gratitude and
begged him for Giuseppe Scalla's address.   He wrote it
down on a piece of paper and signed it with his initials.
'Take this to Giuseppe Scalla and be sure to hand it to him
in person,' he said.   Then he blessed her and left.

At dawn the next morning Grazia took the train to Girgenti.   She had never been in a lawyer's office and felt
very timid when confronted by the secretary.   Noticing
her peasant dress, the young man was brusque with
her and told her that Avvocato Scalla was much too busy
to see her that day.

'I must see him now!' she screamed.   'It is a matter of
life and death.'   Hearing the commotion, Giuseppe Scalla
came out of his office.   Grazia threw herself at his feet,
begging for a few minutes of his time.   When he saw her
note and recognized the handwriting and the initials as
those of the famous jurist, he led her into his office and
listened to her story.

When she was through, he said, 'I'll take the case, but
I shall need five thousand lire.'   It was more money than
she had ever had but she promised to raise the money
for him in three days.   When she returned to Caltanissetta,
she sold what few possessions she had; then she went
from door to door begging for money.   No one turned
her down when she explained how the money was to be
spent.   Before the three days were up, she had collected
the full amount and delivered it to Giuseppe Scalla.

With the trial only a week off, the lawyer decided there was no time to lose. That night he traveled secretly to the jail on the outskirts of Caltanissetta where Giovanni was interned. At first the jailer refused to let him see the prisoner at that late hour, but when he recognized the visitor as the famous Giuseppe Scalla, he became very courteous and said he would be glad to make an exception in his case.

The lawyer came to the point as soon as he was left alone with Giovanni.

'I can't help you unless I know the truth,' he said. 'Now be frank with me, was Signora Puzza speaking the truth when she said that you stabbed Don Alfonso?'

Giovanni nodded. 'Very well,' said Giuseppe Scalla. 'Now listen to the plan I have in mind and do exactly as I say.'

In less than ten minutes the lawyer had finished his talk with Giovanni and returned to the jailer. 'I want you to do me a great favor,' he told him. 'I want you to release Giovanni Cataldo tonight for a half-hour. You have my word of honor that he will be back in his cell within a half-hour.' As he spoke, the lawyer drew five thousand lire from his wallet and put them on the jailer's desk. The jailer protested a little, but the temptation of the money was too great and after a few minutes he agreed.

In the suit of clothes the lawyer gave him to wear, Giovanni found a shiny bread knife similar to the one he had used to stab Don Alfonso. At the appointed time he left the prison and went directly to Signora Puzza's house, making certain that no one saw him along the way.

With the handle of the knife he banged at Signora

Puzza's door and demanded entrance. He banged until
he heard the old lady get out of bed. When he saw her
looking out of her bedroom window, he brandished the
bread knife at her menacingly. As soon as he heard her
screams for help, he darted away. In less than twenty
minutes from the time he had left the prison he was back
in his prison cell.

The trial was one of the briefest murder trials on record
in Caltanissetta. The moment Giovanni entered the
courtroom Signora Puzza jumped up from her chair and,
pointing an hysterical finger at him, screamed: 'There he
is, the man who tried to kill me last night as he killed Don
Alfonso. *Aiutu!* Don't let him come any closer! He
has a bread knife in his pocket. He wants to kill me!'

The Judge tried vainly to restore order. As Giovanni
advanced to the front of the courtroom, she kept shouting
'*Assassinu*' as though she expected to be murdered right
then and there. Then suddenly she fainted. When she
was revived, she got behind a policeman for protection
and insisted at the top of her lungs that Giovanni had
come to her house with a bread knife in the middle of the
night to murder her. It took two policemen to calm her
and keep her quiet.

When it was Giuseppe Scalla's turn to speak, he confined himself to a single point. He asked the court to
consider the scene Signora Puzza had made when she saw
the defendant and declared that the old woman was
obviously out of her mind. 'Giovanni Cataldo has been
in jail since the day he was arrested for the murder of
Alfonso Cavallo. How could he have gone to Signora
Puzza's house last night and threatened her life when he

was locked up in a cell? Your Honor, it is clear that the poor woman is deranged and that the testimony she offered which led to the arrest of Giovanni Cataldo cannot be considered valid. I move the case be dismissed.'

'The Judge was obliged to release Giovanni for lack of sufficient evidence,' my Uncle Nino said, chuckling.

'What happened to Signora Puzza?' my mother wanted to know.

'She spent the rest of her days in an insane asylum. She should have minded her business in the first place. No one ever felt sorry for her. After all, she was an old woman almost through with life. Giovanni was just beginning his. But you can see that if it hadn't been for Giuseppe Scalla he would have died in jail. Didn't I tell you that Giuseppe Scalla was like Darro?'

My relatives enjoyed telling stories about crime in Sicily. For one thing, the stories belonged to a past they had long ago romanticized; for another, they had the extra glamour of dealing with characters my relatives had known personally. All of them were told as true stories and all of them were at least as melodramatic as the one Uncle Nino told about Giuseppe Scalla. Some of them only lacked music to be operas.

To hear a recital of them, you would have imagined that Sicilians were a bloodthirsty lot who spent most of their time killing each other. But if you examined the stories and listened to them carefully, you would realize that each story expressed some profoundly noble sentiment and was always told with the proper amount of moral indignation.

Oddly enough, American crimes seldom intrigued my relatives. The only hair-raising stories I heard about American lawbreaking were those told by relatives who reminisced about the lawless Pennsylvania coal-mining towns they had once worked in. Sometimes a dramatic American crime would remind them of a more dramatic Sicilian one, but on the whole there was little attention paid to the crime stories that crowded the pages of Rochester newspapers, except by sensitive people like my father, who would become concerned if the participants had Sicilian names.

The Sicilian stories entranced me more than the matter-of-fact murder accounts I read in the press, partly because they were more skillfully told but mainly because, as often as not, the real villain in the piece turned out to be the law itself. Being too young to understand the meaning of 'true justice,' I interpreted my relatives' stories with all the literalness that an immature mind can be guilty of. From hearing their stories it was as clear as the light of day that the fat policeman on our block who was supposed to symbolize law and order was actually a villain underneath his uniform. This only confirmed an old and strong suspicion of mine and I began to think that, at last, there was one thing I could see eye to eye with my relatives.

On the strength of this, I went so far as to ask my parents to conspire with me against such representatives of law and order as my school principal and the truant officer. But, unfortunately, my parents' respect for American law and order seemed to have developed with dismal rapidity. I was not only rebuffed but, on one occasion, slapped violently by my mother when I persisted in trying to engage her in a fine bit of collusion.

My parents hardly showed the tolerance of some of the other Sicilian parents in Mount Allegro. There were the parents of Tony and Louie Pazienza, for instance, who were not the least shocked or angered when the boys were caught stealing boxes of oranges and were only saved from arrest through the generosity of the grocery store proprietor. Their attitude seemed to be that as long as the boys had escaped punishment, everything was fine, especially since they had dutifully been bringing home whatever oranges they did not sell. It was only when the boys began to steal from their own relatives that Mr. and Mrs. Pazienza became alarmed and requested the authorities to put their sons in a reform school for a while.

American Pattern

A FEW OF MY RELATIVES BEGAN BREAKING away from Mount Allegro to live on the outskirts of town where they could enjoy the luxury of a vegetable garden. At first they seemed lost in their new American surroundings, where there were no guitar sessions and no storytellers like Uncle Nino. Every few evenings they would come bounding back to the neighborhood with tall stories about the joys of suburban life and bring generous gifts of fruits and vegetables.

But as they became acquainted with their new American neighbors — most of them families of German and Irish origin — their visits to Mount Allegro became less frequent. Some of them grew quite aloof and did their best to forget they had ever lived in a poorer environment. Others, like Compare Calogero and Rosario Alfano, couldn't bear to be away from their Sicilian neighbors and moved back into Mount Allegro.

Those who left it for good developed strange habits and tastes. They took to drinking fruit juices at breakfast and tea with supper. They wore pyjamas to bed, drank whiskey with soda, and learned to play poker.

My relatives pretended to be scandalized by the foreign customs of these renegades, but at heart they were envious and gradually they too adopted some of them. The most popular of all was poker. The Unholy Three began to play less briscola and more *pochero,* as they pronounced it, and my Uncle Luigi shone as a *pochero* expert because he had often watched the game played at his union's headquarters and naturally knew more of the rules than anyone else. He knew what it took to make a *fulla-hausa,* a *straighto,* and a *flosho* long before the others did. For a while he won the most money.

If the children had had their own way, my parents would have dropped all their Sicilian ideas and customs and behaved more like other Americans. That was our childhood dream. Yet, as much as we wanted them to be Americans and as much as we wanted to live an American life, we did not have the vaguest notion as to how to go about it. I used to wonder how it would be if our family moved out of Mount Allegro, as some of the other relatives had done, but the idea of leaving playmates behind was too painful. Besides, it was clear to me that those who had moved into American neighborhoods didn't seem any more American than they ever had, in spite of their tea and pyjamas.

Although no one seemed to approach them in real life, the movie stars came closest to our idea of what Americans were like. I tried to imitate some of my favorite stars, but in the face of having to speak Sicilian and eat Sicilian food it seemed futile. In my imitations, no one pointed to me and said: 'Look, that boy must be American. He has dark eyes and an olive skin, yes, but probably some of his Mayflower ancestors intermarried with the Indians.'

It was obvious that my teachers were true Americans; that was clear from the fuss they made over my name and my big brown eyes. Most of them had eyes that were a hard blue or gray. There was no use imitating them. They knew far too much and I was too scared of them, for they had it within their power to make my life at home either miserable, or ringing with laudatory speeches from my Uncle Nino. I could do without both, for while I understood the ranting of my father when my marks were poor, I was seldom able to understand the pure Italian praises of my uncle when my marks were good.

I was also annoyed by the great expectations teachers had of those of us who were obviously of Italian origin. We were expected to be particularly brilliant in Latin and, of course, in any of the Romance languages. As for such subjects as music and drawing, our teachers were positively insulted if we did not show signs of becoming another Verdi or another Da Vinci.

In the study of languages we could nurture their illusions for a time because the language we spoke at home made it easy for us to guess at the meanings and pronunciations of Latin and French words without having the slightest idea of their grammatical aspects. But when examination time came with its blunt questions about grammar rules and declensions, there could be no guessing, and our teachers were horrified at the poor showings we made, never admitting that they had been completely bluffed up to that point, and, in a sense, victimized by their own propaganda. It is quite possible that if we had been treated as ordinary children, with no extraordinary heritage to give us an automatic mastery of Latin languages, we might have felt more compelled to memorize the dull workings of grammar.

My experiences in drawing and music classes were particularly unhappy and fairly indicative of the delusions some of my teachers had of students with Italian blood. In drawing, I surpassed everyone in the class by my gross ineptness. Despite my teachers' most patient efforts, I could never draw. But while I was the first to admit it, my teachers were the last. One of them was especially unreasonable. I had spent nearly all of an afternoon trying to do the impossible: paint a landscape that looked like a landscape. I simply did not have a landscape in me. My landscapes resembled everything else but landscapes. Most of them looked like scrambled eggs mixed with spinach.

But my teacher was not interested in eggs with spinach; she was determined on a landscape. Gerry Amoroso. An Italian, wasn't I? Then, it was silly for me to say I couldn't paint a landscape. I offered her the scrambled eggs again. She was not interested.

'Unless you paint me a landscape, I shall have to send you to the Principal's office.'

That should have been enough to make me turn out a half-dozen landscapes in five minutes. The Principal was the Devil, a skinny giant with false teeth that rattled when he became angry. Even the teachers were afraid of him.

'I'll never be able to paint a landscape, Miss Oglethorpe.'

'You are being very stubborn, Gerry.'

'No, ma'am. I'm telling the truth. Don't you want me to tell you the truth?'

I should have kept my mouth shut. A few minutes later I was on my way to the Principal's office.

The Principal rubbed his hands and looked me up and down as though he were trying to decide how well I would roast over a fire.

'So you can't paint a landscape, eh?'

'No, sir.'

'Have you *tried* to paint a landscape?'

'Yes, sir, I have, but my landscapes don't look like landscapes.'

I was frightened, but determined to let him know how things were.

'You're being contrary!' he shouted. 'I want you to paint me a landscape this very afternoon.'

'Yes, sir. Miss Oglethorpe wants me to do the same thing. I wish I could.'

'Your parents are Italian. I can tell by your name. Some of the greatest artists the world has ever known were Italian. No reason on earth why you can't paint a simple landscape.'

'No, sir.'

'I shall permit you to return to your class without punishing you if you will promise to paint me a landscape. Any kind of landscape,' he added desperately.

'But I can't.'

'I shall have to whip you if you don't.'

'But I'm telling you the truth,' I protested, at a loss to understand how anyone could possibly be whipped for telling the truth.

The truth, though, was all the incentive he needed.

In a moment he had uncoiled a long snakelike belt.

He put me over his bony knees and began whacking me
with all the gusto of an old man trying to prove that he
is not as old as you think. It was the first time in my life
I had ever been whipped and I made the most of the
opportunity. I must have yelled very loudly because at
the end of a half-dozen strokes he suddenly stopped and
panted, 'Will you paint a landscape now?'

'Can't,' I panted back.

Six more whacks. Six more deafening screams. His
knees began to creak and sag under my weight. He was
obviously exhausted. 'There,' he said in a triumphant
voice that didn't ring true, 'that will certainly teach you
to paint a landscape when your teacher says you must.'

It didn't.

Nor did my Latin heritage do me any good in the field
of music. I had the bad luck to be reared in the player-
piano era, the neurotic years following the First World
War when Sicilian parents considered it a social disgrace
if there was not a player-piano in the house with a complete set of Verdi operas to pump out on it, and a piano
teacher making weekly trips to instruct the children.

It was the first time my relatives came to real grips with
American-made culture, and their zeal was fanatical.
Families went without proper food so that the installments
on the player-piano could be paid. They moved into
larger homes, which they could not afford, so that there
would be room to house the piano, the piano bench, and
the cabinet that held the rolls. Some families, who could
no longer buy on the installment plan, increased the mort-
gage on their homes to raise money for a piano.

Every child tall enough to reach the piano was regarded as a potential concert artist long before anyone heard him play his first scale. The player-piano, supplanting the squeaky phonograph and preceding the popular use of radio by nearly ten years, became a symbol of culture. Until your children were old enough to play the keyboard, you could listen to all the operas and hear old Sicilian songs (with the words written on the rolls) merely by pumping. What more could one ask of America? For my relatives it was the miracle invention of the twentieth century. It gave them a medium for reviving their musical memories of Italy and it was a perfect excuse for forcing a musical education on all their children, something that only the rich had been able to afford in Sicily.

In her passion to make musicians of us, my mother was no less heroic than all the other Sicilian mothers in Mount Allegro. She hoarded nickels from her small allowance to meet the down-payment on our player-piano; then she hoarded more nickels so that she could pay off the music teacher punctually. It was her contribution to the culture of her children, and she was as avid about it as a mother who decides that her young ones need more milk.

It was mainly of music that she thought when she thought at all about culture. Music, and sometimes higher education; not of literature, nor of art. She had an ancient Sicilian prejudice against books and sincerely believed that if you read too many of them, you were bound to go mad. Painting, unless it resembled photography, was of little interest to her. But music was something else. Music was food for the spirit. Without music, there could be no real happiness.

If she could only manage to have her four children –·
or even one – play arias from Verdi and Bellini or play
dance music (how she could dance!).   Or if they did not
prove to be that gifted, if only they could play the accompaniment to the songs such as those we heard during the
long winter evenings from newly arrived Sicilians who
sang to ease their homesickness.   If only they could play
anything, how happy and proud she would be!

As the oldest, I was the first victim of her campaign.   I
turned out to be a bad choice, for instead of practicing
my scales, I hid under the bed and read novels.   In quick
succession, I took up the piano, the violin, and the guitar.
My lack of real patience and the inertia the simplest scales
inspired in me were obvious to everyone but my mother.
She staunchly refused to believe that her eldest son could
have no musical talent.   All my music teachers were immediately struck with my lack of response, but my mother
persevered in believing that if I found the musical instru-
ment that appealed to my special talents, I would surely
master it.   It was a beautiful theory, and I am sure she
still clings to it.

By the time I had convinced several piano teachers and
her that the piano was not my medium, the nickels she
had put aside for my musical education were nearly all
gone.   But my mother did not lose heart, as I had hoped
she would.   This time she decided that it was the violin
that was best suited to my talents.   She borrowed ten
dollars from her brother and bought me a three-quarter-
size violin that still smelled of varnish.   Then she solemnly
promised our relatives that within two years I would be
entertaining them with concerts of the finest Italian music.

I myself became influenced by her propaganda and for the first two weeks I practiced my scales assiduously. My teacher was a gentle and shy Neapolitan who pressed men's suits in a factory during the day and taught the violin evenings. His best advertisement was his four children, who had learned so well from their father that before long they, too, were adding to the family income by teaching. It seemed like a pleasant and clean way of earning a living, and those first few weeks of my life with a violin were motivated more by that idea than by the prospect of playing for my relatives.

My mother's nickels finally gave out and since my violin teacher was not sufficiently impressed with my genius to offer me lessons on credit, she enrolled me in a public-school violin class conducted after regular school hours. There were nearly forty students in the class. This did not discourage my mother; it simply meant that the concerts she planned for me would have to be postponed a year or two.

Despite the size of the class, I quickly became conspicuous as one of its worst students. I weathered the abuses of the instructor, an ex-prodigy with an Anglo-Saxon name and a Latin temperament, and pretended to take his criticism seriously, but outside the class I no longer practiced with the same zest. My career as a violinist came to an abrupt end one afternoon when the instructor was listening to some of the students individually. When I played for him, he blew up.

'Are you, or are you not Italian?' he demanded.

'Yes,' I said, frightened at his violence. 'But I was born here.'

'It makes no difference where you were born!' he roared. 'You have Italian blood in you and should have some aptitude for music. Why can't you play the simplest scales for me?'

I could not very well tell him I had not been practicing. 'I don't know,' I lied.

'What part of Italy do your parents come from?' he asked belligerently.

When I said Sicily, he looked immensely relieved and almost happy. Without another word he went to his desk and wrote rapidly on a pad. Then he gave me the note and told me to report to the school office with my violin.

I had the sickening sensation that the world had ended for me. I had visions of my parents throwing me out of the house and leaving me alone, high and dry in an unfriendly world with no possessions except a violin that I could not play.

At the office a beautiful blue-eyed brunette told me what I already knew: the violin teacher did not want me in his class any longer. The brunette, noting the despair in my eyes and the telltale droop of the violin case under my arm, became sympathetic.

'Now, don't take it too hard, sonny,' she said patting my head. 'It's nothing to worry about. Not all people can play the violin. Look at me, I can't.'

I looked at her. Then she told me what big brown eyes I had, as if that would fix everything, and sent me home.

But I was afraid to go home. I went to see my Uncle Nino instead, figuring that since he had not become a diplomat despite his family's hopes that he would become one, he might understand why I could not become a violinist. I also knew that if I could persuade him to plead my case, my parents might be more inclined to be lenient.

Uncle Nino listened to my story in detail. When I came to the part where the teacher had asked me what section of Italy my parents came from, I took the liberty of embroidering it a bit. 'I told him Sicily and he told me that explained everything because Sicilians didn't know anything about music,' I said. Uncle Nino was indignant. He reached for his hat and announced he was going to tell the instructor exactly what he thought of him and his knowledge of music.

With great difficulty, I was finally able to restrain him and persuade him that the instructor had been joking; that, of course, he knew that Sicilians were as gifted in music as any other kind of Italians. My fervor gave me away. He looked at me suspiciously and then asked that I play one of my exercises. He listened patiently while I went through the simplest exercise I could remember. At the end of it, he looked sad.

'It sounds terrible,' he said gently. 'I can't say I blame your teacher.'

But, having no children of his own, he could be counted on to be generous toward his nephews. He accompanied me home and broke the news of my dismissal to my mother. When he saw how crestfallen she looked, he made the point that the teacher obviously did not like Sicilians, so how in the world could I possibly be expected to learn anything from him?

I think my mother finally realized that I probably could

not learn from anyone. Shortly afterward she announced that inasmuch as I had shown that the violin was not my medium, I would receive guitar lessons. My brother Joe, who had just finished proving that the piano was not his medium, would take my place at the violin. We both made faces. I regret to report that two months later my mother gave both of us up in despair and turned her attention to my sisters Maria and Giustina, who were now tall enough to reach the keyboard.

The problem of educating their children was easily solved by my relatives. If the children were females there was no problem at all. To give a daughter more education than that required by law was considered an extravagant waste of time and money. It was fine if you could afford piano lessons for her; that was something of a luxury but it made sense, for a girl who knew some music was bound to be more *simpatica* than a girl who did not and, of course, everyone knew that when a man wanted to marry he tried to choose a girl who was *simpatica*. But everyone also knew that a man was not interested in a girl who knew much more than he did. So what was the use of spending money on her schooling? Far better for her to learn to sew and cook, or to earn money for the family until the right man came along to marry her. Even if you imitated the Americans and sent your daughter to college, she would end up by marrying anyway, and what was the use of her education to her then? Look at the case of Dunnietta Palermo. Her mother ruined her eyes working in a tailor factory to send her through a teachers' school; then she up and married less than a month after she received her diploma. Now she had three children and spent most of her time in the kitchen. *America pazza!*

It was different with sons. They had the world before them. Not the kitchen. In a country like *l'America*, which had *la Democrazia*, they could go to high school and then to college with a little sacrifice on the part of the parents — and emerge a lawyer or a doctor. *Dottore, Avvocato* — magic words to any Sicilian. All other professions seemed insignificant to them. The *dottori* and the *avvocati* were the men most respected in their homelands — and they were the ones who made the most money.

America bella! Here a poor Sicilian who earned his bread shining shoes could, by shining more shoes, send his son through college and see him become an *avvocato* or *dottore*. It was wonderful because then, presto, the poor Sicilian was no longer poor. He could stop shining shoes and he and his wife could live comfortably for the rest of their lives, confident that the son for whom they had made so many sacrifices would support them and honor them. Not only that — but they would enjoy a great deal more 'respect' among their *paesani*, regardless of whether he had been a shoe-shiner in Rochester or a *cafone* in Sicily. What more could a man want?

My father and mother enjoyed a great deal of 'respect' among their *paesani* because he came from a long line of fine pastrymakers and she could boast of a father who had been the chief architect of Realmonte and of an uncle who was a university professor. But the prospect of making their oldest son an *avvocato* or *dottore* dazzled them, and they started conditioning me for those professions even while I was still young enough to want to be a street-car conductor more than anything else in the world.

But it was obvious to everyone that I would never make an *avvocato*. My Uncle Nino pointed out that I was far too sensitive and too honest. So my mother told me I would be a doctor. That seemed much less exciting than being a streetcar conductor but for a while I accepted her decision. Then I learned that being a doctor was not at all like playing doctor — a game the boys in the gang enjoyed playing with the little girls in the block — and also that, while doctors were supposed to cure people, the doctor who attended my youngest sister, Giuseppina, had been unable to prevent her death. I refused to become a doctor.

My Uncle Luigi came to my parents' rescue by suggesting that the profession I was really fitted for was *farma-cista*. When you were a *farmacista*, people would not call you Mr. Amoroso but Farmacista Amoroso. Pharmacists, he said, were respected almost as much as doctors and they had a far easier time. Their work was clean as well as profitable and they collected their money on the spot. A pharmacist could charge you anything he wished for a few grains of powder or a little medicine and no one would ever dare complain for fear he would put poison in the medicine you bought the next time. Truly, a wonderful profession.

My parents were impressed. My father bought me a chemistry set which was beautiful with its five different-colored liquids and its tall delicate test tubes. He also fixed me a small laboratory in one corner of the cellar and, when I protested that I could do nothing without a

Bunsen burner, he even bought me that.   For several days the gang saw nothing of me.   I spent all my spare moments in the gloom of the cellar playing with liquids, test tubes, and litmus paper.   I toyed with the idea of distilling water.   Then one day I almost set myself and the house on fire when a test tube exploded in my hands. That ended my career as a *farmacista*.   My father looked discouraged and said that maybe I should become a streetcar conductor after all.   My mother lit a candle on Saint Joseph's altar and prayed that I would gather more sense as I grew older.

As far as accepting some of my relatives' habits and notions was concerned, my mother's prayer seemed to be in vain.   The more aware I became of the great differences between their Latin world and the Anglo-Saxon world (I thought of it as 'American' then) the more disturbed I was; nor was I the only child of Sicilian parents who was disturbed.   We sensed the conflict between the two worlds in almost everything our parents did or said. Yet we had to adjust ourselves to their world if we wanted any peace.   At the bottom of our dissatisfaction, of course, was the normal child's passion for conventionality. It wasn't that we wanted to be Americans so much as we wanted to be like most people.   Most people, we realized as we grew older, were not Sicilians.   So we fretted inside.

I was embarrassed by the things my relatives did when in public; most of all by their total indifference to what Americans might be thinking of them.   I mistook their high spirits, their easy naturalness, and their extraverted love of life for vulgarity, never dreaming that these were qualities many Americans envied.   I had a particular dread of picnics in public parks.   Spaghetti, chicken, and wine were consumed with pagan abandon then and the talk and laughter of my relatives filled the park like a warm summer breeze.

A few feet away would be an American family quietly munching neatly cut sandwiches that came out of neatly packed baskets — and drinking, not wine of course, but iced tea with trim slices of lemon stuck into the brims of their glasses to make them look pretty.   It would make me blush to realize how shocked these subdued, well-mannered Americans must be by the circus din of our Sicilian eating festival.

There were other disturbing contrasts.   The women in our picnic would be wearing silken party dresses, the kind usually worn to weddings, because they believed in having their good times in the best clothes they had, regardless of the occasion.   The Americans wore crisp and oh-so-neat dresses especially designed for picnics.   And also the Americans had the sense to leave their infants behind in the care of nurses who fed and cleaned the infants in privacy.

But my Sicilian relatives had little regard for privacy. They brought all their infants with them on their picnics and the women had no inhibitions about baring their breasts to feed them, no matter where they were or how many Americans might be about to watch them.

Never having seen the exposed breasts of an American mother, I imagined they were never as large and as sprawling as Sicilian breasts, but rather neat and delicate, like the food they packed for picnics.   In my prudishness,

I was also confident that the breasts of American mothers were purely ornamental and never used for the messy business of feeding hungry brats.

Our general attitude toward all Americans was bound to be distorted, for, not knowing any of them well, we could not make independent judgments and were influenced by the confused opinions our elders had of them. On one hand, my relatives were cynical about *Americani:* they had no manners; they licked their fingers after a meal and they chewed gum and then played with it as though it were a rubber band. Also, *Americani* were *superbi* (snobs) and looked down on people who didn't speak their language fluently. On the other hand, they feared and respected *Americani* and there were times when they emulated them.

If a Sicilian began to behave like an *Americano,* they said he was putting on airs but, actually, they had great admiration for anyone who achieved any degree of Americanization. After all, to be an *Americano* was a sign that you were getting on in the world. The bosses were Americans. The police were Americans. In fact, nearly anyone who had plenty of money or a good steady job was either an American or was living like one.

You had only to look at the example set by the sons of poor Italians who became doctors or lawyers in the community. As soon as they had established themselves, they married blonde American girls and moved as far as possible from their former neighborhoods. Some of them dropped the vowels from the end of their names, so that people would think they had always been American. They stopped associating with their relatives. Their wives got their pictures in society pages and, instead of having a raft of children, they bought wire-haired terriers and walked them around the block, like many other prosperous Americans. The only times they liked dealing with Italians was when it meant money in their pockets.

In spite of the fact that the word *Americano* was usually preceded by the Sicilian word *fissa*, meaning stupid, Americans were suspected of miraculous shrewdness and dishonesty. Yet once an *Americano* had shown his friendliness to a Sicilian in any way, however trivial, he could expect to be smothered with hospitality and love — never, of course, the love that one Sicilian relative has for another, but enough love to make an American regard his own relatives as so many cold fish for the rest of his life.

My relatives conceded that there were good and bad Americans, just as there were good and bad Sicilians, but they suspected that most of them were inclined to take advantage of a foreigner who could not speak their own tongue. Even before coming to the United States, Sicilians were educated to be suspicious of Americans. From their relatives in America, they received long pathetic accounts of how they had been robbed and cheated. Those who were planning to migrate were warned to beware of Americans from the moment they set foot off the boat.

The first supposedly English word many of my relatives learned even before they landed in America was *girarihir*, meaning 'Get out of here.' Immigrants were solemnly advised to yell this word at any stranger in America who approached them, for it was emphasized that if a Sicilian was identified as a *greenhorno*, some American would surely try to rob him of his money or belongings.

New Bread, Old Wine

AT EIGHTEEN I LEFT MY SICILIAN RELATIVES.
Living among them, I had the sense that though I was
born in America I was not really an American. I decided
to become a part of the outer American world; perhaps
in that way I could rid myself of the feeling that I was
more Sicilian than American. Actually, I was too young
to know exactly what I hoped to accomplish and acted
a great deal on intuition, as the young must do when they
are short of experience. But this much I knew for certain: the influence of my relatives was stronger than that
of my teachers, stronger than all the movies I had seen
and the books I had read.

The jobs I held after school and during summer vacations stimulated my curiosity about the outer American
world. Selling newspapers on street corners, working in
restaurants as a bus boy, ushering in a burlesque show
(when my mother thought I was cashiering in a cigar
store), working in the public library — all that gave me a
glimpse of America. I wanted to see more.

It seemed expedient to go to college first. My relatives

were nettled to hear that instead of studying medicine, law, or pharmacy I planned to study no particular subject but a number of subjects, with the idea of equipping myself for newspaper work. My Aunt Giovanna threw up her hands. *'Ma chi si stupidu!'* she said. 'Such dirty work printing a newspaper. Why don't you take up a cleaner profession?'

I tried to explain how clean the newspaper profession was, and that writing for a newspaper did not mean setting type. She could not understand. 'If you intend to dirty your hands, why waste your hard-earned money and your parents' on a college education? Why not become a *briccoliere* like your Uncle Luigi? When there is work he makes ten dollars a day.'

My mother was not sure what I was talking about when I told her I was going to write for a living. She looked worried and said she should never have permitted me to read so many books. She begged me not to waste my education on something as uncertain as the writing profession. Could I not become a teacher instead; or at least train to be a teacher, so that I would have something to fall back on if I couldn't earn a livelihood as a writer? *Maestro.* It was obviously the fourth item on her list of the most respected professions. I was the oldest, the only one in the family who was going to get a college education. It was important to her that I bring honor to the family by training myself for a profession my relatives recognized and respected. Writing was no profession. Anyone who had any education at all wrote. So she argued. I didn't want to hurt her; I promised I would train myself as a teacher as well as a writer.

My Uncle Nino was the only one impressed with my ambition to write for a living. '*Bravo,* Gerlando,' he said. 'After you learn what there is to know, you will tell me all about it.   Then we will both write a great work for Hollywood.   We will make much money that way and I will take you to Italy and show you the sights.   God's Blood! Do you know that I have never been in Florence, the city of Dante?'

When I broke the news that I was going to an out-of-town university — Syracuse — my relatives were plainly horrified.   Could it be that I was becoming a calloused American?   The idea that I could bear to leave them behind offended some of them.   They began to regard me as a heretic.   A good Sicilian son stuck near his family; the only time he left it was to marry, and even then he lived close by so that he could see his relatives often. Life, after all, was *being* with each other.   You never left your flesh and blood of your own free will.   You left only when it was impossible to earn a living near them, or when you died.

But I was determined to make the break.   I pointed out that they had left many of their relatives behind to come to America, a strange and faraway land, while I was going to a near-by city where the language and customs were the same as they were in Rochester.   The nearness of Syracuse cheered them a little, and on the day I left my father gave a banquet in my honor at which he served *cannoli* and his oldest wine ('My oldest wine for my oldest son,' he said) and my Uncle Nino made a speech about me and Dante.   Then they all accompanied me to the depot and when the train was leaving the station they wept, as though I were going to a war and might never come back.

Except for two or three summer vacations, I never did go back to Rochester to live. And after I went to work in New York my trips home became shorter and fewer. I got caught in the whirlpool of American life.

I began to know America and to feel like an American, and gradually to learn that America did not differ so much from the street I grew up on. The people I met — and I met many — were much like those I had known in Rochester. But now I could see them more distinctly and fit them into the pattern that was America. At the same time, I learned to see my relatives more objectively and, although I still retained my childhood resentment for some of their habits and attitudes, for the first time in my life I began to appreciate their warmth and their talent for living. Through my sisters I kept closely in touch with my family and whenever I could I spent the holidays in Rochester.

Mount Allegro looked more ragged as the Depression wore on and there were even fewer flower gardens. A new gang of boys played near the street light. The Enemy died but Mr. Michelangelo, finding her daughter no more supportable as a neighbor, refused to tear down the spite wall.

There were a few deaths among my relatives. Donna Rosalia fell victim to one of the horrible diseases she had imagined for herself and died after wasting away from a hundred and seventy pounds to eighty. Her husband, Rosario Alfano, left Rochester a month after the funeral to return to his native town of Girgenti, and on his departure my Uncle Nino wept and wished he were going back to Sicily with him.

At the age of eighty-seven, Great-Uncle Minicuzzu died very suddenly one afternoon while his wife was out buying him a gallon of wine. He got an elaborate funeral — the finest send-off my relatives had ever given anyone — and all his children who could afford it had Masses sung for his soul.

The day of my great-uncle's funeral my mother fell down a stairway and was crippled with a bad knee for more than a year. When the doctors admitted they could do nothing for it, she went to a *paesano* in the nearby town of Garbut who had the reputation of being blessed with *mani santi* — sainted hands. With a single twist of his hands, he made her knee as good as new. Another item of news was that Cicca Ricotta married a boy of Sicilian parentage and at the wedding feast Don Antonio got so drunk with joy and wine that he passed out before it was over.

Except for growing older and poorer, my relatives hardly changed. Some of them who had bought homes in the twenties lost them to the banks in the thirties. On the whole, it was surprising news to them that the twenties had been an era of prosperity. In the early years of the Depression many of them lost their jobs. They laid the blame on the 'elections,' a word which by now began to sound synonymous with Destiny, and claimed that the next 'election' would probably make things better. When Roosevelt was elected and several of them got jobs on government projects, they said, 'You see, it is all a matter of having a good election.'

By the middle of the Depression years most of my relatives had become American citizens.   They were proud of their voting privilege, but their general understanding of American politics was still limited to the headlines they could spell out in the newspapers and to the broken promises they heard from ward heelers who came around periodically with cigars and fat smiles.

Uncle Nino continued his boycott of the English language but Aunt Giovanna, stubborn as ever, went to school and tried to learn enough words to become a citizen.   If she learned any English, no one ever heard it. When she came before the Judge in naturalization court, she flickered her beautiful eyes every time he asked her a question and somehow managed to convince him that she knew all the answers but had forgotten them for the moment.   Her naturalization was the only triumph she enjoyed during the Depression; everything else seemed to go wrong.

First, she became so rheumatic that she no longer had the strength to pump her player-piano.   There was no one else to play it.   My Uncle Nino had no interest in music that required such strenuous effort; the piano lost its tone so often from disuse that she finally gave it away.   Then she and my uncle were obliged to let the bank take the two houses they had owned for twenty years and move into a rented apartment that was too small to entertain more than one family at a time.

Worst of all, the tailor factory where she had faithfully sewed for more than thirty years put her on a piecework basis when orders became scarce and she earned only a fraction of her former salary.   Some weeks there were no orders and she earned nothing. Uncle Nino gallantly tried to find a job for the first time in his life, but gave up at the end of three months and became a passionate amateur fisherman. My aunt was too proud to apply for relief, but it became apparent that the fear of not earning enough money to pay for food and shelter was beginning to torment her.

How driven she was by this fear we learned in 1933, when for the first time she failed to take her brood of nephews and nieces to Sea Breeze Park to celebrate Assumption Day. Up till that time it had been her annual custom to pack an enormous lunch and spend many hard-earned dollars treating her young relatives to rides on the roller-coaster and the merry-go-round and buying them such exotic edibles as hot-dogs and ice-cream suckers. It was a most impressive way of observing the miracle of the Virgin Mary being lifted to heaven.

To finance the lark, Aunt Giovanna would go without fruit and pastries for several weeks before Assumption Day — a truly touching sacrifice for a large woman who loved sweets as much as she did. In spite of her job, she had always managed to have that day off. One year she boasted that her department had to close down on Assumption Day because it was unable to operate in her absence.

When one of my young relatives heard that Aunt Giovanna was not taking him and his cousins to Sea Breeze Park on Assumption Day, he was aghast. The annual picnic had become as important to him as Christmas. In his youthful indiscretion, he demanded an explanation. My poor aunt burst into tears. 'Ah, *niputi miu!*' she cried, 'if only I didn't need my miserable job as much as I do, what a wonderful picnic we would have! But my heathen boss wouldn't understand my taking a day off in times like these to celebrate a holy day.'

Although there were fewer jobs and less money, my relatives still congregated frequently and drank to each other's health.   My father kept on giving more banquets than he could afford, and he still deigned to make *cannoli* occasionally.   On my birthdays and at Easter he would never fail to send me a huge box of pastries and his blessings.   And each autumn, as surely as the leaves fell, he wrote me a note in Italian which invariably read as follows:

> My dear Son:
>
> With this note, I am glad to send you news of the excellent health of your mother, of Joe, Giustina, Maria, and myself and to trust that you too are in good health.
>
> The days go fast.   The grape is ripe and it is now time again, my son, to make some new wine.
>
> Having nothing else to report at present, I send you the affectionate embraces and kisses of your mother, Joe, Giustina, Maria, and your dear father who loves you.
>
> PEPPINO

That was all he ever needed to say.   The note would be a signal for me to dispatch him enough money to buy twenty boxes of California grapes and wish him luck with his new wine. He would reply promptly with an enthusiastic account of the grapes he had bought and the hope that my health was fine and that I would be home soon to drink some of the old wine he was saving especially for me. This correspondence took place every year and was all the letter-writing we ever did. Everything else was communicated in English through my sisters.

Uncle Luigi suddenly became old. Rheumatism, the bane of many of my Rochester relatives, got the best of him and at the age of sixty-five he gave up bricklaying. He bought himself a cane and hobbled from one relative's home to another, more garrulous than ever and a little bitter. No widow, rich or slim, had come his way. He complained about his aches, his children, the general condition of the world, but mostly about the size of his old-age pension, which he said was barely enough to pay for the streetcar rides he had to take in order to get around town for free meals.

'*Porca Miseria!*' he complained. 'What kind of system is this when an old man is given only sixteen dollars a month to live on — about fifty cents a day, mind you, to feed and clothe himself? If it were not for my children, I'd starve to death.

He was eloquent on the subject of his youngest son a boy of twenty-three who had never had a job: 'Look at Alfonso. He was born a few years before the last war. He grew up in those terrible years after the war. He has been a jobless adult during the Depression and he probably will be killed in the next war. *Ma chi sistema e chista?* What kind of system is that? If I weren't so old, I would do something about it!'

When I was home one Christmas he pointed a long finger at me and said: 'You know, if people could only understand that Death destroys everything in the end, they would be more humble and treat each other like brothers. But as it is, dog eats dog in this world of ours, and the fatter the rich get, the skinnier become the workers.'

Yet his eyes still danced, and it was rumored that he had been seen in strange neighborhoods, carrying his cane as an adornment rather than support, and wearing his loudest neckties. It was obvious to all the relatives that he was still hunting for widows or any other form of female life that would give him a tumble. '*Luigi Casanova,*' Uncle Nino called him to his face.

My Aunt Giovanna and some of his own children agreed that Uncle Luigi must be entering second childhood. They argued that at his age a man sat in the sun or took care of his grandchildren; or, like Great-Uncle Minicuzzu, *bonarma,* interested himself in church activities. But Uncle Luigi preferred the shade to the sun, showed no inclination to play nursemaid to his grandchildren, and as far as the church was concerned, he was still the man of many religions who submitted wholeheartedly to none.

Compare Calogero was the only one who defended Uncle Luigi with any enthusiasm. He said that 'second childhood' was a misnomer and claimed that my uncle was merely getting his 'second wind.' When the relatives scoffed at such quibbling, he told them a story about an old man in his native town of Messina which quieted them for a while.

'Arturo Nicosia was his name. He was one of the richest men in Messina and the most productive. When his first wife died, he had twenty-three children. He was seventy-three years old then and everyone figured he would spend the rest of his days playing with his grandchildren. But after a year, he announced he couldn't bear sleeping without a woman any longer and let it be known throughout Messina that he had his eye on Mafalda Baccala, a beauty if there ever was one.

'Mafalda Baccala came from a poor family of many girls who had made strange marriages. One of her sisters married a blind man; another a man with one leg. It was not really a bad idea because both men received pensions from the Government. Mafalda's parents did all they could to persuade her to marry Arturo Nicosia. They told her that instead of having to earn her keep as a servant, she would be able to have her own servants, and they said that the old man was sure to die in a short time and leave her a rich widow. As an inducement, Arturo Nicosia actually agreed to make a will leaving all his property to Mafalda. The girl was finally persuaded.

'When I went back to Messina the year before last to see my mother, *bonarma*, before she died, I called on the old man. *Bedda Maria!* Do you know that he had had six more children by Mafalda? The poor girl was still pretty but I thought she looked rather discouraged. As for Arturo Nicosia, he was ninety-two years old now — and he lay in his bed most of the time saying prayers and mumbling thanks to the Lord for the bread He had given him.'

Uncle Luigi obviously did not expect to enjoy his bread that long. On his sixtieth birthday he had thrown a lavish party for the relatives, explaining that since he did not expect to see seventy he wanted to spend what money he had in sharing one final good time with them.   When he became sixty-five and found himself very much alive, he vowed that if he ever reached the age of seventy, he would spend all the money he had on another party.   It seemed like an excellent way of staving off Death.

As he approached seventy, he began to worry.   He thought of his vow and shook his head sadly.   It did not seem right to be that old and not have a celebration — but where was he going to find the money?   Aunt Giovanna suggested that he gamble on Italian lotto, a racket otherwise known as the 'numbers game.'   The game was especially popular among my relatives during the years of the Depression.   No matter how little they earned, they gambled a few pennies every week.

Part of the game's popularity was probably due to the nostalgia it evoked.   A player could bet on Palermo, Bologna, Naples, Rome, Florence, Venice, or Genoa — and if he wished, he could play the board.   My relatives usually put their money on Palermo because it was the city nearest to their home towns.   Uncle Luigi was one of the few who had never become an addict of Italian lotto.

When he had a few extra cents, he preferred to spend them in a card game like poker or briscola.   But he realized he could never win enough money at either game to pay for a party.   The week before his birthday, when he had practically abandoned all hope, he decided to risk five cents on Italian lotto.   He chose three numbers to play on Parlermo.   One of them corresponded to his age; the other to date of his birth; for the third number he consulted a Sicilian numbers dictionary and modestly chose the numerical equivalent of the word *vecchio* – old.

Uncle Luigi's modesty was his salvation. Two days after he made his five-cent investment, the results were published. There in black and white were the three numbers he played. He had won two hundred and fifty dollars. My mother, who was there when the news reached him, said that the excitement almost killed him. He threw away his cane and danced wildly around the room, kissing everyone who was in the way, and making odd and very loud noises.

The first thing he did when he collected the money was to give his children and his sisters ten dollars each. Like most Sicilians, he was superstitious about good luck and felt that unless you shared it with others it would surely turn into bad luck. Then he bought himself a complete outfit of clothes, enough to wear until he was ninety. A few dollars he put aside for poker, and the balance, about fifty dollars, he spent on food and wine for the birthday celebration.

My relatives still talk about the party. There were too many to feed at one time, so Uncle Luigi had two large meals served. His sons and daughters came with their families to the noonday feast; the rest of the family circle attended the buffet supper and ate *pizza*, hot bread with olive oil, roasted chestnuts, and chickpeas, all to the accompaniment of red wine.

Afterward, the adults sat around reminiscing about Sicily; the youngsters danced and listened to jazz, and the Unholy Three found a fourth and spent most of the evening playing briscola and swearing at each other as though they meant every word of it.

Separated though I was from my Sicilian relatives, my bond with them grew stronger through the years. The older I became and the more I appreciated them, the less desire I had to cut myself off from them. The memory of my life in Rochester gave me a *root* feeling, a sense of the past which I seemed to need to make the present more bearable. I found myself admiring my relatives for some of the same qualities I had once disliked, and wishing I could share their warm and easy acceptance of life.

Like a man who becomes interested in the old wine he has been drinking, I tried to trace their origins. First I read the books about Sicily. There were the travel authors who stuffed their sentences with adjectives that glowed with the cheap brilliance of neon signs. There was D. H. Lawrence, who, in his passion for honesty, could never make up his mind whether he loved or hated Sicilians and, in desperation, finally said that 'The Sicilian is an over-cultured, sensitive, ancient soul and he has so many sides to his mind that he hasn't got any definite mind at all.'

There were the historians. They were the most impressive, for they supplied the evidence with which a Sicilian could tell almost anyone afflicted with a genealogical fetish to go climb his family tree. A Sicilian's family tree extended through the foundations of time, even down to the regions of mythology. The tree was both ugly and beautiful. Sicily had been the land of Cyclops, the meeting place of Pluto and Proserpine, and the Gates of Hades were said to be located there, but it was also the home of poets and philosophers like Pindar, Aeschylus, Archimedes, and Empedocles. Sicily had shared generously in Greece's ancient glory.   There was proof of that all over the island, including the classic temples to the Greek gods that still stood in the province of my ancestors.   The Greeks were not the only ones attracted to Sicily.   Among others there were the Phoenicians, the Saracens, the Romans, the Normans, the Spaniards.   For better or worse, they all left their mark.

I also read the books about the American Melting Pot and got the picture of a giant, bubbling cauldron, some three thousand miles wide, in which Italian immigrants dived and swam about until they spoke English with almost no accent and developed a marked preference for potatoes to spaghetti.

Then I began asking myself questions like these: Was it in the chemistry of human life for my relatives to become Anglo-Saxonized — the apparent goal of the melting pot theorists?   So long as they believed in freedom and democracy — and their long history showed those ideals to be as ingrained in them as their religion — was it necessary that they try to change themselves?   Didn't America need their wisdom and their warmth, just as they and their children needed America's youth and vigor?

The books were not enough.   I resolved to go to Sicily and look at the earth of my ancestors and meet some of the uncles, aunts, and cousins my relatives left behind when they came to America.   I would find out for myself what chance the American Melting Pot had with my Rochester relatives.   The only difficulty was that there was Fascism all over Italy.

In my years of becoming an American I had come to understand the evil of Fascism and hate it with all my soul. One or two of my relatives argued with me on the subject because they had a great love for their native land and, like some men in love, they could see nothing wrong. Fascism was only a word to them; Mussolini a patriotic Italian putting his country on its feet. Why did I insist on finding fault with Fascism, they asked, when all the American newspapers were admitting Mussolini was a great man who made the trains run on time?

Most of my relatives had no definite ideas on the subject. My father was one of the few with enough political acumen to make a distinction between a government and its people. When one of the patriots proudly declared that Mussolini had eight million bayonets ready for any emergency, my father snorted: 'Eight million bayonets? *Misca!* Where has he got them? Stuck up his arse?'

I did not have the patience to wait until Fascism was destroyed. In spite of my hate for Fascism, in spite of the gloomy prospect of traveling through a country where free speech was dead, I would go to Sicily. I would know with my own eyes what the flesh of Fascism was like. My chance did not come until the summer of 1936. By then I had saved a few hundred dollars. The publishers who employed me were willing to spare me for two months, and I obtained commissions to write some articles about the trip.

Through the influence of a magazine editor I was also able to equip myself with a valuable bit of camouflage, a letter from the Italian Tourist Office in New York addressed to the Minister of Propaganda in Rome, introducing me as 'a young journalist of Italian parents who plans to write some articles about the ruins of Italy.' Not until several years later when the writer of the note dramatically renounced his connections with the Fascist Government did I realize how far his tongue had been in his cheek when he wrote those words.

I started my trip to Sicily by visiting my relatives in Rochester. It was the dutiful thing to do. My relatives wanted to give me the benefit of their advice as well as messages to deliver to those they had left behind. My parents were anxious to show me off. To all of them the proposed trip was a major achievement of my career, easily equivalent to getting a college degree or landing a steady job.

There was virtually a mass meeting of relatives on hand when I arrived in Rochester. Cousins who had not been on speaking terms with my parents forgot their differences and joined the throng. Relatives who had moved to faraway American neighborhoods were there. My father's *compari* were nearly all there, including Compare Calogero, of course. He had brought with him a number of his own relatives, among them a Mrs. Tripiedi from Auburn, who turned out to be a girlhood playmate of my mother.

The affair had a gay, holiday atmosphere and, if I had not been so much the center of attraction, I might have enjoyed it. My relatives pelted me with questions, messages, and addresses of relations scattered all through Sicily. To visit all of them would have taken at least a year.

They all listened to my itinerary with poignant enthusiasm. Palermo, Girgenti, Porto Empedocle, Realmonte

— the names were like music to them. These were the towns where many of them had spent their childhood and where some of their closest relatives still lived. They looked at my map of Sicily and joked about some of the smaller towns where the population was so small that chickens and goats were said to be included in the count to make the total more impressive.

They were deeply amused by the idea that it was I, instead of them, who was going to Sicily, and they talked of their memories, the beauties of Sicilian scenery, and the relatives I would be meeting for the first time. Some of them wondered if I would be able to make myself understood. Compare Calogero said: 'You may have to talk to them in sign language or hire somebody like Rosario Alfano to be your interpreter. It will certainly take someone who has been in America to understand the strange Sicilian you now speak.' It *was* strange; in the years I had been away from Rochester it had declined to gibberish, but I was not too worried about that since I could still understand everything my relatives said, and I knew that a few weeks of hearing the language would bring back much of my vocabulary.

Many of the relatives asked me to convey their greetings to Rosario Alfano. He was one of the few who had gone back to Sicily after living in America and they were all anxious to know how he liked being in his home town again. My cousin Vincenzo begged me to see his mother in Palermo, whom he had never visited since he left her thirty-five years before. 'She will treat you like a son,' he promised. 'Everyone who brings her news of me becomes her son. I would give my right hand to be able to see her before she dies!'

Mr. Michelangelo took me aside to tell me how happy he was about my trip.   He was more than eighty now but still doing a full day's work.   'If your Great-Uncle Mini-cuzzu, *bonarma*, were still alive he would have been over-joyed to know you were visiting the land where Garibaldi fought so bravely,' he said.

He talked at some length about Garibaldi and urged me to memorize the words of *Bandiera Rossa*, the anthem popular in Garibaldi's day.   'It is superior to this tripe the Fascists call *Giovanezza*,' he said.   'It is even better than a prayer,' he whispered, afraid the others might hear his sacrilege.   When he was about to leave, he kissed me on both cheeks and said: 'I would give you greetings for my friends but most of them are dead by now.   I have lived longer — only the Good Little God knows how, when you consider this terrible American climate I've had to endure.'

Caluzzu, my Verdi-loving cousin, urged me to visit Caruso's birthplace in Naples.   He had some of the tenor's records with him, and insisted on playing them for me. During his concert, he kept growling 'Bing Crosby, bah!' and glaring menacingly at the children of my relatives because they obviously preferred jazz to opera.

Uncle Luigi, impulsive as ever, whipped out a dollar bill from his purse and presented it to me with this speech:

'The last time I was in Palermo my stomach bothered me for nearly three weeks. One afternoon, while I was still in agony, I happened to be passing a liquor shop and was struck by an inspiration.   Your Aunt Giovanna would probably call it a miracle and attribute it to Saint Joseph. I went in, told them to give me a bottle of the best cognac they had. I drank the entire bottle. It made me very drunk and very happy. I found myself a nice park bench under a palm tree and slept for a long time. When I woke up, I was no longer drunk and my stomach no longer bothered me.

'Now, I want you to take this dollar. When you get to Palermo, go to a good liquor shop and ask for a bottle of their best cognac. Drink it — no matter what the condition of your stomach may be — and think of me.'

Explaining that he felt 'deeply melancholy' because he could not go to Sicily with me, my Uncle Nino refused to make a speech. 'I should make you an excellent guide, my nephew,' he told me on the way to the station, 'but it is futile talking this way. You will return and describe to me what you have seen and I will piece the picture together for you with what I know. By the way, I wish you would embrace Rosario Alfano for me when you get to Girgenti and ask him how it feels to have his dream come true. Imagine living in Sicily again!

'Some day,' he added, 'we shall go to Sicily together when you are rich. I hope I am still alive then. My only advice to you now is to bear in mind the Sicilian proverb, "He who fears death, dies of hunger." It is one of my favorite proverbs. You understand it, Gerlando? Fear kills the human spirit as surely as disease kills the body. And without his spirit, a man might as well be dead. Remember that on this journey and in all your journeys.' He put an arm around my shoulder. 'Think of it,' he said slowly, 'you are going to Sicily.' He sounded as though he had just realized it for the first time, and I saw tears in his eyes.

Aunt Giovanna begged me to remember to eat my food slowly and never try to talk while eating. 'Only the other day a *paesano* of mine, *bonarma*, choked to death at the table while he was trying to say "Blessed be God" with a hunk of chicken in his mouth. The poor man left nine children.'

My parents were worried because I might not be able to keep my opinions to myself in Italy. 'Keep your mouth shut and avoid all trouble with the Fascists. Whatever you do, don't let them put you in their army,' my father said. 'Always make it clear that you are an American-born American, and never stray too far from the cities where there are American consuls.'

My mother was the last one to kiss me. Through her tears she said: 'Be careful, Gerlando! But if Mussolini causes you any trouble, send me a telegram.'

(T H I R T E E N)

Welcome to Girgenti

THE TALK OF MY ROCHESTER RELATIVES KEPT
flashing through my mind and made nearly everything in
Sicily seem familiar.   Only two things took me by complete surprise: the poverty and the scenery.   I had heard
and read a great deal about Sicily's poor living conditions
but, without actually coming face to face with them, I
should never have known how shocking they were; I
might never have realized that human beings could live
in such poverty and still preserve their dignity.

The scenery was a revelation because I had come to
Sicily expecting to see green meadows, softly undulating
hills, and long stretches of vegetation.   What I saw made
me understand what time and nostalgia must have done
to my relatives' memories.   Within an hour after I took
the train from Palermo to Girgenti I was plunged into a
Wagnerian maze of naked solid-rock mountains.   Preci-
pices and cliffs arched overhead dangerously, like monsters of mythology frozen, solid, and shaved.   Pluto and
the Gates of Hades, indeed.   It was a wonder that Sicilians were not a cringing people; a wonder that their eyes
and hearts had any softness.

It was better toward the sea, near Girgenti. The blue
of the Mediterranean was like daylight after the dark
terror of the mountains.   There was less nakedness.   You
often spotted patches of green where lemon, almond, and
olive trees bloomed, wonderfully indifferent to the ravages
of Nature around them.   You could see the sky more
easily.   It made everything seem more gentle.

My entrance into Girgenti was as casual as though I
had lived in the city all my life and were coming back
from a weekend jaunt in Palermo.   The conductor actually asked me if I had enjoyed my excursion in Palermo
and when I told him I was from New York, he looked me
over suspiciously and remarked that I 'didn't look like an
American.'   A few phrases of my personal concoction of
Sicilian convinced him that I must be a foreigner; but I
was depressed instead of flattered by his first impression.
I had the terrifying feeling that I was going to be swallowed into this island of rock and never see America again.
It was a worry that stayed with me all the way through
Sicily and even on the mainland of Italy, where there were
plenty of American consuls around.

The fear that the Fascists might get me was not entirely
a product of my imagination.   In the few days I had been
in Italy I had already been severely cross-examined by
Fascist officials in both Naples and Palermo.   My American passport had made no noticeable impression on them.
It was only after I produced the letter to the Minister of
Propaganda that they stopped treating me as though I
might be a spy or a deserter and believed that I was what
I claimed to be.

When we reached the top of the mountain overlooking

Girgenti, the train paused and exchanged whistles with another train. Sicilian trains seemed incapable of meeting each other without stopping and exchanging such endearments. The conductor stuck his head out of the door and called over to the engineer of the other train.

'One of my passengers says he is the son of Peppino Amoroso, the pastrymaker,' he yelled.

The engineer stretched his neck to get a good look at me and I obligingly made myself as conspicuous as possible. 'Ah si, lu figliu di Peppino,' he remarked nonchalantly, as though my father had left Sicily the day before. 'How is your father?' he asked politely. Then, when his engine was puffing away, he said: 'Give him my regards when you see him. Tell him his old friend Cicco Spina was asking about him.'

The train began to descend into Girgenti.

Pindar called the city 'the most beautiful among mortal cities,' and a historian of its Greek period said that its people built as if they would never have to die and ate as though they would die tomorrow. Nature and man must have been more lavish then. All that is left of the Greeks' city is what was formerly the acropolis. Yet it still has beauty. It starts from the top of a long hill and unrolls itself down to a plain of olive trees and Greek temples, continuing down to the edge of the island to Porto Empedocle on the Mediterranean, the port town where my father and Luigi Pirandello were born.

From the hilltop I could see the Mediterranean, with the golden-colored temples in between contrasting their brilliance with the dazzling blue of the sea. Immediately below me, nearly halfway down the slope, were the streets and houses of Girgenti, huddled together as closely as my relatives at a party.   This was the city the Greeks called Akragas, the Romans and the Fascists called Agrigento, and my relatives called Girgenti.   In deference to the latter, I preferred to think of it as Girgenti.

The Fascists also changed the names of the principal streets.   The main street, which was known to my relatives as the Via Atenea, in honor of their Greek forbears, was now the Via Roma.   But the street still overlooked the Greek temples and the sea; apparently, there was nothing the Fascists could do about that.

Most of the city's streets were little more than alleys cutting their way through the sloping huddle of stone houses like so many narrow gulleys.   There was no pattern to them and, like people who try to avoid each other but do not succeed, they met at the most unexpected places.   A local patriot explained to me that the narrowness of the streets and their lack of pattern were part of a grand strategy to resist the numerous armies who tried to take Girgenti.   Civilian defense in those days was highly effective.   From the second-story windows of their homes, the townspeople would empty buckets of scalding water and hot oil onto the swarms of invaders clogged in the streets below.   Many a Carthaginian, I was told, was burned to death that way.

A large committee of uncles and cousins, some of them looking amazingly like me, were waiting for me at the station.   At first they were solemn and polite and, as they took turns kissing and embracing me, they asked the usual questions about my journey and the health of my parents.

I could not make out one relative from another. I kissed and let myself be kissed and knew that each one was closely related in some way, but I was too bewildered by their numbers to identify them.

One of my relatives, a man six feet tall who resembled an Irishman I knew in New York, sensed that I did not know who he was. With tears in his eyes, he caught me in his arms again and asked: 'Don't you know me? I am your father's brother, your Uncle Pitrinu.' He seemed hurt because I had not known it instinctively. I had once seen a photograph of him but it had been so retouched and prettified that it bore little resemblance to him.

I was at once struck by the fact that there were no women present. Later, when I learned to what extent the women of Girgenti were excluded from the lives of their menfolk, it did not seem so strange. I asked them where Rosario Alfano was. They told me he had gone to visit a sick relative in Messina but would be back to see me before I left.

They led me off to the car Uncle Pitrinu had rented especially for the occasion. On the way they stopped everyone they met and said: 'Meet the son of Peppino Amoroso. His name is Gerlando and he is from North America.' They were proud that I had come so far to see them, though a little disturbed by the fact that I had traveled from Palermo third class along with the peasants. As soon as they heard me laugh with them, they dropped their solemnity and treated me as though they had always known me. What did I do for a living? How much did I earn? What did the Americans think of Italy's victory over Ethiopia?

They were disappointed in all my answers to these questions, but cheered up considerably when I showed them the letter to the Minister of Propaganda. After that, I was an important personage and was henceforth introduced to people as 'the son of Peppino Amoroso who has a letter of introduction to the Minister of Propaganda.' Inevitably, of course, I had to produce the letter to prove that the relative who was introducing me was not a liar.

They were amused by my brand of Sicilian. What in the world did I mean by such words as *conduttore, boto, signa?* They had never, of course, heard them. The true origin of *baccauso* first dawned on me then. Fortunately, there were enough authentic Sicilian words in my sentences to carry their meaning. Sometimes I managed to use a Sicilian idiom and then there would be a howl of laughter and congratulations, almost amounting to relief, for I was thereby establishing my identity with them.

They quarreled as to where I should stay. Each relative wanted me to be his guest and threatened to become offended if I did not accept his hospitality. I refused to decide and said I would leave it up to them. After much wrangling, they agreed I should first stay with my father's uncle, Stefano, because he was the oldest and because he had treated my father like a son after his parents died. After that, I was to stay with my Uncle Pitrinu because he was the closest of kin.

There was some dispute about this point. It developed that Uncle Pitrinu had not been on good terms with my father for the past twenty years. My father had loaned him three hundred dollars to come to America, which my uncle used instead to marry and set up a funeral estab-

lishment in Porto Empedocle. He had never returned
the money nor answered my father's letters asking for it.
But my relatives decided that inasmuch as Uncle Pitrinu
had demonstrated his brotherly love by coming all the
way from Porto Empedocle — five miles away — and paying for the rent of the car hired in my honor, he had a
right to extend his hospitality to his American nephew for
a few weeks. After that I could stay with . . .

I interrupted, pointing out that I could only be in
Sicily a short time; and that I planned to visit several
Italian cities to gather material for articles. They had
known me less than a half-hour and already they were
appalled to think that I could bear to leave them. 'You
can come back to Italy some other time and see those
cities. They will still be there. We may not,' they
argued.

And my cousin Nardo said: 'I'll get you all the material
you want for articles. I will introduce you to men in
Girgenti who have read many books. They will tell you
anything you want to know.' They talked of my departure with such eloquence and pain that I wondered
whether they had forgotten I was staying a few weeks and
not leaving that afternoon.

My Uncle Stefano skillfully put an end to the discussion.
'We must remember,' he said solemnly, 'that Gerlando has
a letter to the Minister of Propaganda. He must take it to
Rome and deliver it in person.' They were grateful for
the explanation; it proved that I was not heartless. 'You
just can't afford to keep a Minister waiting too long,' they
explained to each other.

In their eagerness to show how much they loved me,

they deluged me with hospitality. They poured it on me unmercifully, particularly at meal times. Breakfast and the midday meal were simple enough, but the evening repast was usually interspersed with noisy debates. I would insist I had eaten and drunk more than enough; they would tell me I had barely begun and pile my dish high with food again. 'Mangia, mangia,' they urged. 'Eat it without bread, but eat it,' they would finally say in desperation. And, in desperation, I would try to eat more, though my appetite had long since been satisfied, for it was hopeless fighting their obsession to stuff me with food.

They took turns at dining me and each one tried to feed me more than the others. Some of the older relatives who remembered my father's fondness for sea-food and assumed I shared it went out of their way to cook the most exotic species they could buy. It was obvious that none of them could afford the quantities of food they served me, yet each family swore that their meal was but a snack and that I was starving myself before their very eyes. Two or three times I tried to buy some of the provisions, but they became offended at these attempts and forgave me only on the ground that I was an American and must have been brought up among a lot of Indians.

Their poverty made their hospitality seem all the more painful. The most prosperous of my relatives were the few who were civil-service employees and earned about seventy-five dollars a month. Their food and clothing expenses were easily as high as those in an average American city. In addition, they paid many fees and taxes unknown to my Rochester relatives, among them an artisan tax, and taxes on their furniture and even on outdoor stairways (so many lire for each step).   I could not understand how most of my relatives could keep up with their taxes and living expenses; they were masons, carpenters, and laborers who worked only occasionally and did not earn nearly as much as the civil-service employees.

Like bureaucrats the world over, the civil-service workers were the most loquacious and faithful supporters of the Government.   Their boasting was only equaled by that of the college boys who had had Fascism drilled into them from childhood.   Those were days of drunken hope for such patriots, probably the only exultant ones the Fascists had enjoyed since they had come into power.   Ethiopia had just been won and every loyal Fascist felt like a Caesar holding the world by the tail.   'Soon,' a young law student declaimed to me, 'we're going to show the world that the French are an effeminate race who can't fight and the English a weak and treacherous nation always trying to betray Italy.'

One of the most ardent Fascists I talked with was my cousin Nardo, who had a clerical job in the postoffice.   He was fond of bragging that his two sons, eleven and twelve, could handle guns and bayonets like adult soldiers.   The boys were just as proud of themselves and would come to see me in their smart black uniforms, demanding to be photographed.   Their sister Ciccina, a handsome girl of fourteen, kept singing the latest Fascist songs to me and quoting resonant excerpts from Mussolini's speeches.

The children and the parents were disturbed by my lack of enthusiasm.   They dragged out a book that must easily have weighed fifty pounds.   It had been published in celebration of the Fascist Party's tenth anniversary and showed scores of roads, bridges, postoffices, and railway stations built since Mussolini took over. Nearly all of them were constructed in the more northern Italian cities around regions popular with tourists.

I asked why their government was doing nothing to improve some of the small towns I had visited around Girgenti where the housing conditions were disgusting and there was no water supply. I pointed out that even in Girgenti there were one-room homes occupied by an entire family and its livestock.

'That all takes time,' Nardo assured me. 'You must have fish blood in you if you can't respond to the wonderful things Mussolini has done for Italy. Take, for example, the train schedules . . .'

I begged him to spare me that. He showed me another book containing memoirs and souvenirs of the Fascist revolution. On one page was pictured a group of Black Shirts holding up clubs and castor oil bottles as proudly as though they were trophies won at an athletic match.

Nardo's daughter pointed to them and gloated: 'That's how our Duce got rid of the horrible Communists. If they try anything funny again, he'll give them some more whacks and lots of castor oil.' I shuddered, and she laughed. She did not realize I was shuddering for her and the rest of the patriots who would some day have to face the truth about their black-shirted heroes.

The patriots were noisy but relatively few. Most of my relatives showed no inclination to ballyhoo Fascism and were plainly skeptical of the daily newspaper accounts that described Ethiopia as the land of milk and honey.

'If Ethiopia is such a wonderful country, why haven't the English taken it over before?' one of them whispered to me.

The peasants, desperately poor and eager to grasp any straw of hope, were the most gullible. On a bus I heard one say to another, 'It must be wonderful to earn money every day.'

'Lucky dogs,' the other said, referring to some relatives who had been sent to Ethiopia to work. 'Some day they will be riding around in automobiles as they do in Brooklyn and we'll be writing them letters begging for money.'

'*Chi lu sa?*' the first replied. 'Perhaps we too can be sent to Ethiopia. Then our relatives will be writing *us* for money.'

The poverty of the city was nothing compared to that of the little towns around it. You had only to take one look at them to know why their people had flocked in groves to foreign countries where they might eat and live as men should. My mother's home town was typical of such towns. The natives called it Munderialli but its official name was Realmonte. To reach it I climbed a steep hill from the railroad station.

Once I got to the top, the only heartening sight was the Mediterranean coming into a wide inlet about a mile away, with small vine-covered hills popping up gaily in between. The town was arranged on a plateau and completely exposed to the sun. There wasn't a tree or a bit of grass anywhere.

The nearest water supply was seven miles away. Every morning a man with a mule and a cart brought a barrel of water to Realmonte and sold it to the natives in bottles.

An inferior quality of water was sold in barrels for washing purposes — so inferior that it had given many of the natives an eye disease which prevented them from migrating to America when our doors were still wide open.

Except for the rather elegant stone houses built for the priest, the mayor, and a few of the natives who had returned from America with dollars, the buildings had dismally regular features and were built close together. They were mostly of dark yellow stucco and arranged in rows along perfectly straight alleys.   Realmonte had produced many clever masons, among them some of my Rochester relatives, but apparently they had been able to do little for the beauty of the town except to make certain that everything was built in straight lines.

My aunt's house, no better or worse than the dozens of other homes I visited, had two rooms and a small hole in the wall just large enough to hold a stove.   The floors and walls were of rough cement; the beams of the ceiling stuck out like the bones of a skinny man.   There was no toilet in the house and no privy outside.   On the walls were pasted long bulletins distributed by the Government telling Italians what to think of Mussolini and the Versailles Treaty.

My aunt lived there with her two daughters and a thirty-year-old son.   Andrea was eager to marry and was attracted to a girl in town who had the proper amount of linen for her dowry, but the marriage seemed to be out of the question because there was no one else to support his mother and sisters.   One of the sisters was named Annunziata.   On the first day we met she half-playfully suggested that we get married so that I could take her away to America. During the past year she had received as many as four proposals from young men of highly respectable families, but she said she was obliged to turn them down because she did not have the necessary dowry.

'I wish I could go to America,' she said. 'I hear that if a man and woman want to be married there, they simply go to church and then have a feast and that's all there is to it. What a wonderful country! Here she has to have linens and money if she wants to marry a man with a respectable background. And do you know that in Porto Empedocle a girl has to provide all the furniture besides the money and the linen. Do you wonder that there are so many spinsters there?'

My aunt had my mother's combination of strength and gentleness. She was one of the few relatives I met who was bitterly opposed to the 'Government' and did not hesitate to say so. 'The taxes are driving us crazy,' she would say again and again. 'If your mother did not send us clothes now and then, God knows what we should wear. Andrea earns eight lire (sixty cents then) a day when he works. How can a family of four possibly live on that?'

The 'Government' was one thing, but Il Duce was obviously something else in her mind. 'The only people we can be proud of in Italy are our King and our Duce. They are both men of genius and will keep us out of war. Andrea says that only the other day Mussolini in person took an airplane trip around this coast to make certain we were well protected. He must have flown right over our town.'

My aunt and cousins, like my relatives in Girgenti, were

proud of me because I was an American. They put on their Sunday clothes and told everyone that 'Margarita's son' was visiting them.   If anyone dared say that I spoke their language 'almost like a native,' they loudly resented it because they thought it detracted from my prestige as an American.

Andrea wore a suit I recognized as one I had discarded several years ago, and every day I was there my aunt wore the black silk dress I had brought for her from New York. I asked her why she did not wear colors and pointed out that, after all, her husband had died all of five years ago.

'In Munderialli we are cursed with stupid ideas,' she said.   'I'm afraid I shall have to wear black till I die. Then they can dress me in anything they please.   One thing I shall always hold against your uncle, *bonarma,* is that he would never consent to moving to another town. Most of the people here are common peasants who don't know any better and I have to put up with their ideas.'

On a Friday they bought a chicken for me and insisted I eat it while they fed on spaghetti.   I objected so much that the chicken became cold, but in the end I had to eat every bit of it so that they would not be offended.   The youngest daughter, Zina, who was the most devout, was the only one who said she would not eat meat on Fridays. The rest of them agreed that 'If we can afford to buy meat, the good Lord doesn't mind when we eat it.'   Apparently God was as understanding in Sicily as he was in Rochester.

Every afternoon we visited persons who had known my mother when she lived there.   Most of them were related to me.   They all said I looked like my mother and showed me pictures of her as a young girl to prove they were right.

One of them exclaimed: 'How strange Destiny is! A young girl leaves Munderialli for a land across the ocean, and thirty-five years later a young man arrives and tells us he is her son.'

Many of them anxiously asked me if their relatives in America had given me 'a little something' for them. They invariably meant dollar bills. In most instances I had to say no. I tried to explain that times were hard in America; that their relatives there were barely managing to earn a living and could only send their greetings. I could tell from their eyes that they didn't believe me. One particularly disappointed mother, who had received neither money nor greetings, asked me if there was something 'peculiar' about the American air that made people forget easily. Her son had not written her a line for ten years. 'I can't understand it,' she said. 'He used to love me so much. I had all I could do to persuade him to join his brothers in America.'

The townspeople would stare at us from their balconies and dark doorways as we walked along the streets through the chickens and the garbage. There were hardly any men around, and many of the women were gray-haired and dressed in black. My aunt would often stop to introduce me to some 'special friend of the family.' Related or not, they asked the same questions about the health of my mother, my age and my salary, the ages of my brother and sisters and whether or not they were married.

Some of them, when they learned I lived in New York, asked me questions that went something like this: 'Do you know so-and-so? He lives on such-and-such a street. Surely, you must have come across him. He is short and dark and has a funny scar on his forehead.' They took particular pains to round up the three or four natives who had been to America and could speak some English. As soon as I was introduced to one of them, a crowd would form around us and beg us to speak *Americano*. As we tried to say a few sentences, the crowd would laugh uproariously and have a great deal of fun mimicking us.

One of the ex-Americans I met worked in the local post-office. In New York, he had helped dig the Brooklyn subway. 'When there was no more work, I came home and bought myself a job with the money I saved digging the subway. The United States is a nice place but only when you are working.' He was a Fascist and spent considerable time explaining how Mussolini was bringing glory to Italy. He justified Mussolini's imperialism on the ground that Italy was overpopulated.

Why, then, I asked, was he asking for larger families? He laughed mischievously and, pointing his forefinger to the center of his forehead, said, 'Ah, Mussolini is a very smart man.'

The other two ex-Americans were not nearly so patriotic. One of them said he had made a 'big mistake' in leaving the United States and begged me to do what I could to help him get back. 'I returned after I had saved a few dollars beause I thought living expenses here were less. Now they have become higher than they were in America. We'll be paying taxes next for the privilege of breathing.' For more than a year he had been trying to get permission from the American consul in Palermo to return to America. He had even written Mussolini a long letter explaining how impossible it was for him to live in Italy and support his family on the salary he made as a mason, but so far had received no reply. Like my aunt, he blamed his troubles on the 'Government,' not on Mussolini.

The third ex-American had no illusions about Fascism and took great delight in expressing himself on the subject in four-letter Anglo-Saxon words. 'Believe me, fellow, it is better to be dying in America than to be alive and kicking in this country,' he assured me. He had lived in Brooklyn for eight years, until the authorities learned that he had entered the country illegally, and deported him. Now he was scheming to get back. As soon as he had saved some money, he would pretend he wanted to work in Ethiopia. Once he got there he would escape to Egypt. He was confident he would find a ship there on its way to New York with a captain who could be bribed to take him along. 'I'm going to get back to America if it is the last thing I do,' he said.

On my last evening in town, I sat on the piazza with a group of men, exchanging thoughts while we watched the lighthouse in the distance sweeping the Mediterranean with a large round ray. The younger men avoided talking politics and asked questions about Hollywood movie stars and the height of American skyscrapers. In the group was a young policeman named Vincenzo, who was home on leave from his station in Rome. He quizzed me about the New York police, asking where they got their graft now that Prohibition was over; if it was true that most of them had flat feet, and whether or not they were popular with women.

It developed that his last question had a direct bearing

on one of Vincenzo's recent and sad experiences as a policeman. The average Italian, he pointed out, dislikes the *sbirro* (cop) on general principles. Dressed in civilian clothes on a night off, he was strolling about looking for some girl who would respond to his flirtations. In this way he made the acquaintance of a young brunette, who was the daughter of a tobacconist. For the sake of expediency, Vincenzo told her he was a government clerk. Everything progressed nicely until one evening when Vincenzo absent-mindedly walked into her father's store to buy some cigarettes. Behind the counter was the girl. The moment she realized I was a policeman,' he said mournfully, 'it was the end of everything. She has refused to have anything to do with me since.'

The older men preferred to talk of politics, but everything they said was a repetition of what had appeared in the Fascist press. I could almost finish the sentences they began.

'Some day,' one of them said, 'we shall be able to go to Ethiopia and live like kings.'

'That will mean the end of Munderialli,' one of the young men replied. He turned to me. 'Did you know that there are more people of Munderialli in America than there are here? The only reason everyone didn't leave was because they were either too old or had something wrong with their eyes.'

An elderly man resented this attitude. 'Wait until they finish painting the railroad station, then you will see that Munderialli will have a place on the map. And in a couple of years, when Mussolini lays in the water pipes, Munderialli will be quite a nice place to live in.'

'Yes,' answered the young man, 'if the taxes don't get us by that time.'

We talked until the lights went out. The old men told me that Italy and Germany could lick anybody but did not want war, that the Soviet Union was no good, and that the United States was their great friend and ally.

The next day I left town on a train that was a half-hour late.

Blighted Land

EVERYWHERE I SAW REPLICAS OF MY ROCHES-
ter relatives. There was the same wide variety of types.
Some had the coloring and features of Arabs; others
looked like models for El Greco. Sometimes you would
see a Moorish head on a Spartan body; or the raven hair
and lustrous black eyes of a Saracen set off by a Roman
nose. There were redheads, like my Uncle Nino; soft
brunettes, like my mother; and a scattering of blue-eyed
blonds.

Temperamentally, they were so much like my Rochester
relatives that I realized how futile it was for anyone to
believe that Sicilians could become conventional Americans in the course of a single lifetime. There were some
differences, of course, because the life of Sicilians was
tuned to an age that did not know industrial progress.
Farming was the main industry, but the peasants worked
with no more equipment than their ancient ancestors had.
In all the time I was in Sicily I did not see one modern
farm implement.

The greatest difference was that these people were

harassed by poverty and tyranny.   My Rochester relatives
seemed happy and carefree in comparison.   In villages
like Munderialli the long strain of having neither enough
liberty nor enough bread was plainly written on the faces
of the people.   In the larger centers, like Girgenti and
Porto Empedocle, the atmosphere was less gray.   Poverty was not as obvious there and the people's sense of
humor did not seem as lost.   Yet even there you were always conscious of the fear people had of speaking out of
turn.   It lay on their hearts and minds like a heavy poison.
But Sicilians had to talk, for it was in their nature.   Some
talked to me because I was an American relative and
would not give them away.

One of them knew some English and secretly listened
to the news broadcasts from London.   'If I did not know
what was going on in the outside world, I think I should
go crazy,' he told me.

In Palermo there had been the relative who talked to
his horse Garibaldi for want of a better audience.   Filippo's wife, Dolorata, might hear his complaints about the
customers he drove around in his hack, but it was Garibaldi who listened to his more serious talk about philosophy and politics.   He explained it to me this way: 'Women
talk too much.   They blab to their priest or their neighbors.   A woman's tongue is like a spool of thread.   Once
it starts unwinding itself . . .'

I asked Filippo if he would not get more satisfaction
talking to men instead of his horse.   He hastened to assure me that Garibaldi was very intelligent.   'And who
else is there to talk to?   Men used to sit in the cafés and
discuss things, but that is no longer safe.   The Govern-

ment hates criticism of any kind, you know, and that makes it hard for me because I enjoy finding fault with things. It makes me feel more intelligent than I am.'

He paused to comb Garibaldi's tail. 'Now, Garibaldi is all right. He listens to all my ideas and he doesn't go around broadcasting them. He's smarter than a lot of men I know.'

Sometimes a Sicilian's thoughts would explode in public. In a barber shop I heard a fat postal clerk saying: 'We Italians are capable of making great sacrifices for our country. If our Government asks it, we shall tighten our belts further and, if it becomes necessary, live on bread and water.'

At these words a fisherman who was having his hair cut jumped out of the barber's chair. 'Porca Miseria!' he yelled, waving his thin arms in the face of the postal clerk. 'How much further do you think we can tighten our belts? Sacrifices! I tell you if we don't make ourselves be heard soon, this Government is going to squeeze us all to death.' He suddenly stopped, realizing he had said too much, and went back to his chair without another word.

There was some gay talk too. Shortly after I arrived in Girgenti I became the rallying point of a group of young bachelors, most of them first and second cousins of mine. The group was named the Club Latti after the plump and frivolous owner of the only radio store in Girgenti. His store became our chief meeting place. Although Latti hospitably kept the limelight on me, he was the group's natural leader and took the initiative in most of its activities, which consisted mainly of bathing and picnicking.

Latti never permitted his business to interfere with his pleasure, and would unhesitatingly close shop at any hour of the day to join us. To his complaining customers he would explain that he had closed the store because he had felt a strong compulsion to go to church and pray.

Latti was the personification of a perfect salesman. His patter was punctuated with bright quips, and he had a natural genius for demolishing a customer's sales resistance with flattery. His passion for money was literally sensual. He enjoyed letting coins drip from his fingers into the cash register and would cock his ears to hear the ring of the money. In his desk drawer he kept an American dollar bill — for luck. Several times, while he was talking of his yearning to be in New York, he would suddenly kiss the dollar bill with a noisy smack, exclaiming 'Ah, bella America!'

Latti's wide range of gossip scintillated with boasts of his male prowess. According to him, any wife in Girgenti bored with her husband or in need of some extra-marital excitement would be sure to find her way to his door. And because he wanted to show his hospitality in the best way he knew, he offered to introduce me to one of his back-door guests on her next visit. 'She will enjoy the taste of an American,' he said. He could not understand why I would not accept his offer, nor could the other members of the Club Latti. Nor could I, for that matter.

Latti's greeting was always the same. 'La pipa, la pipa!' he would cry out, and I would comply by taking out my pipe and lighting it. The pipe distinguished me from the rest of the smokers in Girgenti, for in Sicily only the very old men ever smoked pipes. The Club Latti never ceased being delighted with what they regarded as my eccentricity and were always asking me to smoke the pipe, as though it were a pleasant reminder to them that I was an *Americano.*

The Club had other remarkable members besides Latti, among them Lazzaro, who was a postoffice clerk by day. At night he was an artist who modeled bas-reliefs on ostrich eggs. His tools were sharply edged scalpels of varying sizes. He used these to describe fine lines on the surface of the eggs. His masterpiece was an egg suspended like a globular map, which was decorated with panel scenes depicting the life of Christ. He was an excellent draftsman and must have had a tremendous amount of patience, for it was obvious that one slip of his scalpel might break the egg-surface and ruin months of work.

Lazzaro had tried to find a buyer for his masterpiece, but had not received an offer large enough to compensate for all the time he had spent on it. A few months before a rich old woman, recuperating and repenting in Girgenti over some mysterious injustice she had done her daughter-in-law, thought of buying the egg and sending it to the Pope as evidence of her penance. But, unfortunately for Lazzaro, there was a reconciliation between the old woman and the daughter-in-law, and she no longer considered it necessary to placate her conscience.

In America Lazzaro would probably have been an immediate success, but in Italy, where artists are taken more for granted, his fame was confined to the province of Girgenti. The Christ egg, as he called it, was admired among many of the peasants and every few days a group of them would call on him, hats in hand as though they were in church, and beg to have a look at the Christ egg. Pleased as Lazzaro was by attention, he was always grumbling about his inability to make money at his art. 'Where does it get me?' he would ask. 'All I get out of my work is a lot of mud that people drag into my house when they come to see the eggs.' I tried to buy one of his eggs but by that time he considered me a close friend and refused to take money. He tried to give me the egg as a gift. In the end, we compromised by my accepting an etching of the local Temple of Concord on a small plaster plaque.

The Club Latti enjoyed storytelling, but no one was as good at it as my Uncle Nino or Uncle Luigi. Perhaps they were too young to have mastered the art; perhaps they would become more talented when they knew the meaning of nostalgia and could color their yarns with it. They were better at discussion, but the subjects they could discuss safely were few. Subjects like the high cost of living and the political situation were out; a stool pigeon might disagree with their opinions and report them. As for repeating what they saw in the newspapers and heard on the radio, that was something for the ignorant and the super-patriots to do; not for skeptics like them.

The safest and most stimulating topics of discussion were automobile accidents and women. You could say whatever you thought about either and no one would ever report you. Any member of the Club Latti could become as excited about an automobile accident (no matter how trivial) as my Great-Uncle Minicuzzu could about a battle of Garibaldi. The automobile drivers in the accident would be developed into protagonists of stupendous proportions; the automobiles themselves would take on the aspect of colliding planets. What they could do with a couple of dented fenders for inspiration! And if by happy chance one of the drivers had so much as bumped his nose or bloodied himself a bit, the story would be whipped into a melodrama that would make an Italian opera libretto sound like something out of A. A. Milne.

But automobiles around Girgenti were scarce and accidents did not happen every day, so sex became the most frequent subject of discussion. My cousin Giuseppe, who was nicknamed Figaro because he was a barber with operatic ambitions, felt he had to defend the club's apparent obsession with the subject.

'We Italians enjoy discussing women because we know how to love them more skillfully than anyone else,' he told me. Figaro could not open his mouth without bragging a little. 'Moreover,' he said, 'it is a topic with no beginning and no ending. Anyone can contribute to its discussion, no matter how little schooling he has had. And if you feel above that' (he winked to assure me he did not think I did), 'you can amuse yourself by listening and trying to figure out how much of what you hear is true and how much of it wish-thinking. Not all of these fellows are as truthful as I am.'

I heard many long and detailed comparisons of intimacies with women. Most of them were calculated to show what Don Juans the participants were. The men usually started with stories involving seductions of tourists and married women, and wound up talking about the women that were immediately available: the latest batch of prostitutes that had arrived in Girgenti.

It was easy to talk about the prostitutes because that was one feature of life in Girgenti that was ever changing. A new group of them arrived punctually every two weeks and were lodged in a house next to a church. The house had a front door for bachelors and a back one for married clients. The girls were managed by the Government and went from town to town like troupers in a road show. At the end of each two-week performance, they would move on to the next city and be replaced by another group.

The new batch generally had the same proportion of blondes, brunettes, redheads, plump and lithe figures, demure and aggressive types, and Frenchwomen — so that customers with different tastes could be kept satisfied all year around. My friends explained that the reason the girls were moved around every two weeks was because the authorities did not want citizens to form attachments with them. Whatever the reason was, the prospect of new women every fortnight was a constant source of stimulation to the Club Latti and must have filled the Government's coffers with many more lire than would have been snared otherwise.

Figaro sounded like the most successful of the Don Juans. Away from the jeers of the others, he would entertain me with long, fantastic tales of his love career. He could not have been more than twenty-five but the achievements he claimed in the field of sex would have done credit to a man twice that age. His life story seemed to consist entirely of a series of overlapping love affairs interrupted by mothers, husbands, and brothers. Somehow, when things were going particularly well an irate relative would suddenly appear and Figaro would find it expedient to leave town for a few days.

He was still bitter about an affair he had had with an English girl a few months before. He had met her at a local hotel where he had been summoned to wash her hair. Although he knew less than a dozen English words, it did not take him long to impress her with his charms. 'It is a power I have in my fingertips,' he explained seriously, holding up his fingers so that I could examine them. 'Once I get these into a woman's scalp she becomes like so much putty.'

The English girl was no exception. When Figaro suggested a tour of the Greek temples by moonlight, she agreed. 'We covered the ground thoroughly,' he said. 'In the few days I was with her I made her understand Greek and Sicilian culture as she had never known it before.' He sighed eloquently. 'The first night I showed her the Temple of Concord. It is the largest, you know, and it took nearly all the night. The following night it was the Temple of Juno. The third night the Temple of Castor and Pollux. As you know, there is not much left to that temple but we managed very well.'

He talked lyrically of the moonbeams shimmering against the golden temples, while the blonde beauty of the girl pressed against him. 'I went to wash her hair the following week but some fellow who had just arrived from London was there — her husband, I suppose — and she pretended she had never seen me before. When he left the room, I suggested another tour — there were still some things we hadn't seen — and she just looked at me scornfully, as though she did not know what I was talking about. Can you imagine anything like that? Tell me, Gerlando, are American girls that hard-hearted?'

Figaro and my relatives had many other questions about American women. Were they passionate — or just good-looking? Did they make good wives, or were most of them unfaithful? Was it true that respectable women were often seen alone on the streets at night? They were shocked by the same things that had once shocked my Rochester relatives.

From the Hollywood movies some of them had seen, they had gathered the notion that American women enjoyed many of the liberties men had. They were surprised to hear me tell them that the movies had not been exaggerating.

'Why, how is it possible for a nation to have so many *strafalarii* and still be as great a country as the United States?' Nardo asked. He was frankly bewildered. When I defended the rights of American women, particularly their right to divorce a man if he wasn't a suitable mate, Nardo turned to Latti and said, 'Didn't I tell you that Americans are crazy?'

They made me feel as though I had come from a strange civilization. If I had been defending the social habits of a tribe of cannibals, they could not have expressed more amazement. For the first time I began to appreciate some of the compromises with American life my relatives in Rochester had succeeded in making.

I did not spare them any details. I told them that their relatives in Rochester let their children choose their own husbands and wives; that the men did not gang together as men did in Sicily, but allowed their women to participate in their discussions and even to play cards with them; also that respectable Sicilian women were often seen alone on the streets and at public places. When I said that I had often taken respectable girls to restaurants and theaters unchaperoned, they looked skeptical. Then Figaro brightened up and exclaimed: 'But, of course, you mean they did not remain respectable after that. Ah, Gerlando, you must be a great one with the girls!'

To my Sicilian relatives there were only two kinds of women: respectable women (*donne oneste*) and *strafalarii*. The latter were fair game for any man. The others were wives and sisters you honored, supported, and protected; but their place was in the kitchen and the bedroom or on a dais far above the crudities and temptations of life. If they slipped from their dais and were found out, their life as respectable women was over. The brothels were filled with such women.

'There is nothing worse than an unfaithful wife,' Nardo said. 'When she gives in to another man, she is giving up everything. But with a man it is different. He can carry on with another woman without getting serious, isn't that so?'

He asked me what I would do if I were married and found my wife in the arms of another man. I said I would probably divorce her, and then asked him what he would do. Nardo shrugged his shoulders. 'I believe I would shoot both of them — my wife first.'

The night after this discussion Nardo accompanied the Club Latti to the brothel where a new group of girls had arrived.

One morning I received a postal card from Rosario

Alfano.   He was still in Messina visiting a very sick *compare.*   Having heard that I planned to leave Sicily shortly, he begged me to stay until he could get back.   'I must see you,' he wrote.   'There are a number of things I am anxious to discuss with you.   Please wait for me as a favor to an old friend.'   I wrote him that I was leaving for Porto Empedocle to stay with my Uncle Pitrinu for a few days but that I would be back in Girgenti and wait there for him.

Porto Empedocle was refreshing after Girgenti.   There were fewer civil-service employees; most of the inhabitants were either miners or fishermen.   There was more space and vitality and it was good to breathe the salt-water tang of the air.   It was not a pretty town yet it had charm. Part of its shore was a wide beach; the rest of it was lined with tall cones of lemon-yellow sulphur.   Although the houses were shabby, many of them looked out on the sea and some of them had back yards with grape arbors.   The docks were gay with small boats and fishing nets.   In the distance you could often see the sailboat fleet of the sardine fishermen.   They were usually so far out that their sails looked like dainty handkerchiefs leaning against the horizon.

Uncle Pitrinu was known as one of the gloomiest men in Porto Empedocle — his position as the town's leading undertaker may have added to that reputation — but he seemed almost exuberant while I was his guest.   I think it cheered him somewhat to be my host; he may have felt that this was his chance to clear his conscience of the money he owed my father.   At least, that was the impression I got from the enormous amount of fish, spaghetti, and wine he tried to force on me several times a day.

But his spirits were even more bolstered by the fact that he had just completed arrangements for the marriage of his eldest son, Turridu, to the daughter of the local bandmaster. Bandmasters rated high in the Sicilian social scale, higher than undertakers, and Uncle Pitrinu was as proud as any business man who has just swung a profitable deal.

Turridu worked for a government agency in Rome and had yet to see the girl his father had selected for his wife. But he had a photograph of Maria and his father's assurance that the marriage would prove an excellent one. Uncle Pitrinu showed me a letter from his son thanking him profusely for arranging the marriage and expressing deep gratitude for his good taste.

'Why hasn't your father picked out a wife for you yet?' my uncle asked me. I tried to explain that I would choose my own wife when I was ready to marry, but he was certain I must be joking to talk that way.

With the details of Turridu's wedding all set, the families of my uncle and the bandmaster were already treating each other with the familiarity of in-laws. I was the guest of honor at one of their banquets and aroused particular interest in the girl's family because of my uncle's insistence that I bore a striking resemblance to his son Turridu. All through the evening Maria kept looking at me and at the photograph she had of Turridu and shaking her head. 'I don't see the resemblance at all,' she said. It was hard to tell whether she was relieved or disappointed.

In Rome a few weeks later I met Turridu and discovered that he was not as confident of his father's choice as he had led Uncle Pitrinu to believe.   But he was a dutiful Sicilian son and, come what may, he was going to marry Maria and be with her the rest of his life.   He explained that was the way of Destiny; nevertheless, he had a burning curiosity to know what Maria actually looked like and would plague me with questions about her physical details.

Did she have good legs?   Was she fatter than a woman should be?   How about her breasts?   Had I noticed the size of her feet?   And he would insist on having me sit with him in sidewalk cafés by the hour while he pointed to women passing by and begged me to compare them with his prospective wife.

Through my Uncle Pitrinu I met nearly everyone in Porto Empedocle who remembered my father, among them a surprising number of women who still had photographs of him as a handsome and gay bachelor of twenty. There was one spinster who kept her photograph of my father on a boudoir table next to a portrait of the Virgin Mary.   She examined me wistfully and conceded there was a general resemblance.   'I do believe he has the same forehead and the same nose, and he certainly looks as underfed as Peppino used to,' she told my uncle.

Uncle Pitrinu took a fiendish delight in telling me things about my father's romantic youth that I had never heard before.   One afternoon while we were eating a *gelato* in front of the pastry shop where my father had once been an apprentice, he suddenly pointed to a buxom woman passing by and whispered: 'Your father almost married that lady thirty years ago. Think of it, she might have been your mother.' I thought of Aunt Giovanna and her love for such dark speculation.

Fearful that I may have inherited some of the romantic traits he so lavishly attributed to my father, Uncle Pitrinu warned me to steer clear of women on the trip. 'If you should feel you need a woman, go to a brothel; it's safer and healthier,' he advised. 'Don't take up with a *strafalaria,* because she will strip you of your money and then leave you.'

To convince me that what he was saying was true, he told me about an American-born young man named Salvatore Bottiglia who had come all the way from Syracuse, New York, to visit his relatives in Girgenti.

'Like you, he planned to make a grand tour of Italy afterward. He had been here less than a week when he met an American dancer who was stopping at a hotel near the temples. You would have thought he had never seen an American girl before the way he went after her. Well, to make a long story short, they left Girgenti together and went to Palermo.

'He was back in about a month. All the money he had saved for his grand tour was gone. She had dug it out of him and when she found he had no more, she disappeared. The only souvenir Mr. Bottiglia had of the experience was a sickness which I can't mention because there are women present. *Lu poveru fissa!* Luckily for him, his relatives took pity on him and got him a doctor. When his health improved, his uncle accompanied him to the boat at Naples to make certain he wouldn't get into any more trouble.'

Back in Girgenti again, I decided to do some sightseeing while I was waiting for Rosario Alfano to return from Messina. My Great-Uncle Stefano was proud to be my guide, but when I suggested a tour of the temples he firmly refused to accompany me. Although he conceded they were beautiful and had brought a great deal of needed tourist trade to Girgenti, he saw no point in interesting himself in glorifications to pagan gods he had no use for.

'I will show you the temples that really matter,' he said, and he took me to see some of the thirty Catholic churches in Girgenti. First we visited the Cathedral of Saint Gerlando, the Norman who had become bishop of Girgenti. Because my name was Gerlando and I had come all the way from North America and had a letter to the Minister of Propaganda, the sacristan permitted me to hold the curved staff Saint Gerlando had once carried and to examine the regal vestments he had worn at his services. In a back room of the church I saw a Reni painting of the Virgin Mary carelessly hung between a cheap portrait of Mussolini and a calendar print of King Emanuele.

In another church my great-uncle showed me an ancient Greek coffin which was now used for baptismal purposes. The carvings on its sides were obviously scenes from the mythology of those heathens, the Greeks. But my great-uncle had no objection to the coffin, since it served so practical a purpose. No doubt he would have changed his attitude toward the temples if they could have been converted into Catholic places of worship.

Like many other Sicilian Catholics I knew, my great-uncle would have denied that the religious customs he

observed had any connection with his non-Catholic ancestors. Yet the evidence was all around, particularly on
the days when the saints were feasted. One morning I
woke to the beating of drum rhythms that took me back
to the Harlem night clubs. Wandering around the streets
were peasants with long, narrow drums hanging from
their necks. They were pounding them all over the city
to announce the annual four-day celebration for Saint
Calogero, the patron saint of Girgenti.

Saint Calogero was famous for his miracles in curing
the sick and the maimed. The story was that he had
been a missionary doctor from Ethiopia who became so
revered for his cures that he was canonized shortly after
his death. No one had ever disputed his Ethiopian ancestry — you had only to look at the features and coloring
of his statue to be convinced of it — but that year some of
the noisier Sicilian Fascists, carried away by the conquest
of Ethiopia, were insisting that Saint Calogero had been a
Sicilian who acquired a heavy coat of tan.

The drumming continued for four days. Every day
there would be processions of gaily decorated mules and
horses bearing food offerings of devout Catholics to the
Church of Saint Calogero. In the evenings the peasants
came to the church with crude but very graphic crayon
drawings illustrating the numerous ways that Saint Calogero had interceded to save their relatives from some
horrible disease or accident.

These they hung next to the altar of the saint, and
Sicilians from the entire province came to look at them
and be reminded of other instances where Saint Calogero
had rescued someone from a terrible fate. One of the

drawings I recall showed a child who had fallen out a window and was suspended in midair. Below was written the explanation that the child fell and would have died from her injuries but for a miracle of Saint Calogero. Another drawing pictured an old woman whose body seemed to be frying on a hot stove; a supplementary drawing showed her alive and healthy — thanks to another miracle by the saint.

On Saint Calogero's Day — the final day of the celebration — sixteen of the strongest peasants available carried the heavy life-size statue of the saint out of the church and through the streets of Girgenti, followed by cheering crowds that yelled 'Viva San Calogero!' as they sucked on cones of sherbet and waved their candy and papier-mâché replicas of the saint's statue.

Latti informed me that up till that year it had always been the custom of the people to throw bread at the saint and at the processions from their balconies. This custom had been abolished by law. Some said it was because bread was becoming scarce; others claimed that the police had discovered that some of the townspeople saved their hardest and stalest bread for the occasion to throw at those they did not like. 'It was surprising how much damage you could do with a hard piece of bread if your aim was good,' Latti mused.

Anxious mothers with sick children waited for the parade to pass their houses. I saw one of them dart out of a doorway with a child in her arms and push her way through the crowd. The peasants stopped their march. A priest took the child from the mother and held him over the open prayer book which Saint Calogero had in one hand.

While the child lay on its back screaming with fright at the sight of the saint's mahogany face and white beard, the priest blessed it and returned it to the mother. Confident now that her baby would soon become well, the mother gratefully kissed the feet of the saint as the peasants took up their burden again. Every few yards the procession stopped again so that another mother could have her sick child cured.

In the evening the celebration came to an end with a huge fireworks exhibition on the edge of town. There were hundreds of bombs, roman candles, and sky rockets spitting stars and flowers. The main feature was portraits in fireworks of Saint Calogero and Mussolini. These two notables blazing prettily in a half-dozen different colors were to climax the exhibit. For some reason that was never determined Mussolini did not come off successfully. While Saint Calogero blazed his full glory, Mussolini glowed doubtfully for two or three seconds; then a pinwheel of green fire jumped out of place and went whirling over the expanse of Il Duce's jaw. The next moment the whole portrait burst into flames and collapsed.

Rosario Alfano returned from his trip to Messina the day after the celebration. He burst into tears when he saw me. 'Please forgive me for this display,' he said embracing me. 'But it is so wonderful to see an old friend from America.' He wiped away his tears, and as he smiled at me the ends of his white mustache curled up around the sides of his nose. 'Also,' he added, 'I've been having a very gloomy time of it. My Compare Gaetano, *bonarma*, died from his illness, and two days after we buried him

his wife passed away from the shock.   I'm afraid I still feel
the effects of watching a great many people weeping.'

I was glad I had waited for him to return for I too felt
good about seeing someone from my past.   Rosario looked
a little more haggard than I remembered him in Rochester
but his eyes still twinkled and, as usual, he wore a black
hat cocked to one side.   He tried to speak to me in
English but he had obviously forgotten what little he knew
of the language.   'It is strange,' he said, 'but ever since
I've been in Sicily I have wished I had taken pains to learn
English when I lived in Rochester.'

Speaking Sicilian with him had its disadvantages.
There were relatives and friends all about us listening
eagerly to what we had to say to each other, and that
made it difficult to exchange frank opinions.   Moreover,
Rosario was so popular in Girgenti that we could not walk
down the street or sit in a café without being joined by some
of his friends.   'They love me because I don't mind paying the bill,' he said, laughing.   'They think I have a pile
of money from living in America, where the streets are
paved in gold.'

Rosario suggested visiting the temples, where we could
talk without interruption.   The next morning we packed
a luncheon of bread, cheese, and wine and, without telling
anyone about our picnic, took a bus down to the valley of
the temples.   'This place is a paradise in the spring,' he
said.   'The almond trees are in flower then and they
form a beautiful garland around the temples.   You must
come back again some Spring and see it with your own
eyes.'

We sat against a column in the Temple of Concord,

looking toward the sea, and drank some of the wine. Rosario talked eagerly, like someone who had not been able to express his thoughts for a long time and was anxious to make up for it. He talked mostly of his memories of Rochester and his life in Sicily, pausing only to hear my answers to his questions about Mount Allegro and his old friends. He asked if my Uncle Nino was still talking of coming back to Sicily to live. 'It is still his dream,' I said.

'Tell him to stay where he is. He would not be happy if he came back to Sicily. There is beauty here but it no longer has the same meaning. I wish I had never left America. Things are not as I expected to find them. There is a blight on the land and the people are unhappier than I ever remember them to be. Sometimes I think they are afraid of each other. They all say there won't be another war but I don't believe it. I can see it coming every day, and every day I curse the moment I decided to leave America.'

I asked him why he did not come back. He sighed. 'It is too late and I am too old. I might as well be buried here where I was born. . . .'

He begged me to stay in Girgenti a few days longer and be his guest, but for some time I had been feeling the same depression he felt about Sicily. I wanted to leave. I was beginning to get lonely for America and I thought how good it would be to be home again.

• • • •

Two weeks later I was back in Mount Allegro drinking my father's oldest wine and telling my relatives about Sicily.

FINALE

YEARS BEFORE AMERICAN CITY NEIGHBOR-
hoods began being destroyed in the name of urban renewal,
Gertrude Stein wrote these words: "When you get there,
there's no there there."

I thought of these prophetic words when I last visited
Mount Allegro, the area that took its name from the title
of this book. Except for a ghostly landmark, St. Bridget's
Church, where I used to confess my sins, Mount Allegro
no longer exists as a neighborhood. That the church is still
there is a miracle of sorts, another testimonial to the
tenacity of Catholicism. Nowadays, with too few parish-
ioners, it stands forlornly, the last physical reminder of a
past which, in 1973, was finally bulldozed into the com-
post of local history. Gone are the clapboard houses
with their front porches that the Jewish, Polish, and
Italian immigrants purchased before World War I from
their fleeing Irish and German owners who wanted no
such neighbors. All the streets have disappeared; there is
not the slightest trace of them. What was once Mount Allegro (a topographical misnomer, chosen for its cheerful
connotation) now resembles a Kansas prairie.

Yet a prairie with a difference, for within a 22-acre tract
that was the core of Mount Allegro stretches a
five-million-dollar Coca-Cola bottling plant, a monument
of sorts to the failure of the city authorities to live up to
their urban renewal promises. The plant is a low-slung

box of a building, not unlike the shape of a coffin, totally surrounded by a formidable barbed-wire fence. Somewhere within the enclosure must be the space that once contained the house and the garden where my family lived, where my relatives came to talk and behave as if they had never left their beloved Sicily while sipping the dark amber wine my father made in his cellar.

It would be unfair to ascribe the death of Mount Allegro to the promoters of urban renewal. The neighborhood began declining in the early fifties with the demise of its oldest residents, the immigrants. The houses also began to die. Some had already been lost to the banks during the Depression years and were suffering badly from the ravages of absentee ownership. The houses of the immigrants, passed down to their children, fared no better. Unwilling to inhabit a neighborhood that was rapidly becoming a black and Puerto Rican ghetto where acts of arson and vandalism were common occurrences, the children hastily disposed of their properties to slum landlords, or became slum landlords themselves by renting them, and retreated to the suburbs. By the mid-sixties, the neighborhood had deteriorated into a dreary scene of dilapidated buildings and rampant weeds, dead ripe for a race riot and, eventually, for the false promises of urban renewal.

The final event to evoke a Mount Allegro of a happier era was the golden wedding anniversary of my parents in 1958. At the altar of St. Bridget's Church, they repeated their marriage vows in the presence of their family, relatives and former neighbors, most of whom no longer lived in the neighborhood.

When my father died four years later, my mother, left alone, refused to move out of the old family house, despite the protests of her children who feared for her safety. She saw no reason for concern; she had made friends with her new black and Puerto Rican neighbors, and she was in daily communication with my brother and his family who operated a corner grocery store less than two blocks away and lived in an apartment attached to the store. For two years she kept reassuring her family that no harm could come to her under these circumstances. Then one evening, while she sat alone in a front room saying her rosary, her hope of remaining in the old house came to a sudden end. A gang of hoodlums speeding by in a car hurled a beer can through a window near her chair. Although the can and the flying glass missed her, she became sick with fright. She offered no resistance when, a few hours later, my brother moved her out of Mount Allegro to the suburban home of her youngest daughter, where she lived the rest of her life.

Shortly after this episode, in the summer of 1964, Rochester experienced its first race riot. It erupted while the police were trying to arrest a drunk at a black street dance, and within hours most of the stores in the vicinity had been smashed and looted. Spreading to other sections of the city, the riot took four lives before it was over. My brother's store, though in the direct path of the looters, was spared, perhaps because he had the reputation of treating his black customers fairly, but more probably because only two days earlier his sons, Charles and Gaspare (better known as Chuck and Gap), had saved the life of a black neighbor's child. When the hysterical mother had burst into the store wailing about the drowning of the child, the two boys dropped what they were doing and sprinted to her apartment. Chuck fished the child out of a bathtub, then Gap applied artificial respiration while his brother summoned a police ambulance. On the night of the riot the word that went out among the looters was: "Don't touch the Mangiones."

The corner grocery store, along with the house attached to it, became a casualty of urban renewal nine years after the riot, in 1973. Exercising their prerogative of eminent domain, the city authorities compelled my brother to sell them the property for a song. He and his family then moved to a suburb not far from the Catholic cemetery where, with the exception of my Protestant uncle Luigi and members of his family, nearly all of my relatives who figure prominently in *Mount Allegro* are buried.

Among the first to go was Uncle Nino, the poet laureate of the clan, who died in 1956, five years after the death of his wife, Aunt Giovanna. He had been living alone in the same apartment they occupied for twenty years. Housekeeping was not one of his talents and within weeks after my aunt's funeral, the apartment was reduced to a nightmare of dirt and disorder. He had alienated most of his relatives by refusing their help and shunning their company, claiming that the mere sight of them reminded him too painfully of the happy years he had known with his wife. This explanation infuriated the relatives, who maintained that in all probability they reminded him of his bad behavior as a husband. "She killed herself for him," they said, "so that he could live like a gentleman." It was true that during most of their married life he had subsisted on what she earned as a button sewer in a tailor factory, a job she held all her immigrant years.

Her husband spent much of his time playing cards with his old cronies, fishing for bullheads in the ponds around Lake Ontario and, in his later years, sitting in the New York Central railroad station watching travelers come and go. He claimed the latter to be his favorite hobby, but there were those who insisted that the main attraction for him was a blonde and friendly Polish waitress, employed at the station. Whatever faults his contemporaries found in him did not diminish his appeal for all the children in our family. Possibly because his imagination was as free as our own, we felt more closely related to him than we did toward most of the other relatives. He was the only one we addressed by his first name without any fear of reprimand, and although his teasing was sometimes little short of sadistic, he, the childless uncle, knew how to listen to our problems without making us feel that the world was coming to an end. To many he may have seemed a useless person, but I continued to regard him with much affection as a poet and philosopher so that when my father telephoned to inform me that Uncle Nino was dying and had asked to see me, I took the next plane to Rochester and went directly to the hospital. What ensued merits, I believe, more than passing mention.

In the waiting room expecting me was my Uncle Luigi, 82 years old and six feet tall. His once powerful body now seemed to be sagging. He embraced me but he had no words of greeting. His first words must have been those gnawing at his soul ever since he realized that his oldest friend was close to death. "I am packed and ready to leave," he said. "Anytime my call comes. After all, it's about time, isn't it?" Now that he had articulated his feeling, he felt better, and at the sight of a pretty nurse waiting for an elevator he was reminded of a "true story" involving a 75-year-old man and a girl of 20 he intended to marry. Aghast, his protesting relatives pointed out that when he was 80, the girl would be 25. "Well, when that happens," he said, "I'll divorce her and marry another

20-year-old." It was an old joke I had heard him tell before, but he was still delighted with it and at the punchline laughed with such vigor that I had no doubt he had packed his bags prematurely.

Together we went up to see Uncle Nino, who looked too furious to be dying. But I could hardly bear to look at him. There was a tube stuck up his nose which was taped to his sunken cheeks; another emerged from his stomach. At least half of his flesh was gone and his wrists were wasted to the bone. A red and gray moustache bristled over his thin, wry lips; his voice came intermittently, abruptly going off and on like a defective radio, while his eyes glared with a rage that was brownish yellow, like the rest of his bile-ridden body.

Ignoring his old friend, he spoke my name; then, directing me to draw my chair closer to his bed, apparently not wanting Uncle Luigi to overhear him, he lost no time conveying the theme of his anger: his pain was intolerable and no one was doing anything to help him, least of all his doctors and nurses. "They want me to die in agony." He cursed them with fierce Sicilian maledictions, then, reducing his voice to a whisper, confided what he wanted of me, "the only one of my nephews with the intelligence to understand my problem." The favor he requested was appalling. I was to buy him a "poison pill," something that would deliver him from his agony quickly; he had secreted five dollars under his pillow for the purchase. The thought of becoming responsible for his death horrified me; moreover, the energy emanating from him led me to rationalize that the doctors might still be able to save him. I pretended that I would try to buy the pill for him and asked him for the money. But I am a poor actor. He looked me in the eye and read my mind, and began shouting that he did not believe me, that I only wanted to deprive him of his only chance to kill his pain.

The noise of his Sicilian brought the nurse, a strong woman twice his present size but obviously afraid of him. Continuing in Sicilian, he ordered her to leave, calling her *"figlia di butana"* and threatening to tear the tubes out of his nose and stomach. Later I learned that he had fought the nurse with his fists when the tubes were first inserted, and that on the morning of his arrival at the hospital he had jumped out of bed and raced up and down the corridors looking for an exit, screaming that he wanted to go home.

Watching him in his torment, I felt miserable for lacking the courage to get him his poison pill. Although the nurse had left, he kept on ranting about her, a diatribe of eloquent obscenities. At last, he leaned back exhausted, though his eyes remained open and moved round the room as if it were packed with enemies. During all this time, he had paid no attention to Uncle Luigi, who, finally unable to contain himself, made a bid for his attention by telling me that Nino had beaten him in the last four games of *briscola* they played; as soon as he was out of the hospital, he was going to play him again and this time get even with him.

Uncle Nino exploded, calling him *"vigliacco"* for wanting to get even, and asking if it wasn't enough that he was going to attend his funeral. Trying to placate him, Uncle Luigi said there wasn't going to be any funeral; it was only a matter of time before he would get well and be discharged from the hospital. Uncle Nino was not placated. "You can talk nonsense like that," he screamed. "You are 82 years old and strong as an ox. You don't have any tubes stuck into you. . . ."

Uncle Luigi seemed to wilt under the tirade. It wasn't his fault that he was 82 years old and healthy, he protested. "I've had nothing to do with that. My bags are packed. I am ready to go. I've had six children and fourteen grandchildren, and I have no unmarried daughters. There's really no reason why I shouldn't go."

Uncle Nino directed his response to me. "He is 82 years old and he has the muscles of an elephant, and all he can do is brag about all the children and grandchildren he has. Why doesn't he help me instead of sitting there bragging?"

His old friend looked mystified. "But Nino, how can I help you?"

"You have the muscles of an elephant. You could help me escape from this place. The pains will go as soon as I leave here. . . ."

He tried to say more but his voice was gone. His lips kept moving and he did a frenzied charade with his skinny hands, which I suppose was intended to describe the method of escape but which I could not follow; nor, apparently, could his old friend. There was a long and dreadful silence, then the nurse came in to whisper in my ear that my mother was downstairs waiting for her turn to come up; no more than two visitors were allowed at the same time. Uncle Nino kept glaring at her, muttering "butana, figlia di butana."

After the nurse left, I explained what she had said and held out my hand to him, promising to return the next day. His grip was surprisingly firm but his eyes were moist as he whispered "addio." He no longer seemed angry with me. At that moment I wanted to embrace him, tubes and all, and ask his forgiveness for denying him his poison pill. Instead I kissed one of his sunken cheeks, and departed.

I never saw him again. The next day he fell into a coma
from which he never emerged. He had provided his own
means of escape. A few days later he was dead.

Uncle Luigi regretted not having tried to spirit his old
friend out of the hospital. "After all, at my age what difference would it have made if they had sent me to jail for
it?" He survived Uncle Nino by five more years, still expressing surprise that death had not claimed him sooner. I
mourned his passing. From childhood I had admired his
iconoclastic turn of mind and his candidness. He was ever
willing to engage my relatives in forensic combat with his
un-Sicilian ideas and conduct. Apart from his flirtations
with a wide variety of American religious sects—he was
the first of his clan to break with the Catholic Church—he
had a genuine craving for venturing beyond his cir-
cumscribed Sicilian world in order to expose himself to
ideas and customs foreign to his own culture. Yet, as I
gradually came to realize, except for dropping one religious sect for another, or acquiring a new American mistress
with interests different from those of the previous one, he
would not venture far. With his brains and brawn, he
might have become a Moses of his people leading them
through the exile of their self-imposed boundaries, but his
lack of English, together with his inability to think of himself as anything more than a master bricklayer, precluded
any such future; he would remain nothing more than a
gadfly philosopher who enjoyed taunting his relatives for
their fear of the new.

My father died a year later, in 1962, at the age of 78,
after six years of failing health. Although I had no
difficulty understanding my mother and uncles from the
start, it was not until I became an adult that I was able to
regard my father as a fellow human being rather than as
the Sicilian authoritative head of our family. When that

happened, we became close friends but, unfortunately, he had begun to die before our friendship could fully transcend our father and son relationship. Living in separate cities and seeing each other mainly during the hubbub of holidays did not allow us enough hours together. Our best times occurred when he and my mother would visit with me. Once they came to Washington for almost a month while I was convalescing from an almost fatal bout with pneumonia (it was during that time that I resolved to write *Mount Allegro*); much later, in Philadelphia, he came alone for several weeks to help my wife paint and repair an old Victorian house we had purchased. He could fix almost anything.

He could also make friends almost at will. Unhampered by the limitations of his English (he never lost his habit of using the pronoun "she" for all genders), within a few days after each arrival he would be on cordial terms with the neighboring storekeepers and even with a few of our less than cordial neighbors. The educational gap between him and some of my highly sophisticated friends did not deter him—nor my mother, for that matter—from establishing an easy rapport with a number of them. In one instance, the rapport grew into a lifelong friendship with a scholarly Sicilian aristocrat, Prince Corrado Niscemi, who in the late forties entertained him and my mother at his Palermo palazzo.

It was Niscemi who, fathoming the brilliance that went beyond my father's culinary skills, pronounced him a modern-day Ulysses capable of surviving in any situation. There was some truth to the compliment; he was ingeniously resourceful and unafraid, and though Niscemi never knew it, he had, like Ulysses, journeyed away from his family for an extended period, presumably to explore the

possibility of setting up a pastry shop in California (a plan
he never realized), but also, I suspect, to search for a self
that must have been swamped with the concerns of
fatherhood. Unlike Ulysses, however, he failed to attain
any measure of fulfillment commensurate with his intelligence and imagination. As must have happened to
thousands of other immigrants with little or no education
and much talent struggling to earn a livelihood in an alien
land, his commitment to his family obliged him to spend
most of his working years as a lowly wage earner in a factory.

The father presented in *Mount Allegro* is not nearly as
complex as he actually was. For all of his vitality, he suffered from periods of black despair that tortured our
childhood with the fear of losing him. It was a subject that
was never discussed, but during the anxious hours of
waiting for him whenever he was unduly late or unex-
pectedly absent, we could not help but recall the fate of
his own father who, on a Christmas Eve, had drowned himself in the Mediterranean, leaving behind a family of several young children of which he was the youngest. Deprived of a father model early in life, it was remarkable that
he could cope with his role of father as well as he did. But
he was unlike the other Sicilian fathers we knew. While
he never let his children forget that they were living
under a dictatorship, albeit a loving one, he shocked his
peers by allowing us to address him and my mother with
the informal *tu,* an unheard of concession in a Sicilian
household. And instead of spending his free time away
from home playing cards and drinking with his friends, as
is the tribal habit of Sicilian fathers, he preferred the
company of his wife and children and would rarely
socialize without them.

The doctors had a medical name for the illness that took his life, but the actual cause of death may have been the half dozen years of boredom he suffered after his first stroke. He recovered from it quickly enough, but it must have robbed him of his zest for living. No longer was he the vital participant in the life around him; he became instead an apathetic onlooker, a role that flagrantly misrepresented what he had been. He must have brooded about that a great deal. With his death, the full meaning of death overwhelmed me for the first time.

My mother was buried next to him seven years later, at the age of 84, the last of the main protagonists of *Mount Allegro* and the most valiant. For her husband and their children she had been a constant and generous source of love and assurance. My father reigned as the dominant family figure but it was she, with her gift of insight and earthy wisdom, that kept the rest of us on a more or less even keel. She was a woman of strong spirit yet compassionate and with a liberal turn of mind that seemed surprising in one with only a couple of years of elementary school education. For her there were anxieties but not despair. As much as she had loved my father, his death did not release her hold on life. Shortly after she became a widow I began receiving letters from her, the first she had ever written. They were penned in her own invented phonetic Sicilian which I had only to read aloud to hear what she was saying. Having always considered her incapable of writing anything, I expressed amazement at her new and unexpected accomplishment. She explained that, with my father gone, she came to realize that she could not very well expect to receive letters unless she started writing them, adding that she needed to receive letters to avoid worrying about me.

Mount Allegro may not suggest it, but anxiety was a

constant factor in our family life, mostly anxiety about one another. Neither my brother nor I ever learned how to swim because my father, a powerful swimmer who had acquired the skill in the salty waters of the Mediterranean which provide buoyancy, was fearful that his sons might drown in the unsalted waters of Lake Ontario which, of course, offer no buoyancy. Whenever either of us ventured into the lake, his shouts would bring us back to shore. By the time there were opportunities to take swimming lessons, our fear of water was so deeply inculcated into our psyche as to make swimming seem completely beyond our abilities. In my mother the sense of anxiety was honed to the point of clairvoyance. On one occasion, during a snowy, windy morning when my father was in our garage trying to start his Ford and my mother was in an upstairs bedroom of the house, it saved his life. After the wind blew the garage doors shut, my mother heard the faint blare of the car horn as his body, unconscious from carbon monoxide, collapsed over the steering wheel. Without any notion of what was happening (she had never heard of carbon monoxide), she frantically dashed out into the snow in her nightgown, flung open the garage doors, and dragged my father into the open air, just in time. It was nearly a month before the doctor pronounced him well enough to leave his bed.

Notwithstanding three tragedies in her lifetime that could not be averted—the accidental murder of a favorite brother and the loss of two young daughters before either one could reach school age—as well as serious illnesses that threatened her own life several times, my mother managed to remain undefeated; to the end, her years as a mother and wife were a glowing affirmation of her attitude that, despite all the suffering and anxiety, life is a variegated pleasure. If she experienced disappointment, it may have been in the failure of her three eldest children (the youngest was denied the chance) to manifest any musical talent whatever despite her heroic efforts to stimulate it with lessons financed by the nickels, dimes and quarters she hoarded for that purpose. Yet her insistence that there must be musical talent in the family (our love of dancing was proof enough for her) was not in vain. Somehow it became transmitted to my brother, who made certain that his sons, Gap and Chuck, received a thorough musical education. To her delight they achieved some measure of fame as composers and instrumentalists during her lifetime. That their music may not have been exactly what she had in mind did not seem to disturb her. It also pleased her that her eldest son finally acquired the profession she had long wished for him, *professore.* Devoutly religious, she attributed all such agreeable developments to her faith in the power of prayer.

Also answered was the prayer that she visit Sicily while there was still time to embrace her octogenarian sister, Rosina, who had breast-fed her on the death of their mother. After an absence of more than 45 years, she and my father returned to their native land for a three-month sojourn which, appropriately enough, was financed with royalties of *Mount Allegro.* To be reunited with many of the close relatives and friends they had left behind in Agrigento, Porto Empedocle, and Realmonte was one of the brightest highlights of their lives.* Yet they had no wish to prolong their stay and were genuinely glad to return to their

*My own reunions with relatives in Sicily are described in two other books: *Reunion in Sicily* (1950) and *A Passion for Sicilians: The World Around Danilo Dolci* (1968). These books, along with *Mount Allegro* (1943) and its companion volume, *An Ethnic at Large: A Memoir of America in the Thirties and Forties* (1978), are all interrelated.

adopted country. With all its faults, *l'America*, not *l'Italia*, had become the country they preferred. "Sicily and many parts of Italy are more beautiful," my mother said, "but America is better in other ways." To which my father added, "Once you have children in this country, how can you go back?"

It was true that their roots were firmly planted here, but I could discern no radical change in the Sicilian way of life they and my other Rochester relatives pursued. Whatever changes had occurred were mainly ones of attitude. By the middle of the century, for example, they no longer maintained that it was impossible to have a good marriage with a non-Italian woman. They were no longer alarmed when their children chose a mate of another religious faith or of a different nationality background. And by that time they were permitting their daughters to socialize with young men to whom they were not betrothed and without benefit of chaperones. There were also some changes in their own social life. Now that their children's families were claiming more of their attention, the immigrants were no longer as hungry for one another's company as they had been in the heyday of Mount Allegro. The storytelling sessions had virtually disappeared, either because they had run out of stories or, more likely, because television by then had reared its voracious head and seemingly swallowed their tongues.

They made few friends with the *Americani;* mainly they kept to themselves, shopping in Italian stores and frequenting Italian dentists, doctors, lawyers, shoemakers, and barbers. Much of their social and business life was conducted in their own language. Contrary to the advocates of the melting pot theory, they did not "melt down." While they learned to appreciate the economic and political advantages of their adopted country and to develop a staunch sense of loyalty toward it, which was strikingly evident in the years we were at war with Italy, they showed little inclination to embrace the dominant Anglo-Saxon culture, as had been predicted they would. However, they did become "Americanized" in one significant respect: slowly but surely their faith in *Destino* began to wither. The longer they lived here the more they sensed that they themselves, not destiny, had the power to change their lives. For most of them this awareness came too late to do anything about it.

Perhaps the overriding motive in writing *Mount Allegro* was to recapture the world from which I had escaped while it was still fresh in my memory. There was also the hope that I could produce a work that might help dispel some of the more spurious clichés pinned to the image of Italian Americans by an uninformed American public. The book was intended to be primarily informative, quite sedate in tone. It did not work out that way. After several false starts, it seemed best to present my material as a memoir, but before long my chief protagonists were asserting themselves in a manner that exceeded the etiquette of the conventional memoir.* I thought it wise to let them have their say, as long as I could have mine.

For reasons apart from the self-doubts that assail one's first attempt to produce a book-length manuscript, *Mount Allegro* was not easy to write. After I had finally hit on a style that would let me tell my story without sounding

---

*It came as a shock when the book's original publishers, who had accepted the work as nonfiction, decided to publish the memoir as fiction—a decision dictated by the belief that more copies could be sold that way. My protests were of no avail and, in defeat, I gave my protagonists fictitious names.

either like a sociologist or a fiction writer, I began to question the validity of choosing a project that did not mesh with the times—we were about to go to war with the native country of the very people I was writing about. I also wondered who else besides Sicilians, few of whom could read English, would possibly be interested in a book about my relatives.

I need not have worried. Although *Mount Allegro* was issued only a few months before the American invasion of Sicily, the reception it had was anything but inimical. There was an avalanche of intoxicatingly enthusiastic reviews, and several hundred letters from readers of diverse background (including Anglo-Saxons and nothern Italians), who expressed their pleasure in identifying with some of my Sicilian relatives. A particularly gratifying appreciation came from the Italian historian Gaetano Salvemini, an antifascist hero of mine, who was then teaching at Harvard. He wrote that reading *Mount Allegro* was "reliving my childhood in Apulia 60 years ago. I could see in each of your characters some person who is still alive in my memory. Your feelings are a strong mixture of fun, respect and tenderness that recalls Dickens at his best."

Not everyone shared his opinion that I was respectful. Uncle Nino's wife was hurt that I, a favorite nephew, had given her the name of Giovanna, which I learned— too late, alas—was the name of a Sicilian queen notorious for her sexual excesses. (I was more astute in changing my family name Mangione to "Amoroso.") She was not the only one who felt slandered by the book. Two enclaves of angry Sicilian Americans, though unable to read it, became convinced that I had vilified their native village. At a mass meeting instigated by a Rochester lawyer who had put the idea into their heads, their sense of outrage pro-

duced a three-pronged plan of attack: suing me and my
publishers for libel, sending a petition to the Immigration
and Naturalization Service, my then employer, demanding my immediate dismissal, and circulating a spite book
in which each of the aggrieved *paesani* could express his
personal opinion of me. Tempted though I was to create
some juicy publicity (which might improve the sales of the
book) by letting matters take their course, I squelched the
whole enterprise with a letter that expressed my own
Sicilian anger for being grossly misinterpreted; I also
pointed out that should they enact their plan they would
be lending credence to the canard that Sicilians are by
nature a revengeful people.

From a retired social worker who had worked among
the Sicilian immigrants of Rochester about the time that I
was born I received valuable information about their local
history which I would have incorporated into the text of
Mount Allegro had I known of it in time. She was Mrs.
Florence Kitchelt Cross, who sent me her scrapbook of
clippings and photographs that documented a unique effort on the part of the Sicilians to inform the people of
Rochester that, contrary to the impression contantly generated by the local press that the Sicilians were a criminal
and sinister lot, they were mostly a decent and law-
abiding people well deserving of the community's respect.

Encouraged by Mrs. Cross, a group of them formed an
acting company to stage "The Passion Play," the dramati-
zation of the suffering, death and resurrection of Christ, as
evidence of their good character. The large cast included
milkmen, bakers, masons, ditchdiggers, shoemakers,
tailors, and a variety of factory workers, among whom
were several of my relatives. During their months of re-
hearsals the actors were joined by other Italians who

sewed costumes, built sets, and collected contributions toward the cost of the production.

The date selected for the performance was Columbus Day (1908), possibly in the hope that the Americans in the community would "discover" the real character of the Italians. Invitations were mailed to hundreds of community leaders and their spouses, but the audience was disappointingly small and almost entirely Italian. Fortunately, the actors' performance generated such excitement as to create a demand for an encore. This time the auditorium was packed with both Americans and Italians and, though the lines of the play were in Italian, the entire audience rose to give the actors a standing ovation when it was over.

The next day the newspapers that had been featuring Italian crime on front pages devoted the same space to reviews and editorials praising the production and thanking the Italian community for having enriched the cultural life of the city. But, as Mrs. Cross acknowledged in our correspondence, it takes more than a theater production to change public opinion for long. Before the year was out, the press was back to its old habit of giving prominent space to any crime committed by anyone with an Italian name.

My parents and several other relatives were in the audience when "The Passion Play" was performed for the second time, but none of them had ever told me about the production and the motive behind it. My parents may have felt it unnecessary to burden their children unduly with the worry that they belonged to a stigmatized people. All during childhood we were aware, of course, that there must be a certain amount of prejudice against Italians, particularly against Sicilians—it was implicit in

my father's concern with the local press's attitude toward
them and in the fact that his own brother felt compelled to
change his name to an Anglo-Saxon one in order to in-
crease his chances of employment. We were also aware
that Rochester's two largest factories maintained a strict
policy of not hiring persons of Italian background. But the
extent to which anti-Italian prejudice had long existed
throughout the nation was unknown to me until a quarter
of a century after the publication of *Mount Allegro*, while
researching the Italian American experience for a brief
history of the subject (*America Is Also Italian* [1969]).

The intensity of the hatred and abuse directed against
the immigrants in the years when they were pouring into
the country by the millions included everything from
lynchings in the South to denial of police protection in the
New York slums. The general antagonism toward them inspired one editorial writer to describe the immigrants as
"a horde of steerage slime." Could I have written as
even-tempered a book as *Mount Allegro* with such knowledge in mind? I doubt it. But perhaps my ignorance
served me well, for I might have attributed to my relatives a sense of outrage which was mine, not theirs. The
outrage I heard them express was usually directed against
the failure of the American school system to teach students the meaning of respect, and the prevalence of
American social customs which struck them as immoral.

A *New York Times* reviewer of *Mount Allegro* marvelled
that its appreciation of the Sicilian immigrants was that of
a grandson rather than a son, adding that I had "succeeded in telescoping the experience of two generations in
one." The "telescoping" would not have been possible, of
course, without the perspective that evolved from having
put considerable time and distance between me and my

Sicilian world. Only then could I begin to grasp the reasons for my relatives' attitudes and conduct and also to perceive how, inadvertently, they engendered problems of identity among their offspring who, reared in a bicultural situation—Sicilian at home, American on the street and in the classroom—were seldom sure who they were.

Psychologically, at least, the immigrants were better off than their children. *They* had no identity problem. With their old-world pragmatism ground into them by centuries of foreign domination, they could accept the difficulties of living among foreigners with foreign customs; hence their lack of outrage at anti-Italian bigotry. Yet for all their wisdom, they failed to see the dilemma of their American-born children who were constantly being pulled in two opposite directions: by the parents with their insistence on their own philosophy and customs, and by the teachers who promoted ideas diametrically opposed to theirs.

In this incessant tug-of-war, the influence of the parents often prevailed, and the offspring were left with confused impressions of identity that made them reluctant to venture into the American mainstream. Their alienation from the rest of the community was further aggravated by the persistence of the media, through its exploitative treatment of Italian American crime, in conveying the impression that the great majority of Italian Americans must somehow have underworld connections. How readily this impression lends itself to further calumnious generalization is publicly documented in a White House tape that surfaced during the Watergate affair. After agreeing with his aides that it would be politically wise to appoint some Italian American to a top level federal post, Richard Nixon asks: "Yes, but where would we find an honest Italian American?"

The grandchildren of the immigrants, while not indifferent to such maligning, have a far easier time than their
parents. In increasing numbers they have acquired formal
education and become more objective about their ethnic
situation. Unlike their parents, they can relate to the culture of the immigrants without any sense of conflict. For
them and their children their Italian roots often become a
source of psychic sustenance, not embarrassment. And
they are not at all reluctant to become part of the American mainstream.

This healthier state of affairs began flourishing in the
fifties when enlightened parents of my generation were
able to shake off the old-world view of the immigrants that
if money could be found for a college education, only sons
should be educated and only those traditional professions
which promised the greatest degree of prestige and
affluence—doctor, lawyer, dentist, pharmacist—should be
pursued. From my own observations, Italian American
parents tend to send both their male and female offspring
to college and permit them to choose whatever studies
appeal to them, enabling more and more of the new generation to participate in every sector of American enterprise. In the case of the family in *Mount Allegro*, it may
be worth noting that, whereas I was the only one of my
relatives to attend college, six of my parents' seven grandchildren (two females, four males) have college degrees,
and there isn't a doctor, lawyer, dentist, or pharmacist
among them.

Except as a place-name for a place no longer there,
Mount Allegro has become a memory. Yet, to a surprising
degree, it is a memory with an influence that remains
verdant. The immigrants all are buried and their children
and grandchildren are scattered in various suburbs and

cities, some with spouses of non-Italian ancestry, but the bond between the living and the dead stays intact. Although the family reunions, which still take place in Rochester, are not as frequent as they were in my parents' time, nor quite as noisy and prolonged, the spirit of gregarious conviviality reigns as of old.

There are some differences, of course. No Uncle Nino to deliver orations. No one to emulate my father's feat of toasting with rhyming puns each guest around the table. No Uncle Luigi to start a game of *briscola* or *pochero*. Gone are the sounds pumped from a player piano, along with the opera recordings that would pierce the atmosphere with their histrionic sopranos and tenors. On the other hand, the food courses virtually duplicate those once prepared by my parents, even to the extent of including *cannoli*, which are astonishingly like my father's but just miss his artist's touch. And throughout each gathering, as in my youth, there is the cacaphony of young children, the upcoming fourth generation, squirming, giggling, teasing one another endlessly, harboring secrets they do not share with adults.

It all evokes my yesterdays and, in the poignancy of remembering, I hear my parents, uncles, aunts, and cousins talking in Sicilian at the top of their voices, sometimes simultaneously, pausing only long enough to shout commands at their young which are generally ignored. All the while I listen for my father's laughter and luxuriate in the warmth of my mother's eyes, as I try to efface the image of the bottling plant and the barbed-wire fence.

Mt. San Angelo
Sweet Briar, Virginia
January 1981

ABOUT THE AUTHOR

Jerre Mangione was born in Rochester, New York, of Sicilian immigrant parents. He is the former national coordinating editor of the Federal Writers' Project and professor emeritus of English at the University of Pennsylvania. Besides *Mount Allegro*, his ten works of fiction and nonfiction include *The Dream and the Deal: The Federal Writers' Project, 1935–1943* (Syracuse University Press), *An Ethnic at Large: A Memoir of America in the Thirties and Forties, Reunion in Sicily*, and *A Passion for Sicilians: The World Around Danilo Dolci*. He is coauthor of *La Storia: Five Centuries of the Italian American Experience*.

New York Classics
Frank Bergmann, *Series Editor*